SPIRITUALLY-ENGAGED KNOWLEDGE

In a supposedly 'global age,' which not everyone accepts, the late Dr Jennifer Crawford has brought together a range of disciplines in her creation of a unified, sensitive 'way of knowing' for the global era. Drawing upon her academic and lived experience in philosophy, environmental science, social work and feminism, together with a deep spiritual commitment, Jennifer Crawford has deftly woven together complex ideas in her reconceptualisation of global justice.

Spiritually-Engaged Knowledge: The Attentive Heart is framed within the author's troubling encounters in India recounted in the Prologue and Epilogue. These transformative experiences inspired her multi-disciplinary exploration, which took her beyond the boundaries of Western epistemology.

Locating the global, the author defines what it is to be a member of a global community in which cross-cultural encounters bring forth the possibility of new genre of knowledge. Crawford situates her argument within contemporary philiosohpical contexts, drawing upon postmodern discourse, globalisation theory and the realisation of shared horizon for all human knowledge, which offers up a potential for 'knowing globally'.

Crawford takes the reader through feminist theory, the ethic of care, the craft of 'othering', surrender to the 'other' and to our relationship with the earth which, she argues, can be reconfigured into an ethically-based way of knowing.

Drawing on a range of belief systems, inlcuding Australian Aboriginal spirituality, Christianity, Buddhism, Hinduism, metaphysics and Western philosophy Crawford rebuilds an inclusive, compassionate, redefinition of care for the new millennium, which she calls spiritually-engaged knowledge.

Jennifer Crawford worked as a field officer for the United Nations Food Programme in India, Sri Lanka and Bangladesh before returning to Australia for a Masters in Environmental Studies and her Doctoral Studies in Philosophy, achieving her PhD which forms the basis of this book.

To the memory of
Jennifer Crawford (1950-2000)
Sheila Crawford (1920-1987) and Harry Crawford (1916-1999)
and for
Kiran Dunkley-Crawford

Spiritually-Engaged Knowledge
The Attentive Heart

JENNIFER CRAWFORD

ASHGATE

© Jennifer Crawford 2005

All rights reserved. No part of this publication may be reproduced, stored in a retrieval system or transmitted in any form or by any means, electronic, mechanical, photocopying, recording or otherwise without the prior permission of the publisher.

Jennifer Crawford has asserted her moral right under the Copyright, Designs and Patents Act, 1988, to be identified as the author of this work.

Published by
Ashgate Publishing Limited
Gower House
Croft Road
Aldershot
Hampshire GU11 3HR
England

Ashgate Publishing Company
Suite 420
101 Cherry Street
Burlington, VT 05401-4405
USA

Ashgate website: http://www.ashgate.com

British Library Cataloguing in Publication Data
Crawford, Jennifer, 1950-2000
  Spiritually-engaged knowledge : the attentive heart
  1. Social justice – Religious aspects 2. Self – Religious aspects 3. Knowledge, Theory of (Religion) 4. Other (Philosophy) 5. Life 6. Spirituality
  I. Title II. Dunkley, Graham, 1946- III. Percival-Wood, Sally
  205.6'97

Library of Congress Cataloging-in-Publication Data
Crawford, Jennifer, 1950-2000.
  Spiritually-engaged knowledge : the attentive heart / Jennifer Crawford.
    p. cm.
  Includes bibliographical references and index.
  ISBN 0-7546-5377-3 (hardcover : alk. paper)
  1. Internationalism. 2. Globalization. 3. Human rights. 4. World citizenship. 5. Spirituality. 6. Social justice. I. Title.

  JZ1318.C72 2005
  303.48'2—dc2

2005004117

ISBN 0 7546 5377 3

Contents

A Dedication	*ix*
Foreword	*xi*
Preface	*xiii*
Prologue	
Meeting I	*xv*
Meeting II	*xvii*

PART I: LOCATING THE GLOBAL

1. Understanding in a Global Era	3
Global Conversations	5
Exploring a Global Idiom	9
Methodological Issues	13

PART II: LOGIC OF INQUIRY

2. Contemporary Contexts	21
The Global Context	23
Globalisation Theory	23
The Return of the Sacred	29
Being Globally	31
Knowing Globally	36
The Postmodern Context	46

PART III: GENRE ANALYSIS

3. Facing the Other: An Ethic of Meeting	65
Before the Face of the Other	67
A Post-deconstructive Ethic	67
Beyond the Other	71
An Ethic of Care	71
Reframing Subjectivity: Who Cares Anyway?	73
The Craft of Othering	77
I-Thou Relationship	79
Direct Seeing	80
Surrendering to the Other	81
De-automatising Perception	83

Earthcraft	84
Meeting Earth Others	85
The Earth as Other	87
Earth Selves, Other Selves, No Selves	90
Knowing Other Wise	92
The Muddle of the Middle	94
The Idea of Injunctions	96
4. Attentive Love	**107**
A Feminine Craft	109
Attentiveness as a Way of Looking	109
Attentiveness as Maternal Practice	113
Attentiveness as Objectivity	115
Attentiveness as Interconnection	117
Attentiveness as Meditative Awareness	119
An Interactive Energy	123
Positive and Negative Attention	123
An Economy of Energy	126
Constructing the Ego's Boundaries	128
Gendered Identities	130
Cutting the Ties that Bind	132
A Spiritual Practice	133
Dadirri – An Indigenous Australian Gift	134
Altering the Tone of Consciousness	135
The Unfixed Imprint	136
5. The Spiritual Heart	**145**
Glimpses of Mindfulness	147
Christian Contemplation	148
Advaitic Awareness	152
Buddhist Mindfulness	154
Sapiential Knowledge	156
Non-representational Psychology	158
Perennialism vs Constructivism	159
Incomplete Constructivism	160
Perennial States of Being	162
A Unified Theory of Meditation	167
Postmodern Spirituality	171
Re-defining the Spiritual	171
The Way of Not-Knowing	172
Knowledge and Tradition	176

PART IV: CONCLUSION

6. A Handful of Leaven   189
   The Rise of Spiritually-engaged Knowledge   190
   Spiritually-engaged Global Politics   197
      A Politics of Conscience   198
      An Inclusive Earth Community   204
      Citizen Sadhaks   207
   Not By Bread Alone   210

Epilogue
   Meeting I   215
   Meeting II   216

Appendix: Female Infanticide in India   *219*
Select Bibliography   *231*
Index   *237*

A Dedication

The publication of this book is both a happy and a sad event. My partner, Jenny Crawford, began her PhD at LaTrobe University in Melbourne, Australia, during 1992 and spent the next eight years completing it, a period which also saw the birth of our daughter, Kiran. In November 1999 we heard that the thesis had been passed, subject to minor corrections, with high acclaim from the examiners.

Within days we left for India and an extended stay at the ashram of Jenny's long-time guru, Sri Satya Sai Baba. Whilst there we learned of the sudden death of Jenny's father, Harry Crawford. Then, literally on the eve of the new millennium, Jenny noticed a lump which proved to be an horrifically aggressive breast cancer and which, on 20 July 2000, took her life.

The minor corrections were completed by Jenny's co-supervisor, Dr Harry Aveling, and the thesis passed in 2000. Originally titled *The Attentive Heart: A Way of Knowing for a Global Era*, Jenny's thesis has been lightly edited by Sally Percival-Wood and myself to create this book. I am greatly indebted to Sally and to Soni Stecker for assistance in this task. Unfortunately, at the request of the publishers, this book contains only an abbreviated bibliography, all other references being available on the Ashgate website. I am also grateful to Angela Tassone and Naomi Underwood for assistance in rectifying the depredations of a rogue scanner. For initiatives in having the thesis passed and published I thank Harry Aveling, Freya Mathews, Purushottama Bilimoria and the late Renuka Sharma, whose tragic death in 2002, also from cancer, adds an additional sad note to the project.

I wish to thank Anne Keirby and Sarah Lloyd of Ashgate Publishing for agreeing to give Jenny's book to the world, as well as to Adrian Marshall for his productions work. The editing and production costs were met from a generous legacy left by Jenny's late father Harry Crawford. Finally, I extend my profound gratitude to Erica Bader, for her indispensable support after Jenny's death; and for her intimate friendship with Jenny for much of their adult lives.

Jenny Crawford's work was inevitably an out-growth of her remarkable, rather adventurous, life. After graduating in science from Monash University (Melbourne) she worked, variously, on a pasture research project in East Africa, an indigenous crafts programme in Thailand, with the UN in South Asia and as a social worker in Australia and Asia. As a field worker for the World Food Programme in India, Sri Lanka and Bangladesh, she saw as much misery and deprivation as any human could. But after leaving the UN out of ire at the corruption, and the neglect of her reports, she saw the beautiful, devout side of India by living for several years in ashrams and other traditional institutions. This period included employment in one of Mother Teresa's Calcutta ashrams as a social worker where she reported directly to Mother Teresa herself. Jenny greatly admired the Mother and her mission despite many deficiencies in processes and treatment she found in the ashrams.

But the main import of this period for Jenny's work lay in her studies of Eastern traditions, both scholastic and spiritual, garnering her wisdom variously in universities, ashram libraries and at the feet of the gurus named in her acknowledgements, among others. At different times she followed both the 'path of contemplation' (*nyani*) and the 'path of devotion' (*bhakti*), thus seeing how they diverged from the Western rationalistic path with which she began in Australia.

The greatest influence upon her was the *bhakti* path of Sri Satya Sai Baba who teaches to 'love all, serve all', to 'be in the world but not of it' and to place the human/spiritual values of Truth, Love, Peace, Right Action and Non-violence above, without necessarily precluding, Western-inspired rationality and 'tricknology', as Sai Baba puts it. Other influences included Father Bede Griffiths, the British-born priest who sought to meld Eastern and Western traditions, and the late Ram Surat Kumar, the guru of her Meetings, who laughed loudly and disported simple widom. I was present at a later Meeting whence he still laughed and disported, but now in a cavernous, empty, unfinished, Western-influenced ashram hall which his devotees decided to inflict upon him.

A variety of feminist, environmental and other social activism completed the streams Jenny sought to blend with Eastern spirituality in a 'way of knowing' alternative to that of exclusivist Western rationality. Jenny was of both the West and the East, always believing that the twain should meet. She did not advocate dogmatic traditions as such, arguing that discernment and modern standards of justice, equity and sustainability should be used to test the validity of traditions, perhaps reflecting what I elsewhere have called 'adaptive traditionalism'. Nevertheless, she saw spiritual traditions as important for her alternative way of knowing, returning to Sai Baba's ashram for relief from the cancer which ultimately took her life, tragically early.

Jenny Crawford's life (1950-2000), exactly coincided with the last half century of the Second Millennium AD, an era which saw, in her view, the continuation, even exacerbation, of a range of world-wide inequities and excessive materialism. This book is about alternative ways of seeing these problems and seeking solutions thereto. It is my hope that our daughter, Kiran, will see an age of new thinking about such issues, to which her mother will have profoundly contributed.

I dedicate this book to Jenny, her parents and to Kiran.

Graham Dunkley
Gladysdale, Victoria
June 2005

Foreword

This is a book about meeting – the meeting of self and other – and it starts with two significant meetings, meetings which posed questions which became lodestars for the author's life. It therefore seems appropriate to introduce the book with another story of meeting – my meeting with the book's author. When Jenny Crawford first came to see me about supervision for her doctorate, she brought with her a breadth of experience and training and a depth of seriousness that was rare and impressive. She had just completed a Masters degree in environmental science and had studied social work in earlier days but during the many years between these two stretches of study she had roamed India and other parts of Asia, working on aid projects and in ashrams and other centres of spiritual training. This particular blend of training and experience furnished her with four different well-articulated but also cross-cutting critical perspectives, namely environmentalism, feminism, Hindu spirituality and development studies. The problematic on which these four perspectives converged was, simply, human injustice – the inequalities and fault lines of oppression within and between societies and between humankind and the larger community of life.

Jenny envisaged her doctoral thesis as her response to this problematic, and she felt that she could not write from any one of the four perspectives without also, equally, drawing on the other three. This was, to say the least, an ambitious call for a doctoral thesis, and calculated to make even the most optimistic prospective supervisor nervous! But I felt that if anyone could do it, Jenny could. She had the experience. She had the ability. And she had the need. It was as if she sought, in this single project, to bring together into some kind of unitive focus the deep but still disparate streams that had been the sources of meaning, but also of perplexity, in her life. The project was not merely an academic outing or the envisaged prelude to a comfortable career but an existential exercise in which Jenny sought, from the evidence available to her and for reasons intrinsic to her very being, definitive remedies for the monumental fact of injustice in this world.

An intellectual journey pursued with the rigour and thoroughness which Jenny brought to her task was inevitably not a short or always a smooth one, and it lasted for the best part of ten years. Sadly, when the epic was complete, Jenny passed away. There is perhaps some consolation for this tragic loss in the fact that a 'life's work' is condensed into this book that she has left us. Jenny sought answers to the basic riddle of injustice and, as far as any individual can, she found them. Whether we accept her answers or not, we are all beneficiaries of her search.

Freya Mathews
La Trobe University
Melbourne

Preface

Summary

Different historical eras are characterised by different governing forms of knowledge and identity. This book argues that the contemporary, postmodern, global context creates the conditions for an emerging genre of knowledge, described here as 'spiritually-engaged', which reframes the project of knowledge within ethical and spiritual horizons. The argument is divided into two main parts. The first part explains why this spiritually-engaged knowledge is emerging in the present era. Globalisation theory and postmodernism are explored, and it is argued that while both lead to the relativisation of socio-cultural systems of knowledge, they also point beyond relativism to reflexivity and beyond that again to a transformative way of knowing appropriate to the contemporary context.

The second part of the argument is concerned with identifying the proposed genre of spiritually-engaged knowledge. The approach taken is interdisciplinary and involves an exploration across various domains – postmodern ethics, feminism, psychology, environmentalism and spirituality – in which this post-discursive way of knowing has emerged. I identify a genre of spiritually-engaged, or sapiential, knowledge that is a form of radical empiricism. Arising out of the meeting with the Other, it is ethically based. Its epistemological strategy is a form of attentiveness described in feminist discourse as 'attentive love'. This attentiveness is a contemplative or meditative praxis that allows for a re-engagement between spirituality and Western intellectual discourse. The book argues that spiritually-engaged knowledge constitutes a nondual way of knowing that has long been recognised in religious traditions. Since nonduality is associated with an expanded mode of consciousness, spiritually-engaged knowledge has radical implications for our understanding of subjectivity. Whilst the scope of the thesis is primarily philosophical, it is argued that spiritually-engaged knowledge does not imply disengagement from the socio-political domain, but offers the possibility of a spiritually-engaged politics.

Prologue

> You will not experience the arbitrary nature of your beliefs by reading more scientific, analytical books, or by just thinking about them. Something or someone outside of yourself must jolt you into opening your eyes, perhaps just for a moment, to an aspect of reality that doesn't fit comfortably into your present belief structure. If this happens, hang onto it! Expand on it, explore it. Don't suppress it and deny it. Rather ask whether some of your previously held beliefs need to be opened up to make room for a richer reality.
>
> Taylor[1]

Meeting I

Strange the images which memory grasps and refuses to relinquish . . . a scene more than twenty years ago in a small Indian village during a period of drought: a woman standing on a bridge above a dried-up river bed throws a small cloth bundle off the bridge onto the hot stones below. The cloth parts, revealing a baby girl who struggles briefly, cries and dies. Many people, including myself, watch, and not knowing what to do, do nothing. Backpacker, foreigner . . . not speaking the language . . . what could I, should I, have done? From the scattered English of local onlookers, a story emerges: drought, poverty and a fifth female child in a family that cannot afford dowries Only one thing is unusual. Infanticide is generally a private matter – the child smothered or poisoned at home by her mother, grandmother or aunt – this woman made the private, public.

I have carried this tale with me for a long time, pondering and enacting various responses to it. The woman, gaunt and crying, wrapped only in a torn sari, was one of the dispossessed, living on the margins (or perhaps at 'the silent, silenced centre') of the global system, excluded by intermeshing grids of 'oppression' from the economic and political exchanges of that system. So finely are the excluding webs of 'oppression' woven that some commentators such as Spivak (1988) have even asked whether there is any possibility that this woman *can* speak and be heard?[2] Yet it always seemed to me that the woman in the scene I witnessed did 'speak'. It is true that she used no words, nor could I have understood them if she had, but by enacting her story in public space she refused silence. She posed a question that both defied and demanded response. Whichever way I turned, her question precipitated a crisis. To pretend not to have seen her is no solution. As Spivak (1988:298) says, 'to ignore the subaltern today is willy-nilly, to continue the imperialist project'.

To ignore the woman on the bridge, to leave her river-bed and wells dry, her daughter dead, leaves few external obstacles in the present path of global development through a capitalist market system. To notice her precipitates a crisis, not just in what we might do, but in who we are.

> But what would it be to be noticed? We are noticed when you realize that we are mirrors in which you can see yourselves as no other mirror shows you. When you see us without boomerang perception It is not that we are the only faithful mirrors, but I think we *are* faithful mirrors. Not that we show you as you *really* are; we just show you as one of the people you are. What we reveal to you is that you are many – something that may itself be frightening to you. But the self we reveal to you is also one that you are not eager to know for reasons that one may conjecture. (Lugones 1991:41-2)

To remember the woman on the bridge is to recall not only a visual image, but also the uncomfortable knot of contradictory emotions that was my own response. I was appalled, outraged, horrified. I was angry at both herself and myself for the silence, the failure to find the words that might call a halt to this. I wanted to rage at the barbarism, the superstition, the poverty, the ignorance that would allow me to dismiss this woman as totally Other, to blame her as alien, outside the field of my concern or attention. Perhaps it was her tears, or the touch of defiance, that kept me from such dishonesty, making both the subterfuge of difference and the high moral ground of judgement unavailable. We shared too much, and anger was countered by an empathy that forced me to acknowledge that this woman was not silent. She had grasped the only degree of freedom available to her. By killing her daughter in public she had announced her question to anyone who would listen. It was I who was silent. Though my hand reached for money to give her, and my arm reached to comfort her, I knew that such benevolence was impossible. I turned to climb back on the local bus and continued my journey, pondering the answer to her question.

In the years that followed, I tried to 'help'.[3] I became involved in the deceptively labelled practice of 'development', and my path took me back to India. Through a diversity of aid projects the woman was offered chickens to generate income; soy-fortified bulgur wheat to feed herself and her children; wells to provide water; employment planting trees to regenerate her environment; credit cooperatives to draw her into the markets of economic exchange; women's groups to raise her political consciousness . . . but she remained intransigent. Several decades of 'development' failed to touch her. When rescued from the bridge in one village, she reappeared on the bridge in another. Her question remains unanswered. She challenges the supposed benefits of 'development' juxtaposing the modern liberal dream of universal well-being with the harsher realities of the contemporary global market place. The woman on the bridge tears the veil of modernity, revealing its internal contradictions.

Like a silent Master initiating disciples into the mysteries of a spiritual tradition, this woman and her daughter initiated me into the koan of the global system. To stop speaking for, or about, the dispossessed, to call for a pause in our projects of benevolence through which we try to absorb them into our system, allows us, finally, to turn around and notice them. We then discover that 'to confront them is not to represent *(vertreten)* them but to learn to represent *(darstellen)* ourselves' (Spivak 1988:289).

Meeting II

But the woman on the bridge is not the only image that my memory refuses to relinquish.

> *Another scene in an Indian town some twenty years ago: a man dressed in rags. The dhoti and various lengths of cloth which cover him are dirty and torn, a soiled turban, loosely wound around his head reveals matted grey hair. The yogi – for such he is reputed to be – is fanning himself with an outrageously large fan made of palm leaves. He sits on a mat, in a small room stacked high with old newspapers, facing several people who have come to see him. I sit down with the others, all of whom have their eyes closed in meditation. 'Why have you come to see this beggar?' the yogi demands, staring intently at one of the meditators. Unsure whether the question is directed at me, I make no response. Eventually he looks at me, asks my name and inquires what kind of work I do. When I reply that I am a social worker he responds with another question. 'What is social work?' Without thinking, or perhaps revealing more about myself than I care to admit, I say 'Trying to help people'. The yogi roars with laughter. 'Do you mean that Jenny does not need any help?' he guffaws. Later, when I get up to go, he comes to the door too. As custom requires, I kneel to touch his feet. He stretches out his arm above my head and says : 'Father's blessing! Father is everything. Father's blessing!' The odd thing is that as he does this, I completely lose awareness of the room. I am engulfed in what I can only describe later as a feeling of bliss. After some minutes, awareness of my surroundings returns and I struggle to my feet to leave. But the extraordinary feeling of bliss does not leave. It continues for several days like a powerful field of love that reconstitutes my entire world. The next week I go to see the yogi again, but he will not allow me in.*

This tale too I have carried with me for a long time, enacting various responses to it. From his dress and surroundings the yogi could almost have been mistaken for one of the dispossessed. But, like the woman on the bridge, he refused silence. He too posed a question that both defied and demanded response. To pretend not to have seen him was no solution and in the years that followed I met him again several times.

To remember the yogi with the fan is to recall the knot of contradictory emotions that I felt at the time. My belief in my work, in my self and in the assumed superiority that unnoticed walks hand in hand with the desire to help, all crumbled, to be replaced by an intense yearning. To ignore the yogi was impossible. A Master initiating disciples into a spiritual tradition, he offered a glimpse of something so numinous that everything else faded before it.

To notice the yogi precipitated a crisis. His laughter continued what the woman's tears had begun. The centuries of colonisation and 'development' surrounded him but did not touch him. Nor was he alone. When I climbed onto the local bus to continue my journey, others like him appeared in different parts of India. Yogis and siddhas, rishis and avataras, both men and women, they sustained a world, which though strange to me, I could enter. They proffered a way of knowing that if accepted, dismantled me and my world.

> To open to another civilisational universe of discourse is to risk one's self.
> One cannot emerge unchanged!

Notes

1. Taylor (1980).
2. I refer here to Spivak's (1988) well known article 'Can the Subaltern Speak?'. My reference to 'the silent, silenced centre' also comes from this article (p. 283). Spivak, and other commentators (particularly the *Subaltern Studies* group headed by Ranajit Guha – see Spivak's note 39), use the term 'subaltern' to refer to 'men and women among the illiterate peasantry, the tribals, the lowest strata of the urban subproletariat' (ibid). The question of representation for the subaltern is a complex one because of his/her exclusion from the dominant educational, political and economic systems. Spivak rightly warns of the danger of 'the first-world intellectual' who is entrenched within these systems, 'masquerading as the absent nonrepresenter who lets the oppressed speak for themselves' (p. 292). But, we must ask, is the position of a third-world intellectual elite any more transparent? And if not, then, as I ask in chapter two, who will speak for the world's 'poor'?
3. Although Spivak critiques the benevolence involved in 'development', it was the earlier analyses of Freire (1970), Illich (1971) and, to a lesser extent, Schumacher (1973a, 1973b, 1978) which really had an impact in development circles. Some of the more forward-thinking non-government organisations (NGOs) on the basis of these analyses shifted their programs from charitable benevolence to 'conscientisation' and people-centred development. See, for example Black's (1992) account of Oxfam's first fifty years.

PART I:
LOCATING THE GLOBAL

Chapter 1

Understanding in a Global Era

> Myself when young did eagerly frequent
> Doctor and Saint, and heard great argument
> About it and about; but evermore
> Came out by the same door as in I went
> *Omar Khayyam*[1]

My meetings with the yogi and the woman on the bridge were not unusual in themselves. They are examples of cross-cultural meetings that occur more and more frequently in our world. These encounters with those perceived as 'global others' occur in the contemporary era with an intensity and frequency that make our time unique. The process of globalisation that characterises the present era – the mass movements of peoples (through migration, labour exchange and tourism) and the inter-penetration of cultures and markets unceasingly confronts us with alterity and with opportunities to meet with the Other. It is my contention that the global encounters to which we are being called, are bringing forth a new genre of knowledge. This book is an exploration of that genre, which emerges from the particularity of my own interactions with the woman on the bridge and the yogi with the fan, and reaches towards the universality of the global domain.

It is appropriate perhaps to be writing of a new genre of knowledge at a time when, on the one hand the technocrats tell us that the entire sum of human knowledge doubles every few years,[2] while on the other hand intellectuals inform us that the postmodern critique has called all knowledge into question. The contradiction between these two statements points to the crisis of knowledge occurring within the contemporary Western episteme. The extraordinary accumulation of knowledge to which the technocrats refer is largely due to the revolution in information technology. It reflects a rapid growth in information, which has left its recipients overwhelmed and bewildered, unable to direct this flood of facts in a way that impacts positively on the contemporary global crises.

But what kind of knowledge *is* needed in our globalising context? If not more facts, then what is it that we need to know in order to respond to the present crises? I propose that the kind of knowledge which we need is in fact emerging in the global context, but it is a way of knowing that is so different from our present understanding of knowledge that it is not at first easily recognised. As we have become more acutely aware of the ways in which our knowing is a socio-linguistic construction, a play of signifiers within a system of representation, the term knowledge has increasingly been placed in inverted commas. The genre of knowledge that I seek to identify here must therefore be thought of as 'knowledge', or perhaps, ~~knowledge~~ – knowledge under erasure. Heidegger employed this practice of erasure in his attempts to go beyond Being.[3] Just as ~~Being~~ for Heidegger was not a negative denial, but a pointing towards something more immediate and originary, so the ~~knowledge~~ I seek to identify involves a way of knowing, a kind of awareness, that because of its immediacy is overlooked.[4] Whilst ~~knowledge~~ may alert us to the dilemmas of signification, it does not offer an accurate representation of the way of knowing which I seek to define here. Ultimately erasure only replaces one inaccurate signifier – knowledge – with another – ~~knowledge~~. What is really at stake is not a change of signifier, but a reframing of our modern Western understanding of what it means to know.

Rather than employ the strategy of erasure (and create a word-processing nightmare!), I have chosen instead to qualify the word 'knowledge' with the description 'spiritually-engaged', which to some degree situates this way of knowing within the Western tradition. In the following chapters I argued that this genre of knowledge exceeds the reach of the rational, conceptual discursivity that we have, in the modern Western episteme, come to refer to as 'knowledge'. By contrast spiritually-engaged knowledge is concerned with a nondual mode of awareness that, since it collapses the subject/object duality inherent in all modern 'knowing', cannot really be said to 'know' anything in the modern understanding of the word. It is not therefore a 'genre of knowledge', in the sense of another particular pattern of signification that can be identified within the dualistic structure of modern knowing. Rather it is a kind of knowledge that stands outside the modern understanding of knowledge. This way of knowing has been recessive rather than absent from the Western tradition, where it is more readily identified within the domain of religion or spirituality than philosophy. It has certainly been present in other cultural traditions of knowledge, particularly those which have not suffered from the modern split between philosophy and religion.

Spiritually-engaged knowledge not only reframes our understanding of what it means to know, but it brings about a total reorientation of the ground of identification of the knowing subject. Such a claim might be considered audacious and it must certainly be approached with care. As I understand it now, it was this kind of spiritually-engaged knowledge that the yogi offered me, though I could not accept it at the time. When something unrecognisable enters our world for the first time we cannot always grasp it. We may eventually approach it via a conversational method that compares and contrasts it with that which is already known and named in our world, until at last it is integrated into our world view. When that which is proffered comes from another tradition of knowledge, this process of integration involves both anamnesis and translation. The former task of anamnesis is concerned with rediscovering, within one's own knowledge tradition, the recessive strands that resemble the new knowledge that is being offered. The latter task of translation involves finding ways of expressing this newly acquired knowledge in the idiom of one's own culture. A similar technique is adopted in the following chapters as this emerging genre of knowledge is investigated.

The fields chosen for exploration can be broadly delineated by the terms 'globalisation', 'postmodernism', 'environmentalism', 'feminism', 'psychology' and 'spirituality'. Not only did each of these seem relevant to my meetings with the woman and the yogi, but each articulates to a greater or lesser degree a submerged aspect of modernity. Elements within each of these fields, I suggest, offer more or less coherent glimpses of the (re-)emerging knowledge referred to as 'spiritually-engaged'. If the contemporary socio-political context of this (re-)emerging knowledge is defined by globalisation, its theoretical context, at least in the West, is defined by postmodernity. The remainder of this chapter introduces the genre of knowledge which I want to identify, and the next chapter explores the interdependent global and postmodern contexts that are facilitating its (re)-emergence.

Global Conversations

Extrapolating from the past, Samuel Huntington (1997) in a well-known essay suggested that the global future was likely to be characterised by a 'clash of civilizations' in which civilisational blocs, rather than nation states, would be the main players in a continuing saga of conflict and domination. Whilst this certainly maps one possible global future, there are aspects of both the globalisation process, and of postmodernity, which suggest other alternatives. In contrast to Huntington's 'clash of civilizations' other more optimistic commentators (Nandy, 1983, 1987a,b; Kavolis, 1991; Blaney and Inayatullah, 1994) have proffered the alternative of a 'conversation of cultures' which offers a path between incommensurability and conflict on the one hand, and global hegemony and homogeneity on the other. It also offers the possibility that the Western episteme might recognise and acquire, through contact with other cultural traditions, the knowledge needed both to avert its own current crisis of knowledge and to participate effectively in the solution of the contemporary global crises.

Although the global context creates many opportunities for exchange with others of the global domain, most of these meetings do not result in conversation. The historical record bears witness to the way encounters between the West[5] and other civilisations have been largely determined by an attitude of superiority which, in the socio-political arena, has translated into conquest, colonisation or conversion, but not conversation. In the colonial era, for example, female infanticide was one of a number of cultural practices used as a means of constructing the superiority of the British over the Indians in order to justify the imposition of Britain's 'civilising influence'. Mani (1990:35) ironically sums up the colonial subterfuge as: 'we came, we saw, we were horrified, and we intervened'. Female infanticide was identified as one of those practices that, dutifully assuming the 'White Man's Burden', the British needed to eradicate.[6] The 'necessity' to intervene in the 'dreadful practices' of female infanticide, *sati* and child marriage, provided legitimisation for the 'civilising mission' of British administrators, missionaries and the British public alike.

Missionary activity also played an important role in the colonial enterprise. The superiority of Western religious and theological discourse was assumed and the world of the yogis, fakirs and rishis was dismissed as a chimera, a variant of the Indian rope trick from which the unwitting populace needed 'saving'. It was several centuries before the philosophical discourses and meditative praxes which constructed that world would be 'taken seriously' by the West. There is no doubt that the various schools of Indian philosophy differed greatly from the Western analytical tradition, but this difference was interpreted as inferiority, an interpretation that was essential to maintain the momentum of 'converting the heathen' and 'expanding the empire'. Early this century, in language that today seems more associated with humour than hubris, the historian La Vallée Poussin (1917:110-112),[7] referring to Indian philosophy, wrote of 'Indian "philosophumena" concocted by ascetics . . . men exhausted by a severe diet and often stupefied by the practice of ecstasy'.[8]

Today evangelical missionary activity in the Third World has been curtailed, but contemporary interpretations of female infanticide can still be used to legitimise 'development' or 'aid' programs that inexorably extend the reach of the global market. Verhelst (1990:86-8) warns of the dangers of 'development pornography', those tragic images of the Third World that are used, not only to construct a picture of the harsh reality of poverty, but also to rationalise intervention into Third World economies in ways which maintain, rather than rupture, global patterns of power and privilege. Economic intervention generally implies cultural intervention and in situations of inequitable power relations, cultural intervention often implies cultural destruction (Verhelst 1990:84).

A conversational rather than conflictual model of the future offers the possibility of a multicultural globalism. All models are subversive one way or another,[9] and Blaney and Inayatullah (1994) consciously develop their model of 'conversation' as a way of countering the dominant view of both past and future as narratives of conflict. Much has already been written about dialogue and the possibility of a dialogic future.[10] It is not my intention to adopt an adversarial stance towards this dialogic approach, nor to split hairs over the difference between 'dialogue' and 'conversation', although such a distinction can be made.[11] What is being explored here is an aspect that has been underemphasised in dialogic approaches. It is concerned with a praxis, or a kind of knowledge, that must be present if a meeting is to evolve into conversation rather than conflict. This praxis is identified as spiritually-engaged knowledge.

Blaney and Inayatullah (1994) relate the possibility of conversation to a spectrum of otherness, a range of different self/other constructions, some of which enable us to meet the other in ways that facilitate conversation, some of which so inhibit conversation that the outcome is conflict. How must the other be encountered in order to enter into conversation? In the following chapters I try to answer this question, suggesting that the genre of knowledge needed represents a submerged way of knowing within the modern episteme. Unlike the dominant form of modern knowledge, this way of knowing exceeds both rationality and discursivity. Since it is concerned with the relation between self and other this knowledge is ethically based, but since it involves re-negotiating the self/other boundary it is also transformative, concerned with re-presenting both self and other.

In conversation the other becomes more than a mirror passively reflecting us to ourselves. The process of conversation involves finding and engaging, not only with the external other, but also with the other within oneself. In this way the other – both internal and external – becomes an ally in a process of critical self and cultural reflection (Blaney and Inayatullah, 1994:31). Within both the personal and the cultural frames of reference, conversation encourages each participant to deepen their understanding of their own distinctiveness by engaging, from their unique position, with the distinctiveness of the other (Kavolis, 1991:130). On the personal level we discover the other within, while on the civilisation level we are drawn into a 'process of "mutual criticism" that allows each civilisation to rediscover and reinvigorate its own vision, including the recovery of lost or submerged knowledges' (Blaney and Inayatullah, 1994:41).

In the contemporary global context where the hegemony of Western modernity is being challenged, conversations between submerged Western knowledges and strands of other cultural traditions have the potential to create alliances by establishing 'a "common horizon" for thought and action' (Blaney and Inayatullah, 1994:37). By way of example, Nandy (1983:49;51) offers Gandhi's capacity, during the Indian struggle for independence, to draw together recessive elements of Christianity with elements of Hinduism and Buddhism in a successful common horizon for ethical, non-violent action. By engaging these apparently disparate discourses in conversation, Gandhi reframed the struggle for independence within ethical and spiritual horizons that could be translated as effectively into the idiom of the British colonisers, or of the Hindu masses.[12]

This work attempts to draw together elements of the secular Western discourses of globalisation, postmodernism (particularly postmodern ethics), psychology, feminism, and environmentalism, with spirituality. In so doing I seek to express in Western idiom a more universal genre of knowledge, which might offer a common horizon for ethical action within the contemporary global domain. My earlier drafts were syncretic, based on the desire to somehow amalgamate the discourses of feminism, environmentalism, and alternative development in order to weave a new conceptual metanarrative in response to the woman on the bridge. Karen Warren has called this metanarrative that arises from the interconnections between all systems of oppression 'transformative feminism' (Warren, 1987:18-20), and in some ways my project here might have come under that banner, for my concern with the woman on the bridge certainly pointed to an interconnected system of oppressions that operated both locally and globally.

But it was my conversation with the yogi that in the end proved more transformative, and which demanded inclusion. That conversation pointed beyond analyses of domination and oppression, and beyond the material needs of the woman on the bridge, however urgent. It demanded that all traces of superiority be dropped, moral or otherwise, and a process of *mutual* critique be entered by acknowledging that the universe of Indian culture may contain some corrective, some knowledge that the secular Western episteme badly needs.

And so spirituality became a participant in the process, pointing towards a kind of knowledge that was submerged or recessive within the contemporary Western episteme. My exploration of the proposed genre of spiritually-engaged knowledge is not intended to be an exercise in syncretism. It is not argued that each of the discourses considered articulates different aspects of spiritually-engaged knowledge which can somehow be brought together to form a transcultural, or universal, whole. Rather, the identification of a contemporary idiom for spiritually-engaged knowledge is sought, by pointing out that this kind of knowledge *already* plays, to a greater or lesser extent, within each of the discursive universes with which I engage. Sometimes one aspect, sometimes another will be represented, but it is present as a recessive strand in the contemporary Western discourses of postmodernism, environmentalism, feminism, and psychology, just as it is present as a dominant strand in the discourses of traditional spirituality.

Bringing together these different discursive universes in a cross-cultural, global context that seeks to identify a more universal form of knowledge is a controversial enterprise. The constructivist understanding of knowledge[13] has created an intellectual climate in which cross-cultural enterprises are problematic, and universal metanarratives are highly suspect. Though current trends favour particularity and narrativity, the tension between universal, transcultural knowledge and particular cultural expressions of knowledge remains a significant feature of both globalisation and postmodern theory. Some, though by no means all, of this tension can be relieved by carefully distinguishing between two different meanings of 'universal' which are often confused. Sharma (1993a:60) clarifies this distinction with a useful example: 'The term universal language may either mean that language is a universal phenomenon or that one language, say English, is spoken by people all over the world.' The former usage identifies a transcendent, or metalevel, species-specific human praxis which is transcultural and transhistorical, and which finds various and diverse expression in a multiplicity of particular, local, historical forms. I refer to this usage as universality. The latter usage involves the absolutisation of a particular, in which the local praxis of a particular group so extends its reach as to be considered a 'universal' norm or ideal. This usage I refer to as universalism.

It is true that at first glance the category of universality, which I apply to spiritually-engaged knowledge, runs counter to the contemporary understanding that all knowledge is culturally mediated. But what I am seeking is a transcultural metalevel of praxis that does not obliterate particularity or diversity, but which recognises that any universal praxis is embodied, or lived out, through a diversity of particular socio-cultural systems. The deconstructive postmodern insight that all propositional knowledge is constructed by the play of signifiers within a socio-linguistic system of signs is itself (paradoxically) an example of a metalevel of knowledge that seeks to escape cultural specificity by grounding itself in the universal human praxis of signification and knowledge-making.

As Sharma's linguistic example makes clear, language (or signification) can be thought of as a transcultural human praxis. The question is, whether or not we can validly begin to build up a universal, human discourse based on species-specific universals which extend from empirical or biological universals – such as our human need for water and food (Spretnak, 1991:17[14]) – through a range of psycho-physiological universals – such as our human cognitive capacities for speech, rational thought, emotion or self-reflexive consciousness (Lonergan, 1972; Gellner, 1992; Webb, 1988,1993) – to transpersonal psycho-social universals – such as ethical values (Kung, 1988, 1991; and Kuschel, 1993) or contemplative capacities (Wilber, 1985, 1990; 1997a; Forman, 1990, 1993, 1996). Whilst the Cartesian mind-body split of the secular modern Western view would probably lead us to agreement on the universality of certain human physiological praxes, it would have us view the psycho-physiological and psycho-social domains with increasing suspicion in the search for transcendent universals. This book is situated in the field of suspicion created by the tension between the universal and the particular.

Exploring a Global Idiom

The broad discursive fields used to translate spiritually-engaged knowledge into the contemporary Western idiom have above been delineated. They are globalisation, postmodernism, feminism, environmentalism, psychology and spirituality. It is helpful to define them in more detail by explaining my use of the terms 'feminism', 'environmentalism', 'psychology' and 'spirituality'.

Globalisation and postmodernism are explored in more detail in the next chapter.

Feminism and environmentalism are both fields of discourse that in the last few decades have gained not only popular, but academic, recognition. Both are clusters of heterogeneous discourses that offer critiques of modernity from different perspectives – environmentalism deconstructs the culture/nature dualism, and feminism the male/female dualism. As well as offering critiques of the governing forms of identity and knowledge, there are discursive streams within both feminism and environmentalism that offer alternative constructions of identity and knowledge. The relational self of certain streams of feminism, and the ecological self of the deep ecological streams of environmentalism, provide examples of alternate identity constructs that challenge the bounded, masculine self that governs modernity. Chapters three and four consider in more detail the alternative forms of knowledge proposed in environmentalism and feminism.

It is important to note here that the discourses of feminism and environmentalism are not simply new discourses formulated around different, previously unnoticed, axes of analysis articulated by the dominant epistemic community. They are, I suggest, discourses of the Other emerging from different sites of representation within previously silenced communities of knowers that are themselves heterogeneous.[15] Conversation between these discourses offers the possibility of alliances between previously unrelated communities of knowers, as ecofeminism so clearly demonstrates. Being concerned with the preservation of alterity and diversity they stand in opposition to modernity's 'Empire of the Selfsame' (Cixous and Clement cited in Sampson 1993:4) that is enshrined globally by the dominant Western nations. The heterogeneous discourses of feminism and environmentalism are not the only discourses that stand in opposition to the hegemonic monologue of modernity, but as Brennan (1993a:vii) (with particular reference to feminism) points out:

> Currently, there are no theoretical means, except for fine sentiments and good will, that enable feminism to ally itself with other social movements that oppose the power networks that sustain the white, masculine universal subject.

I suggest that the spiritually-engaged knowledge identified in this work offers a theoretical means of allying social movements that oppose the individualistic, independent, contained subject of Western modernity.[16] It is, however, a means that allies, not by placing theoretical means in opposition to 'fine sentiments and good will', but by theorising those 'fine sentiments' themselves, and by analysing the praxes involved in deciding to will the good of the Other.

Clearly this impinges on the domain of psychology. With the burgeoning of trans-disciplinary discourse there are now quite well recognised schools of both feminist and environmental psychology and much of the psychological discourse with which I engage later can be subsumed under these two headings. There is, however, a third school of psychological discourse – transpersonal psychology – with which I engage. Transpersonal psychology has three 'roots': (i) humanistic psychology's concern with 'peak experiences';[17] (ii) the cross-cultural exchange, particularly with Asian spiritual traditions that emphasise meditative practices; and (iii) the experiments and experiences with mind-expanding drugs.

Psychology's role within the modern universe of discourse has always carried a hint of subversion as its notions of the subconscious and unconscious have contributed to undermining the modern myth of the rational, individual self. With transpersonal psychology the focus shifts to an explicit concern with experiences and forms of identity that exceed the boundaries of the individual self 'to encompass wider aspects of humankind, life, *psyche*, and cosmos' (Walsh and Vaughan, 1993a:3). Since these transpersonal experiences have often (though not exclusively) been connected with spirituality, transpersonal psychology inhabits the borderlands between religion, spirituality and psychology. As such, it offers a means of constructing 'spiritual' experience in the discourse of psychology, rather than in the discourse of religion, thus freeing spirituality from much of its religio-cultural trappings.

Thus far I have referred to 'spiritual' and 'spiritually-engaged knowledge' without offering any definition of the referent 'spirituality'. This book distinguishes spirituality from religion, although what is identified as 'spirituality' is a component of all extant religious traditions. Wilber (1981, 1983, 1997a, 1997b) argues that a religious tradition performs at least two distinct functions. Firstly, 'it acts as a way of creating *meaning* for the separate self . . . it consoles the self, fortifies the self, defends the self, promotes the self' (Wilber, 1997b:24). Secondly, albeit sometimes for only a small minority, a religious tradition serves 'the function of radical transformation and liberation. This function of religion does not fortify the separate self, but utterly shatters it [offering] not a conventional bolstering of consciousness but a radical transmutation and transformation at the deepest seat of consciousness itself' (Wilber, 1997b:24). The former function Wilber refers to as 'translation' – 'the self is simply given a new way to think or feel about reality . . . a new belief – perhaps holistic instead of atomistic'. The latter function Wilber terms 'transformation' – 'the very process of translation is itself challenged . . . the self itself is inquired into . . . and . . . throttled to death' (Wilber, 1997b:24-5). It is the transformative religious function that I refer to in this work as 'spirituality'.

This 'spirituality' is certainly concerned with 'spirit', but not spirit as opposed to matter, rather 'spirit' in Kovel's (1991:1) sense of the word as '*what happens to us as the boundaries of the self give way*'. Spirituality can thus be defined as the deconstruction of the self/other dualism. Spirituality therefore encompasses both feminism and environmentalism, since both gender and species constitute significant aspects of our self-construction. Spirituality, understood in this way, can also be read as a critique of modernity, and particularly of the individualistic, bounded identity construct that is the dominant form of self within the modern universe of discourse.

This understanding of spirituality brings into view a continuity that exists between postmodernity and modernity. Since it is rendered no less unspeakable by the rationality of modernity than by the discursivity of postmodernity, spirituality is constructed as the Other of *both* modern and postmodern knowledge. The sacred/secular boundary established to divide the modern era from the earlier traditional era remains for the most part unbreached in the contemporary postmodern period. Spirituality lies outside both the modern and postmodern systems of knowledge. Edward Said (1979) critically noted the way that spirituality was projected, justifiably or otherwise, outside the Western episteme onto 'the East', the yogi, the Oriental Other. By identifying common elements in feminism, environmentalism, postmodern ethics and spirituality I hope to bring some of these projections home to the Western episteme and deconstruct the sacred/secular boundary that has characterised both modernity and postmodernity.

What is referred to in this work as 'spirituality', therefore, is a transformative way of both being and knowing, whose working definition therefore has two components, one relating to identity or ontology, and the other to epistemology. The former, as already mentioned, is taken from Kovel (1991:1) who suggests that spirituality is 'what happens to us as the boundaries of the self give way'. In this sense, spirituality is concerned with the deconstruction of the bounded, individual, human identity, and with undoing the self/other divide. Much has been made in feminism, environmentalism and postmodernism of the hierarchically paired dualisms that define the value structure of modernity.[18] Spiritual discourses, particularly in Eastern traditions, have also deconstructed these dualisms. For example, Ramana Maharshi, one of the foremost practitioners of the *advaitic* tradition of Hinduism, argued that the founding dualism which supports the entire hierarchy of knowledge, is the self/other dualism.[19]

Concern with the relationship between self and other provides fertile ground for conversation between the discourses of spirituality, psychology, feminism, environmentalism, globalisation and postmodernity.[20] But it also provides the key to understanding the ethical nature of spiritually-engaged knowledge. Wyschogrod (1990:xv) argues that 'ethics is the sphere of transactions between "self" and "Other"', and, since this emerging spiritually-engaged knowledge is concerned with revisioning the self/other dualism, it also carries significant ethical implications. The ethical dimension of spiritually-engaged knowledge is considered in detail in chapter three.

The second component of my definition of spirituality is epistemological. Philippa Berry (1992:5) suggests that there is emerging in our contemporary era:

a new understanding of spirit, not as the opposite term of a binary couple, but rather as facilitating a wholly new mode of awareness, which not only invites the thinker to abandon their residual attachment to dualistic thinking, but also offers a potent challenge to their desire for subjective mastery and knowledge.

Spirituality on this account is concerned with a mode of awareness, though I would not describe it as 'new', which challenges the dualism and mastery that lie at the heart of modernity. The epistemological strategy associated with spiritually-engaged knowledge is later explored and I suggest that it is best described as 'attentiveness' or 'attentive love'. Although this falls within the domain of philosophy, it is less concerned with philosophy's traditional love of wisdom, than with giving theoretical articulation to the wisdom and universality of attentive love. It seems that what is most needed in the contemporary global domain is not more rational discursive knowledge, of which we already suffer a surfeit, but an understanding of an older wisdom. Although I have already described the aim of this book as the identification of an emerging genre of spiritually-engaged knowledge, it might alternatively be described as an attempt to articulate a philosophy of attentive love.

Methodological Issues

I have already intimated in broad strokes the method which I adopt. I have suggested that it is a 'conversational' method that garners different examples of post-rational, post-discursive knowledge from fields as diverse as postmodernism, feminism, environmentalism, psychology, and spirituality. I do not engage in a critique of these examples, but direct the focus of my analysis towards identifying the common elements between them in order to define an emerging genre of knowledge which I refer to as 'spiritually-engaged'. There is no suggestion that these alternative ways of knowing are identical, but by holding in tension their similarities and differences I argue that it is possible to identify the family resemblance expected of a genre.

This conversational method can be described in more academic language as genre analysis. In describing their methodology for identifying a genre of knowledge, McCann and Strain (1985) advocate the use of two distinct approaches: logic of inquiry and genre analysis. These can be summed up by the two questions: Why is this genre emerging? and What is the genre? (McCann and Strain, 1985:14).[21] The logic of inquiry approach explores the conditions that make the emergence of the genre possible. This approach acknowledges the contextuality and historicity of the genre, and seeks to relate both the emergence and purpose of the genre to its socio-historical context. The second approach of genre analysis, as described by McCann and Strain (1985:12), 'proceeds by drawing inductively a composite picture of the underlying structure of a given form of discourse from an analysis of a wealth of fragmentary realizations'. As in conversation, these diverse fragments are held in tension by the common thread of the emerging genre.

Chapter two follows the logic of inquiry approach, exploring both globalisation and postmodernism which constitute the inter-related contexts of the emerging genre. In the first section of the chapter I explore the processes of globalisation in order to identify those factors which are contributing to the (re)-emergence of a spiritually-engaged genre of knowledge. I utilise Robertson's (1985 *et al*; 1989a,b; 1990a,b; 1992) culturally-oriented model of globalisation theory as a means of describing the contemporary global context, and try within that context to identify the significance of the spiritually-engaged genre, including its implications for identity and discourse formation. In the later part of chapter two, I discuss the postmodern context as it relates to the emergence of submerged knowledges. Since postmodernity has often been read as standing in opposition to spirituality I re-examine the relationship between postmodernism and spirituality demonstrating how postmodernity can be interpreted as providing a context favourable to the emergence of spiritually-engaged knowledge.

Chapters three, four and five are directed towards genre analysis and as such, are concerned with answering the question: 'What is this genre?'. In these chapters I try to identify the 'rules' of the genre. Lyotard (1988:xii) suggested that a genre is not a signification of a new orthodoxy, but a new set of 'rules for linking together heterogeneous phrases, rules that are proper for attaining certain goals'. In these chapters I draw fragments from a variety of sources and compare the ways in which they demonstrate the characteristic processes or rules of the genre I wish to identify. In most cases I do not offer a critique of these fragments, but, following the method of McCann and Strain (1985), use them simply as a means for identifying the defining features of the genre.

As might be expected with this methodology, chapters three, four and five do not present a linear progression through a rational argument. The relationship of these chapters one to another is more like the relationship between the parts of a jigsaw puzzle as they are fitted together in non-linear fashion to constitute a complete picture. Since the encounter with the woman on the bridge seemed to demand an ethical response, I begin the task of genre analysis by focusing, in chapter three, on postmodern ethics. I consider the meeting with the Other as the starting point of spiritually-engaged knowledge, and explore an 'ethic of meeting', called forth through encounter with the Other. The ethical imperatives involved in this ethic of meeting are not universal moral laws that dictate how everyone must behave, but arise out of empirical, ethical experiences to which everyone has access. The ethical encounter with the Other is thus described by a radical empiricism that involves a turning towards the Other.

Whilst this radical empiricism describes the encounter with the Other, in chapter four, I explore the epistemological strategy associated with that encounter. In chapter three, attention or attentive love emerges as the necessary means for genuine encounter with the Other. In chapter four, I explore attentive love, particularly as it has been developed in feminist thought. This chapter is concerned with understanding attentive love as a virtue-based, epistemological strategy associated with a particular mode of awareness, and I explore its application in a diversity of fields through the work of women commentators.

In chapter five, I follow attentive love into the domain of spirituality where it can be considered to find its fullest expression in a form of nondual awareness which I suggest can be found across religious traditions. The implications of this nondual awareness deserve serious consideration in the light of the postmodern critique of knowledge. These implications challenge the materialist bias of Western knowledge by pointing towards the primacy of consciousness. The result however is not an ethereal other-worldly spirituality but a re-sacralisation of the world that has much to offer us in the contemporary global context.

In chapter six, I retrace the path I have taken, briefly considering the application of spiritually-engaged knowledge, and its distinctive epistemology of attentive love, to the domain of politics. I explore the possibilities of a spiritually-engaged politics. I argue for both a politics of conscience and a politics of consciousness, which find expression in the new social and religious movements that have emerged in the global domain. I then explore the possibilities of a global civil community, and consider a form of identity, the citizen sadhak, that might constitute such a community.

Notes

1. Quatrain 27 from *The Rubaiyat of Omar Khayyam*, translated by Edward Fitzgerald, edited G. Maine (1965), Collins, London.
2. This statement was made by Al Gore at the World Economic Forum in Davos (reported in Melbourne newspaper, *The Age*, 6.2.1999, p. 22).
3. See Heidegger (1958).
4. Spivak's (1976:xiii-xix) *Translator's Preface* in Derrida's *Of Grammatology* offers an explanation of this practice of writing 'under erasure'. She makes a distinction between Heidegger's use of the practice and Derrida's, which I do not wish to debate here (p. xvii). I do, however, want to make use of Derrida's reasons for employing erasure and, although I do not employ the strategy of writing under erasure, apply them to my alternative strategy of describing this way of knowing as 'spiritually-engaged'. Like Derrida's use of erasure, this description is intended to suggest that in order to 'grasp' this way of knowing, it is necessary to 'change certain habits of mind'. The description 'spiritually-engaged' is intended to provide a continual reminder that 'the authority of the text is provisional' and that 'we must learn to use and erase our language at the same time' (p. xviii).
5. Although I use terms such as 'the West', 'the modern West', 'the Western episteme', or 'modern Western discourse', it is not my intention to suggest that there is one 'integrated Western culture' or a 'fixed Western identity' (Asad, 1993:18) that characterises all modern or Western persons. I do, however, believe that some

notion of 'the West' is useful to describe a particular pattern of identity construction and a distinctive cultural flow. These might be characterised respectively: as 'a singular collective identity that defines itself in terms of a unique historicity in contrast to all others' (Asad, 1993:19); and as a 'certain set of assumptions about the world and ... knowledge of the world' that arises from that unique historicity that has 'become deeply rooted in the consciousness of modern human beings ... decisively [shaping] our expectations, our actions, and our experience ... [and] constituting our real modern collective unconscious' (Sloan, 1994:42-3). As Asad (1993:18) argues:

> the 'West' is not a mere Hegelian myth, not a mere representation ready to be unmasked by a handful of talented critics. For good or ill, it informs innumerable intentions, practices, and discourses in systematic ways

There is, therefore, both utility and meaning in the referent 'West'. It signifies a particular cultural flow, described by Asad (1993:19) as 'a historicity that shifts from place to place – Greece, Rome, Latin Christendom, the Americas – until it embraces the world'. Thus some theorists in the latter part of the twentieth century conflate Westernisation and modernisation and attempt to universalise, both under the rubric of development and progress. I discuss the validity of this approach in the next chapter.

I also make use, later in this work, of the other term in the 'East/West' dualism. When referring to 'the East' and its variants, I am again not trying to suggest an integrated Eastern or Asian cultural bloc. Indeed, since 'the East' is generally used to refer to the grouping of both Sino- and Indo-traditional cultures, this would be even less correct than the homogeneity implied by the term 'West'. I am, however, suggesting that the Eastern or Asian traditions stand in marked contrast to those of the West since they trace historicities that began in China or the Indian sub-continent and which have similarly shifted from place to place until experiencing a global diaspora in the present day.

6. In order to grasp the subterfuge involved in the British position, it is important to note that during the same period infanticide was common in England.
7. Poussin was primarily interested in Indian Buddhism rather than Hinduism, but he himself does not seem to discriminate between the two in this passage.
8. Poussin continued, arguing that 'Indians do not make a clear distinction between facts and ideas, between ideas and words; they have never clearly recognised the principle of contradiction'. It is interesting just how much these distinctions between 'facts and ideas' and between 'ideas and words' have been called into question by the linguistic turn of postmodern philosophy.
9. Posing as descriptive, or 'neutral', models function normatively to shape societies and the people who constitute them. When a model is widely accepted it becomes a form of control, a way of disciplining people's understanding, perceptions and expectations. The formulation of a model is therefore never simply a theoretical exercise but an attempt to mould the future.
10. Jurgen Habermas is probably the best known proponent of dialogic or discourse ethics (see his *Moral Consciousness and Communicative Action*, 1990). Benhabib and Dallmayr (1990) provide an overview of 'the communicative ethics controversy' in their book of the same name. Sampson (1993) provides an excellent account of the implications of a dialogic approach for the construction of the self.
11. Both in its everyday use and in its theoretical elaboration, 'dialogue' seems to imply a process that is more rational, serious and goal-oriented than 'conversation'. Dialogue is conducted by heads of government and delegates at conferences, people in authority who wish to negotiate their differences. Conversation is the

quotidian art of the 'average person'. It occurs between friends and acquaintances who, while regarding each other as equals, enjoy the differences that play between them. This element of playfulness in conversation sits well within the postmodern context. Conversations do not necessarily prove hypotheses or reach conclusions. Rather, they map a changing panorama of similarity and difference, holding the two in balance, in order to maintain sufficient similarity to sustain the conversation.

12. Gandhi's discourse was not as effectively translated into the idiom of Islam, as evidenced by the historical outcome of partition. However, from the sapiential perspective (which I introduce in chapter five) it can be argued that Hinduism and Islam do, in fact, share a universal, sapiential knowledge that can be articulated by those familiar with the esoteric aspects of both traditions.

13. This constructivist viewpoint found classical expression with Berger and Luckmann's 1967 publication *The Social Construction of Knowledge* but is, of course, the result of many influences, amongst which might be considered: Wittgenstein (1953) and Quine (1969) in philosophy; Geertz (1983) and Sperber (1985) in anthropology; Kuhn (1970) and Feyerabend (1974) in philosophy of science; Code (1987, 1991) and Harding (1986, 1987, 1991, 1993) in feminist thought; the pervasive influence of Derrida in postmodern theory, see de Man (1979). In chapter five I explore some of the shortcomings of the constructivist thesis.

14. I refer here to an example that Spretnak (1991) uses in her argument. In fact, Spretnak's book offers critiques of deconstructive postmodernism from several perspectives, appendices A and B are particularly worth noting.

15. The ambiguity of environmentalism on this point needs to be acknowledged as it always involves the double hermeneutic of a particular group of people speaking on behalf of the Other as 'nature' or as disappearing/exploited species. Authenticity in the case of environmental discourse therefore presents a particularly knotty problem, which I explore in chapter three.

16. The modern subject is generally referred to as masculine but this needs to be understood in the sense that the masculine construction of subject can map onto either a male or female person. This is discussed further in chapter four. It should also be noted that from the perspective that I am adopting here, the governing forms of both masculinity and femininity are regarded as deficient if not pathological.

17. The work of Maslow was particularly important in this. See, for example, Maslow (1968).

18. See Plumwood (1993) for an excellent explanation.

19. See Godman (1985), particularly chapter 4, pp. 47-69. Sri Ramana's thesis was that the separate self was constructed by thoughts which, taken together, might be referred to collectively as the 'I-thought'. This I-thought then provides the point of reference which makes possible the objectivication of the 'external world'. By dissolving, or deconstructing, (the nexus of thoughts which together constitute) the I-thought, that reference point is dissolved and the process of objectivication is undone.

20. The difficulty of naming! There are, of course, postmodern feminisms, environmentalisms and (though I suggest they are still being formulated) postmodern spiritualities. I am using the term 'postmodern' here to indicate a theoretical body of work formulated by theorists such as Derrida, Lyotard and Foucault, which operates as a general critique of the discursive nature of modern knowledge. It functions primarily as a deconstructive critique and as such is useful to those transdisciplinary formations that seek to go beyond critique and deconstruction to tackle the more demanding task of reconstruction. My understanding of the term 'postmodern' is discussed in more detail in chapter two.

21. See Todorov (1975) in connection with these issues.

PART II:
LOGIC OF INQUIRY

Chapter 2

Contemporary Contexts

> Since the late 1960s, another image of 'one world' has edged its way into contemporary consciousness – the globe in its physical finiteness. We share in 'humanity', we are connected by the 'world market', but we are condemned to one destiny because we are inhabitants of one planet. This is the message conveyed by the first photograph of the 'one world', taken from outer space, which has irresistibly emerged as the icon of our age. We all depend on the one biosphere for sustaining our lives. What used to be conceived of as a historical endeavour – to accomplish the unity of mankind – now reveals itself as a menacing fate.
>
> *Sachs*[1]

Why is this genre of spiritually-engaged knowledge emerging in the contemporary context? Since it was the global context of environmental destruction and social injustice that first provided a way of framing the image of the woman on the bridge, let us begin with a consideration of this global domain. Within the broader context defined by the global horizon, the governing forms of both knowledge and identity are relativised. The common horizon of the global context places limits on this relativism and thus challenges us to move beyond relativism to reflexivity, and beyond reflexivity to transformation of our ways of knowing and being within the global domain.

There are, needless to say, different schools of thought within the broad framework of globalisation theory. Beyer (1994:14-44) provides a useful summary, distinguishing four approaches to globalisation as exemplified in the work of four of the principal globalisation theorists. He suggests that these variants are 'distinct but mutually reinforcing directions for conceiving global order, based on analyses of a global economy, a global polity, a global culture, and a global society' (Beyer, 1994:15). These four approaches to the global order are exemplified by the work of Immanuel Wallerstein, John Meyer, Roland Robertson and Niklas Luhmann respectively.[2] This chapter draws most heavily on the work of Robertson, adopting his cultural orientation to globalisation.

In the popular media, the term 'globalisation' has unfortunately become associated with the creation of unregulated global markets.[3] Whilst transnational corporations and national governments seem intent on moving towards this economic goal, some commentators, and it would seem many 'ordinary' citizens, are concerned about this push towards economic deregulation, viewing it as Sach's 'menacing fate'.[4] Whilst I agree that the move to unregulated trade seems likely to exacerbate rather than abate the global problems of environmental destruction and inordinate social inequity, I do not think that this particular form of economic rationalism is the only possible global economic system, nor do I consider that it exhausts the opportunities that globalisation offers. Indeed, as I argue below, unregulated global markets actually work against globalisation, understood as an increasing awareness of the world as a whole, by establishing two worlds, the world of those who participate in the global market, and the world of those who are marginalised and excluded from it.

I suggest, however, that it is by exploring the positive potential of globalisation that we may be able to muster the resources, both intellectual and political, to challenge the present form of global corporate economics and to establish a more equitable and environmentally benign global community. Perhaps the greatest resource available to us in this project is the combined cultural wealth of humanity. If only the west could learn to enter into conversation with other cultures and civilisations, there is at present an extraordinary opportunity to share the intellectual wealth of diverse cultures to, as it were, sift through the wisdom of ages in order to find the kind of alternative knowledge that is needed today. It is for this reason that I have concentrated on Robertson's account of globalisation, because he engages, not only with the cultural, but also with the religious aspects of the process (though these are often deeply intertwined).

I will now explore some different ways of knowing which are emerging in the global context, and which move towards one world, accompanied by a return of the sacred and by increased interest in religion and spirituality. I then consider postmodernism as the other significant aspect of the contemporary context which, from the point of view of those who are emerging from modernity, creates the conditions for spiritually-engaged knowledge. Unlike globalisation theory, postmodern theory is concerned with the subjective pole of knowledge. It breaks with the materialist Western tradition of objective knowledge, and offers the chance of a new engagement with Asian traditions[5] – new possibilities for conversation with the yogi.

Postmodern theory and globalisation theory exist in tension with each other. The postmodern critique relativises discursive theoretical constructs and, from the postmodern perspective, we must place globalisation theory in inverted commas as a socio-linguistic construction, a play of signifiers within a particular episteme. From the perspective of globalisation theory however, it is postmodernism that is relativised in the global domain, where it is revealed as a Western cultural construct. In this chapter it is not my intention to tackle, let alone answer, the thorny question of whether postmodernism's deconstruction of globalisation theory has precedence over globalisation's relativisation of postmodern theory. What I do want to show is that *both* globalisation theory and postmodern theory lead initially to the relativisation of all discursive knowledge, but, at their best, they also lead out of this relativism, via reflexivity, towards a different kind of knowing which I have called 'spiritually-engaged'. It is my contention that an alternative universe of spiritually-engaged discourse, which is both postmodern and appropriate to the global domain, is beginning to emerge from the conversations that globalisation and postmodernity have made possible.

The Global Context

Globalisation Theory

The global domain, it can be argued, increasingly constitutes the essential and shared horizon for all human knowledge. If this is so then we need to have some understanding of this global context, and of what Garrett (1992:299) refers to as the 'dynamics of the emerging global order', in order to be sensitive to the vectors of change operating on our ways of knowing. In the contemporary world, through factors such as the increasing integration of global economic markets, the global network of communications, the availability of rapid international travel and the multiplication of transnational companies and international agencies, we are experiencing a compression of the world system that affects not just our lifestyles, but also the terms in which we understand ourselves. This process of globalisation challenges the governing forms of identity and knowledge that have both created, and been created by, the conditions of modernity. It simultaneously calls forth new ways of knowing and being more appropriate to the contemporary global situation.

Modernisation theory's promise of universal development and well-being stands in stark contrast to the contemporary reality of environmental destruction, and intra- and inter-national inequities that divide the globe's human population so dramatically into rich and poor.[6] This global bifurcation is so pronounced that some commentators[7] suggest 'global apartheid' as the most appropriate analogy for the widening gulf between the privileged market participants and the marginalised majority. These human injustices exist side-by-side with unprecedented destruction of the environment. According to Thomas Berry (1992:4), 'we' (humanity) simply do not grasp 'the order of magnitude of our situation'.

> No other people at any time were dealing with the survival of the planet's geological structures, major biosystems, or chemical constitution to have the whole planet at stake, and to have the power to explode it and literally demolish it – and to be actually in the process of doing that – is something that no one faced in former centuries.

These stresses occurring at the human/global interface constitute one of the unique features of our times, drawing, for the first time, all human discourse into a common domain. The ecological and equity issues that the global context bring into view confront us with the necessity of grounding a transcultural discourse in the physical limitations of humanity's shared social and ecological reality.

Some commentators, such as Kothari (1993:121), interpret the current trend as 'an unprecedented consolidation of the imperial era, of world capitalism and techno-hegemony'. Others, such as Laclau and Mouffe (1985) or Carroll (1992), are more optimistic, suggesting that the new social movements such as feminism and environmentalism can play a significant role in articulating a non-hegemonic global future. Still other theorists, such as Wallerstein (1995:18), suggest that the present inequitable and unjust world system is in a state of 'terminal crisis', a 'point of bifurcation' from which it is 'intrinsically impossible to predict the outcome'. What does seem certain however is that the conceptual frameworks of the Cold War era have crumbled and the fluidity and uncertainties within the global domain demand new conceptual frameworks for understanding our global predicament (Tarock, 1995:5; Wallerstein, 1995:19).

Increasingly, globalisation is seen as the theory, or metatheory, that displaces modernisation, in explaining the current state of the global-human condition. Contrary to a common misperception, globalisation theory is not essentially concerned with world government, but with understanding the '*basic and shifting terms* of the contemporary world order' (Robertson, 1990a:22). Globalisation theory suggests that we are currently caught up in an intensification of a process which involves 'both ... the compression of the world and the intensification of consciousness of the world as a whole' (Robertson, 1992:8). Under conditions of globalisation we experience 'a coalescence of varied transnational processes and domestic structures, allowing the economy, politics, culture and ideology of one country to penetrate another' (Mittelman, 1994:428). This interpenetration of cultures, which characterises our contemporary world, simultaneously defines an inescapable interdependence. As Grewal and Kaplan (1994:13) suggest: 'transnational linkages influence every level of existence'. This web of transnational social, economic and ecological interdependence generates its own demands for transnational cultural formation, for it continually confronts the West with the others with whom it shares the globe.

Globalisation theory draws a distinction between the process of globalisation and the global spread of modernity and capitalism as a process of Western expansion. Although our current form of globalisation is the *result* of the global spread of modernity as the dominant form of the social, it is also distinct from it. According to Beyer (1994:8) 'globalization *begins* in all parts of the globe except the West as an exogenous process, meaning that it would not have happened had it not first occurred in the West. In this sense, globalization *is* Western imperialism', and there have been numerous historical examples, from the civilising mission of the British Empire, to the liberal theories of development, in which the West has attempted to universalise its own culture. But as Beyer (1994:9) continues:

> Globalization, however, is more than the spread of one historically existing culture at the expense of all others. It is also the creation of a new global culture with its attendant social structures, one which increasingly becomes the broader social context of *all* particular cultures in the world, including those of the West. The spread of the global social reality is therefore quite as much at the 'expense' of the latter as it is of non-Western cultures. Globalization theories cannot describe contemporary global society as simply the extension of a particular society and its culture (that is, as one part becoming the whole) because these also change dramatically in the process. Equally critically, however, the emergent 'global culture' cannot itself become a new overarching particularism because it would then be subject to the same relativization as its predecessors.

Despite the ubiquity of Coca Cola, Nike and McDonalds, globalisation theory is not about the emergence of one homogeneous global culture. It is about 'the globalisation of culture', where culture is taken in the broad sense as a set of processes that is influenced by 'the exchange and flow of goods, people, information, knowledge and images which give rise to communication processes' (Featherstone, 1990:1). Globalisation theory suggests that in the present world system, these flows are best understood as occurring, not only within and between states, but also within a larger transnational global domain, or system, that is more than the sum of inter-state (or inter-national) interactions. Since 'it takes as its primary unit of social analysis the entire globe' (Beyer, 1994:14), globalisation theory contextualises and relativises sub-global regional, cultural, and national units with respect to this more encompassing global whole.

In globalisation theory the perceived global spread of a secularised, capitalist Western culture is recast within a new framework as only one side of the story. The other side, now emerging in response to the threat of homogenisation, consists of the multifarious voices of diverse cultures and epistemic communities defining and defending themselves against the threat of hegemony: we see, for example, the world-wide resurgence of non-secular discourses in a variety of forms, from fundamentalism to New-Ageism, which confounds modernisation's prophecy of a homogenising secularism;[8] we see the adoption of culture as a site of representation and resistance, leading, on the one hand, to the splintering of nation states into ethnic communities often with aspirations of independence, and on the other, to their melding into regional blocs, both of which undermine the pivotal position of the nation state as the focus of power and identity within modernity; and we see the universalist aspirations of the women's movement, the peace movement, the environmental movement, concerns with universal human rights and global governance, all of which attempt to transform modern identities and to reclaim, in the name of a humanity defined by difference, the global domain that has been so rapidly colonised by transnational corporate capitalism.

Globalisation theory replaces the earlier centre-periphery models of modernisation theory with a systemic understanding that is multi-polar, and allows for multidirectional flows between different nation states and cultures.⁹ Gone is the *univers cloisonnée*, which might have described the cultural condition of the globe prior to the formation of a world system (Abu-Lughod, 1991:134). Now there are no cloistered cultures. All of us are swept along by these multi-directional global cultural flows. Objectively our lives are changed by their shifting currents, subjectively our understanding of ourselves is destabilised by the changing tides of discursive forms that sweep away old certainties and offer real or illusory choices of identity and lifestyle. Robertson's model of globalisation brings into focus 'the inevitable reciprocity of cultural interaction that is overlooked in models which interpret globalisation only as the universalisation of the most powerful local, and therefore as simply the latest, American (as opposed to European colonial), phase of capitalism'.¹⁰

This reciprocity is articulated in what Robertson identifies as the 'central *dynamic* [of globalisation which] involves the twofold process of the particularization of the universal and the universalization of the particular' (1992:178). Globalisation theory, as presented by Robertson, does not attempt to set these dichotomies of universal vs particular, or global vs local, in the mould of polar opposites. Rather it attempts to theorise 'the simultaneity of the universal and the particular' (Robertson, 1992:172). The particular, in all of its diversity, defines itself against the universal, and has meaning only in the context of the universal, while the universal, conversely is dialectically defined by the particular. To clarify this, Robertson (1992:102) offers the example of Japan's encounters with Confucianism and Mahayana Buddhism. He suggests that in each case Japan, by 'nativistic' modifications, was able to identify the universal within the culturally particular expressions of Confucianism and Mahayana Buddhism, and then, as it were, re-particularise that universal giving it a Japanese form of expression. This unique Japanese construct of the universal could then be returned to the global domain where it contributed that distinctively Japanese expression of the universal in the particular form of Zen Buddhism.¹¹

As with the universal/particular dichotomy, the centre/periphery, and global/local, dichotomies are no longer perceived in globalisation theory as pairs of binary opposites, but as mutually constituting terms which *simultaneously* give rise to specific domains of identity, discourse, power and politics. Thus the centre/periphery model characteristic of modernisation theory is recast as a dialectic because, as Abu-Lughod (1991:142-3) puts it, the periphery 'has powerfully shaped the centre, [and] sweats from its pores'. Globalisation theory provides a framework for understanding why 'marginality has become a powerful space' in which to be (Hall, 1991:34). Likewise the global/local dichotomy is reframed by the understanding that the global interpenetrates the local. As Giddens writes:

localities are thoroughly penetrated by distanciated influences. The appearance, personality and policies of a world political leader may be better known to a given individual than those of his next-door neighbour. A person may be more familiar with the debate over global warming than with why the tap in the kitchen leaks (Giddens, 1991:188-189).

Effective political praxis in the global domain has responded to this 'globalisation' (Robertson, 1992:173) by using the global to either discipline or defend the local. The world-wide campaign against female genital mutilation provides an interesting example of the use of a global network to eliminate specific local practices. Whilst the practice mainly affects specific communities of African women, the campaign was undertaken on a global basis utilising the United Nations system within the global domain, the fund-raising, educative and legal resources of women's movements in non-African countries and the legal, educative and political experience of African women themselves. The campaign was directed not only towards those African nations where female circumcision was still practised, but also towards the diaspora community of Africans living abroad.[12] This globalised campaign operated globally to discipline particularity, changing discriminatory and harmful practices in local cultures.

Robertson (1992:171-2) provides a different example in which the local, in its own defence, gives rise to the global. He points to the strategic global alliance of the more than five thousand nations of indigenous peoples which directs the globalisation dynamic towards the defence of the local. There is now a World Council of Indigenous Peoples, and a declaration of rights for indigenous people is being formulated under United Nations auspices.[13] Robertson (1992:177) argues that globalisation theory undermines the adequacy of the environmental slogan 'Think globally, act locally'. Since the local has been institutionalised globally, we also need to 'Think locally and act globally' in order to defend and preserve what is local.

The picture presented in globalisation theory then, is not one of uniformity where one hegemonic economic-cultural system sweeps away all alternatives. It is rather a complex picture of heterogeneity, of peoples living in diverse situations, which take different forms in different localities depending on the way in which local cultural formations resist, appropriate, or transform the pressures to integrate into the world system. Within this context Robertson (1992:28) argues 'for the moral acceptance of . . . complexity. In other words, complexity becomes something like a moral issue in its own right'.

I suggest that one of the positive features of Robertson's version of globalisation theory is that it facilitates a change of focus, shifting our attention from the foreground – the event-filled world of conflicting interests played out in the economic battles of the global marketplace and the political clashes of the global arena – to the background – the worlds of ordinary citizens and marginalised peoples who, constituting the majority of the globe's population, continue to exist almost unnoticed by the global media networks. By expanding the theoretical horizon, Robertson's culturally oriented globalisation theory makes visible alternative trends emerging between the interstices of transnational capitalism's network that might ground visions of qualitatively different futures focussed on universal human interests.

It is by decentring modernity's subject, *Homo economicus*, and deprivileging economic theory in favour of a dynamic socio-cultural perspective, that Robertson's version of globalisation theory provides space for the recognition of the struggle and suffering of those most victimised by the present world system. It provides a framework for grappling with the increasing number of discourses generated by environmentalists, feminists, indigenous people, postcolonialists, peace workers and a wide range of activists who, escaping the confines of national identities and interests, seek to productively transcend the global/local, universal/particularist dichotomies of modernity. These new social movements can be thought of as constructing new forms of 'global communities' that can be described as 'colloidal' – geographically dispersed through a multiplicity of localities but globally united around a broadly accepted common cause.[14] They provide the possibility of an alliance with the woman on the bridge within the context of a global polis.

However it is not only the new social movements that emerge as 'levers for change' within the framework of culturally oriented globalisation theory. Robertson's culturally oriented globalisation theory also brings into view 'the religious factor' as a potent lever for change in a globalising world. As Tiryakian (1992:308) observes:

> Roland Robertson in the early 1970s was only one of a handful of social scientists on either side of the Atlantic who in effect wagered on the religious factor as having significance for post-industrial, post-1968 society. Within ten to 15 years this intellectual wager was won, as religious forces and movements unexpectedly erupted from the private sphere (to which they had been assigned by secularization theory) into the civic sphere More than any other single factor, it is this unexpected appearance of the religious factor on the world scene (an aspect of the 'return of the sacred' as a feature of modernity) that has been an important stimulus of globalization analysis (Shupe, 1990), precisely because this factor, as a lever for change, has no place in the strictly economic or political accounting of the world system. It thus became an anomaly that called for a different logic of explanation.

Before we explore the impact of globalisation on our governing forms of identity and knowledge, some of the reasons for the re-emergence of religious and spiritual discourse within a globalising world should be considered.

The Return of the Sacred

As already suggested, the global domain confronts us with the problem of discerning universality. Once we take as the focus of analysis the world-as-a-whole, which includes humanity-as-a-whole, then we are drawn into 'the formulation of what Robertson calls "humanitic" or, drawing on Parsons, "telic" concerns: global discourse on the ends of humanity in the light of the relativization of particularisms' (Beyer, 1994:27). The shared social context of the world-as-a-whole unavoidably confronts us with teleological questions concerning our relationship to the biosphere and all of its inhabitants. 'We' (as particular socio-cultural identities which are relativised in the global context of humanity) are forced to consider, firstly, our role in relation to the whole of humanity and, secondly, our role (as humanity) in relation to the global whole. This 'crystallization of global or telic concern' (Robertson and Chiroco, 1985:234) confronts us with what Robertson (1989a:14) refers to as 'the deep issues' – the ultimate questions concerning the meaning and purpose of human life. Until the modern era these telic concerns were addressed by 'religious' discourse,[15] and their re-emergence therefore provides a fertile atmosphere for the re-emergence of religion as people seek to orient themselves within the rapidly changing global domain.

In the global context the secularism of modernity stands out as a feature of the West's deviation from the other knowledge systems of the global domain. Comparison with other cultures reveals the West's extraordinary proliferation of objective theoretical knowledge and its paucity of knowledge in the subjective, or interior, and transcendent domains.[16] In contrast to the prediction of modernisation theory that we should see a convergence of all cultures towards the secular model of Western modernity, we can now reflect on the very different convergence revealed by global domain where there seems to be a resurgence of religious discourse.

In the previous chapter, the distinction was made between the translational and transformative aspects of religions. The former was described as creating meaning for the separate self, and initially it would seem that it is this translational aspect of religious discourse that is summoned by the telic concerns of the global domain. I suggest, however, that the spiritual or transformative aspect is also summoned, perhaps even more strongly. The relativisation of knowledge that occurs in the global domain is particularly challenging for religions which, like modernity, have often claimed universality for their particular inscriptions of meaning. As with other discursive universes within the global domain, the response of religions to relativisation can be constructive or otherwise, and this accounts for the two different faces of the contemporary religious resurgence – ecumenicism and fundamentalism.

The constructive response to relativisation leads, I suggest, to ecumenicism which accepts the relativisation of the socio-historical aspects of one's own particular tradition while staying open to the exploration of what Rothberg (1990:165) calls 'spiritual universals' that are common to one's own and other religious traditions. This move towards understanding the particular as, at least in part, imbued with the universal has two implications. Firstly, it encourages ecumenicists to think in 'human' or 'universal' terms which relativise the particularity of their socio-historical identity and push them towards an expansion of identity. They must engage, in other words, with the transformative or spiritual aspect of religion. Secondly, the exploration of universality requires an engagement in inter-religious conversation that is only possible if there is a move away from the bounded, separate self to a self that is at least porous to the other. This shift from boundedness to 'world-openness' (Turner, 1992:316-8) also requires that the boundaries of the self give way to at least some degree, and this again takes the ecumenicists into the domain of transformation of the self which, I argue, is the concern of the spiritual or transformative aspect of religious traditions. Thus a constructive response to the relativisation implicit in globalisation may begin with the translational aspect of religion, but it will, of necessity, also engage with the transformative or spiritual aspect and can therefore be described with some accuracy as 'spiritually-engaged'.

Ecumenical, or spiritually-engaged, discourse orients itself towards the global whole and attempts to identify that which is universal within its own tradition. Ecumenicists do not reject the specificity of the particular culture(s) in which their tradition arose and with which it has identified in the past. Rather, they seek to make this particularity porous to the universal demands of the global domain. 'The World Council of Churches' (WCC) 'Justice, Peace and Integrity of Creation' program which was launched in 1983, is one example of this kind of spiritual discourse which preserves a diverse Christian base while making that base porous to universal demands (Beyer, 1994:206-224). The Global Ethic that emerged from the 1993 World Parliament of Religions (Kung and Kuschel, 1993) provides another example of ecumenical discourse in which many different religious traditions found a measure of agreement on universal human values.

Whilst modernity privileged the secular, this constructive ecumenical response operates within a transcendent or transcultural horizon which, I suggest, constitutes the essential horizon of any globally inclusive genre of discourse that would respect and foster diversity.[17] This can be contrasted with the fundamentalist response to the relativisation of religious discourse which tends towards universalism rather than universality. Fundamentalists seek to convert the other, while ecumenicists seek to converse with the other. Theologian Hans Kung argues that the fundamentalist discourses remain within the modern paradigm of the (European) Enlightenment, while the ecumenical religious discourses are part of the contemporary 'postmodern', or 'global' paradigm (Kung, 1990:123).

Fundamentalists resist the relativisation of the global domain and direct themselves towards what Beyer (1994:10) refers to as a 'particularistic revitalization of [their] tradition'. Their concern is not that the boundaries of their socio-historical particular self-construct become more porous to others. Rather, they are concerned with the preservation, and if possible the geographic spread, of this particularist self-construct. Fundamentalism is primarily concerned with the translational aspect of religion. It responds to the relativisation of the global domain by resisting engagement with the transformative, or spiritual, aspect of religion. It is therefore more appropriately described as 'religious' rather than 'spiritual' discourse. The Catholic re-Christianisation movement, Communion and Liberation, which was begun in Milan in the 1950s offers an example of this kind of discursive universe that seeks to reaffirm and expand its traditional base within the global domain (Kepel, 1994:47-100).

This brief digression on the return of the sacred provides specific examples of the ways religious/spiritual discourse has utilised the opening provided by globalisation to modify governing forms of identity and knowledge. The relativisation provoked by globalisation offers an opportunity for reflexivity which can be directed constructively towards the larger global context in which we are now placed, or can be utilised defensively to shore up systems of knowledge and identity that belong to pre-global socio-historical contexts. The impact of globalisation on identity will be explored in more political terms later.

Being Globally

Just as modernisation was dialectically dependent on a governing form of modern identity, so we might expect globalisation to produce, and be produced by, a characteristic form or cluster of identities. The libratory potential of these global identities as loci of subjectivity and representation will be investigate below.

Returning to my starting point of the Indian woman on the bridge, I have suggested that the possibility of constructing an identity alliance, which includes both this woman and myself, emerges in the changing identity spaces created by globalisation. In these spaces modern identity constructs of national selves, First/Third World selves, or modern/traditional selves are relativised and loosened from their geo-political moorings. I am not suggesting an immediate or simplistic fall into a universalising identification with humanity that infiltrates many of the proposals for world governance and obscures their neo-imperialist implications, but I am suggesting the strategic use of identity as the basis of imagined global communities of resistance.

Robertson describes globalisation as involving relativisation along several dimensions. He and Chiroco define relativisation as 'a process involving the placing of socio-cultural or psychic entities in larger categorical contexts such that the relativised entities are constrained to be more self-reflexive relative to other entities in the larger context (which does not mean that they will be "constructively" self-reflexive)' (Robertson and Chiroco, 1985:234). With this understanding, Robertson and Chiroco suggest that there are four dominant processes of relativisation, 'two having to do with the relativisation of societies (trans-socialisation) and two having to do with the relativisation of persons, or selves (trans-personalisation)'. Individual selves are relativised within the 'more inclusive and fundamental' contexts of humanity and the world system of societies,[18] and (national) societies are also relativised by the same two global referents (ibid).

National identity, essential to modernity's construction of nation states, is put into context as simply one (albeit still a dominant) alternative in the flux and flow of possible identity constructs within the global domain. Identities based on markers other than geo-political national difference – ethnic identities, regional identities, civilisational identities, gendered identities, religious identities – are also relativised in the global domain. Identity constructs can become delinked from their originating geographical locations and communities so that diaspora or 'colloidal' imagined global communities are created.[19] At least two of the 'ethical revolutions' of this century identified by Mazrui (1995), the racial revolution and the gender revolution, can be conceptualised in terms of changing identity constructs and 'colloidal' global communities.

Significantly, the pervasive relativisation of globalisation induces a 'permanent reflectiveness' (Turner, 1992:317) which makes it difficult to maintain the stable narrative of self required for individuality. And by destabilising the two most significant bases of modern identity – nationality and individuality – globalisation cracks the boundaries of the self and opens the way for new modes of socialisation. At least two alternatives emerge. As I have already discussed with reference to the relativisation of religion, the first alternative seeks to reconstruct a clear identity boundary (fundamentalism), while the second alternative moves towards a more porous identity boundary (ecumenicism). Within the political domain, the weakening of national identity may, on the one hand, move citizens towards re-establishing a non-porous identity boundary by identifying with a different, particular, absolutised construct (which might be either quantitatively 'smaller' or 'greater' than the national construct). There might, as Huntington (1993) suggests be a trend towards civilisational identities, a trend towards ethnic identities or even a trend towards a rigid global identity construct. Regardless of the 'size' or geographic expanse of the identity construct, this alternative involves the maintenance of a non-porous self/other boundary through the reification of a particular concept, such as 'woman', 'worker', 'Croatian', 'Western', 'Chinese' or even 'global', in order to maintain a bounded self (Spivak, 1993:3).

On the other hand, globalisation opens the possibility of moving towards a more complex 'porous' identity that accepts the relativisation of all identity constructs and reflexively uses identity in politically strategic ways. This porous identity resists the temptation to define and defend a rigid bounded self, instead maintaining a stance of openness, refusing the dichotomising of global/local, by remaining simultaneously linked to the local and porous as well as to the global. The porous self is concerned with the self-reflexive adoption of terms such as 'woman', 'worker', 'Croatian', 'Western', 'Chinese', or even 'global', as a means of facilitating the development of a particular imagined community. This kind of porous identity can be conceived, as Mouffe (1992:10) suggests, 'as the articulation of an ensemble of subject positions' which variously come into play according to particular conditions.[20] In order to 'play' with identity in this way, its ultimate emptiness must, however, be understood.

To clarify this concept of porous identity with an example, we might consider the second wave of Western feminism which, with its dreams of a global sisterhood, initially conflated *Woman* with women and, losing sight of its own racial particularity, attempted to construct a homogeneous transnational community. In response to the challenge by women of colour and Third World women, a different kind of transnational feminist community is now emerging that is defined, not by the reification of *Woman,* but by the diversity of ways that term is embodied in different localities. This 'porous' option understands that the term 'woman' is empty, having no definitive meaning, and yet it uses that term self-reflexively as a political strategy to overcome oppression based on gender wherever that may occur within the global domain. By contrast the term 'global' can be used, and has been, used to create an imagined global community that is homogeneous and consistent with the interests of existing elites. This kind of exclusive, hegemonic global community poses perhaps the greatest threat to diversity and to a sustainable future. But the term 'global' can also be used self-reflexively as a strategy to promote a heterogeneous community, a global civil society that resists domination. We might distinguish these global alternatives, respectively, as 'top-down' vs 'bottom-up' globalisation or as 'corporate' vs 'community' cosmopolitanism. The former is a construct of high modernity, while the latter is, I believe, worth exploring as both a construct and constructor of an alternative, postmodern, global future. It offers the possibility of a porous global self constructed through socialisation into a global civil society.[21]

As I discuss in more detail in chapter six, Richard Falk (1992, 1993a,b) has used the term 'citizen-pilgrim' to capture what he sees as the essentially 'spiritually-engaged' character of this emerging global identity. Another commentator, Marc Nerfin (1987), uses the capitalised 'Citizen' to signify a similar global identity. He stresses that Citizenship (as he utilises the term) is a process, rather than a given right, which is earned by engaging in an active process of mobilisation. Nerfin (1987, 173) suggests that there are only 'a few deep-seated mobilising themes: peace, women's liberation, human and people's rights, environment, local self-reliance, alternative lifestyles and personal transformation, consumers' self-defence, and in some industrialised countries, solidarity with people of the Third World, including refugees and immigrants'.

These mobilising themes are, I suggest, concerned with universal human interests and as such they facilitate the construction of wider identities experienced in solidarity with others. They seek to make national and social identity constructs more porous to the demands of variously imagined global communities. The process involves allowing the boundaries of the self to give way in order to recognise and honour perceived patterns of inter-connection and dependence. Such action might be described as 'spiritually-engaged politics'.[22] Operating within the socio-political domain, this kind of mobilisation demands a degree of self-transcendence that calls forth a spiritual horizon within which the division between the needs of the self and the needs of the other begins to disintegrate.

For example, the ecological self, suggested by deep ecologists, identifies with nature and acts in conformity with the preservation, or interests, of nature. This porous ecological identity involves a change in consciousness so that one acts in the interests of a larger ecologically interconnected self.[23] But the co-option of environmental discourse by corporate discourse highlights again the dilemma, discussed above, of accurately discerning universal or global interests. In particular this involves distinguishing between the globally extended self of, for example, the transnational corporate executive and the interconnected global self of, say, the deep ecologist. In the case of the corporate executive, the modern autonomous identity construct is neither transformed nor made more porous to the realities of its universal social and ecological inter-connections, but merely extends the field of its cumulative operation into the global domain. In the case of the deep ecologist, the existing modern identity construct is transformed through accountability to an external referent, namely the environment.

Robertson (1992:106-7) claims 'that globalisation has involved and continues to involve the *institutionalised construction* of the individual'. Provided we understand 'individual' in this context to mean the particularity of an identity construct, then we can see how globalisation frees identity from the often rigid constraints of traditional socio-historical forms and reveals it as a (potentially) reflexive choice concerning the locus of subjectivity at any given time. Reflexive awareness of this choice, combined with the despatialisation of otherness that results from globalisation, calls forth the 'celebration of subjective identity' that 'has played a major part in the virtually globe-wide establishment of various "minority" forms of personal and collective identification' (p. 107), amongst which Robertson includes gender.[24] Thus we see around the globe the emergence of a variety of movements concerned with particular ethnic, religious, gendered or regional identities based on the re-emergence of 'old' (pre-modern) identity markers (such as indigeneity, ethnicity or religion) and the emergence of 'new' (postmodern) markers (Nerfin's universal mobilising themes). When these new social and religious movements orient themselves constructively towards the global context they are concerned with articulating porous identities open to diversity, that simultaneously seek to preserve that diversity. From this positive perspective, globalisation can be seen as facilitating the construction of transformative or spiritually-engaged identities. It is only such identities that offer the possibility of constructing an inclusive global community.

Postmodern feminism provides an example of this. I have already mentioned the move in feminist discourse away from the early constructs of global sisterhood towards more porous structures of identity that strategically employ the universal term 'women' as a means of defending the diversity and particularity of women around the globe. We now see the emergence of a *heterogeneous* discourse that maintains a focus on the universal practice of gender construction, while seeking to understand the diverse local variations of this practice and the ways in which they may lead to inequity or oppression. Such feminism offers an example of the way in which globalisation calls forth, not only a more porous or spiritually-engaged identity, but also a more nuanced approach to knowledge. It is this relationship between globalisation and a different way of knowing that I want to explore.

Referring specifically to feminism, Grewal and Kaplan (1994:19) suggest that 'the question becomes how to link diverse feminisms without requiring either equivalence or a master theory'. This is the fundamental question for the construction of knowledge in the global domain. Is it possible to construct a discourse of resistance that does not replicate existing cultural and economic hegemonies? Basu (1995:20) answers, with respect to feminism:

> In fighting for what appear to be particular goals – finding their voices, setting their own agendas, and creating their own social spaces – women's movements are seeking the most universal objectives. But note that at such moments when the particular and the universal coincide, the subject may no longer be women. Thus, the tensions between local and global feminisms reverberate within the relationship between women's movements and the movements of other oppressed groups. The strengths of women's movements lie in their insights into that which distinguishes them and that which joins them to others who have suffered. And from these encounters come the most exquisite knowledge, vitality, and power.

Whilst the articulation of this 'most exquisite knowledge' that I have called 'spiritually-engaged' is explored shortly, the notions of identity and knowledge, ontology and epistemology, are so closely intertwined that I will return to questions of identity. Before moving on I want to briefly sum up the implications of globalisation for the construction of identity.

The global domain relativises all socio-historical identity constructs. This relativisation leads to reflexivity which may or may not be directed constructively. Constructive reflexivity (with which I am concerned here) adopts a stance of 'world-openness' which is made possible through the construction of a 'porous' self. Since this porosity results from the deconstruction and release of the rigid boundaries of the bounded individual, I suggest that the resultant identity can be referred to as 'spiritually-engaged' and that it represents the ontological aspect of spiritually-engaged knowledge. Constructive reflexivity opens the interior domain within which particularist modes of identity are revealed as a choice. It is the coalescence of identity around universal human values which identifies the spiritually-engaged identity. The recognition of universal human values, or 'shared sensibilities', is therefore an essential part of the construction of identity and knowledge within the global domain, for it is just these 'common commitments [that] . . . serve as a base for solidarity and coalition' (hooks, 1990:27) and make the difference between a clash of civilisations and a conversation of cultures.

Knowing Globally

The emergence of a 'global ecumene' (Grewal and Kaplan, 1994:9) raises acute epistemological problems. Given the diversity of peoples, let alone species, on the globe, we are confronted more immediately than ever with the issue of epistemological authority.[25] I have advocated solidarity with those who are disadvantaged within the global system but the epistemological conundrums associated with global solidarity are myriad. Who speaks for whom? Who can legitimately claim to represent some, let alone all of these global peoples? Who can speak for the 'oppressed', or for the 'privileged'? For women, or for men? Who can possibly speak for humanity, or the world? The issues of epistemology and authority within a domain as vast and varied as the globe are complex and difficult, yet they are intimately related to the issues of justice and sustainable development conjured by the woman on the bridge. Who will speak for her? Who will join voices with her to protect her daughter, her environment and her livelihood? The United Nations Development Programme, in its *Human Development Report 1992*, (p. 74) raises just this question:

> For the first time in human history, the world is close to creating a single, unified global system. But an agreed and participatory system of global governance remains a distant dream. This has left an urgent and disturbing question wandering unanswered round the corridors of power: In a period of rapid economic globalization, who will protect the interests of the world's poor?

By generating 'a universal social context' (Beyer, 1994:11) the global domain relativises, not only identity, but *all* socio-historical knowledge systems. Although itself emerging from the Western episteme, globalisation theory points towards an expansion of the horizon of knowledge beyond the limits of the Western episteme. This global ecumene defines an inclusive context that contains and relativises both modernity and postmodernity, holding them in tension with the other, diverse life-worlds occupied by humanity. By framing this relativism within the bounded global system, however, external referents are brought to bear which limit relativism. The global domain inexorably confronts us, not only with alterity, but also with the finite limits of that domain, challenging us to move beyond relativism, beyond even reflexivity, to another epistemological strategy that enables us to formulate universal horizons of co-operation. As Featherstone (1990:2) argues 'a new level of conceptualization is necessary'.

If, as Robertson (1990a:17) suggests, globalisation theory attempts to 'indicate the structure of any viable discourse about the shape and "meaning" of the world-as-a-whole', there must also be a viable epistemological stance that underpins this emerging genre of discourse and which provides a means of discerning valid and viable global discourse from the variety of discursive forms available. Whilst a supposedly neutral position of the 'objective' discursive subject is adopted here, I must acknowledge more explicitly the Western origin of globalisation theories, and recognise that the epistemological changes which I discuss relate primarily to the postmodern Western episteme as it reluctantly emerges from its position of hegemony and privilege.

Relating globalisation theory to modernity and postmodernity is not as straightforward as it might seem. Robertson claims a discontinuity exists between modernity and globalisation.[26] In this view globalisation did not arise out of modernity, but was set in motion long before the modern era.[27] Whilst the modern era has left its own distinctive mark on both the kind and intensity of the present globalisation, it was not essential to globalisation and we might have reached a different form of globalisation via another path, such as a pan-Islamic global order. Be that as it may, if we explicitly recognise these theories as Western-encoded descriptions of the West's encounters with other cultures in the global domain, then it might be possible to outline a sociology of knowledge that maps both the changing epistemological stance of the various positions of the West and the development of an epistemological stance appropriate for global discourse.

Building on work by Cantwell-Smith (1984) and Robert Bellah (1980), I present a four-stage framework which distinguishes different epistemological positions available to the Western episteme within the global domain. This framework not only allows us to locate both modernity and postmodernity within the broader global context, but also enables us to see more clearly the epistemological, ontological and ethical demands that result from the intensification of inter-cultural contact which characterises globalisation. The four steps considered below, represent increasingly subtle epistemological strategies for dealing with diversity and integration in a world of cultural plurality. They represent alternative strategies for constructing knowledge and subjectivity within a context of difference and they map a pathway that moves beyond domination to genuine encounter with our global others.

The first two stages – superiority and relativism – correspond, from the Western point of view, to modernity, and what I refer to as ludic postmodernity.[28] These epistemological strategies give rise to monologic knowledge because in both, the cognitive structures and categories of the knowing subject remain essentially unchanged and unchallenged. They represent the two options that currently dominate in the Western episteme and which, I contend, the finite global domain reveals as inadequate. I believe however, that an adequate stance for dealing with the simultaneous demands of differentiation and integration within the global domain is possible. It requires a passage through the two later stages of reflexivity and transformation to reach a spiritually-engaged knowledge that transforms, or even ultimately dissolves, the individual knowing subject.

(a) Superiority

The first stage of superiority is based on the assumption that modern Western culture is normative and other cultures are judged on the basis of how closely they approach the Western paradigm of rationality and progress. This epistemological stance adopts a strategy of objectivity which, using Gellner's (1992) term, might be described as 'rationalist fundamentalism'.[29] The socio-historical dimension of knowledge is ignored and the universal/particular dichotomy is collapsed by universalising the dominant particular. The governing ways of knowing and being of the dominant epistemic community are presented, or imposed, as the universal norm or ideal.[30] Thus the primary intellectual categories of the dominant group are understood as cosmic categories that reveal the world-as-it-really-is, rather than being understood as index symbols that sustain a particular cultural narrative. The dominant knowledge is understood as literally expressing universality, rather than being thought of as a particular narrative that is porous or transparent to a metalevel of universality. Literalism, as Hillman (1983:3) warns, is sickness! It kills 'the imaginative metaphorical perspective to ourselves and our world'. An epistemological stance of superiority leads individuals and societies into personal and political stances of domination.

On a global scale, both the environmental destruction and the crisis of social justice bear witness in a poignant and inescapable way to the pathology of a modernity that understands its knowledge as objective 'truth'. In the global context the cultural fingerprints that identify modern knowledge as the product of a particular, privileged epistemic community become apparent. If, however, Robertson's theory of globalisation is taken as both descriptive and prescriptive, then the increasingly apparent generation of 'two worlds' (the over-advantaged and the under-advantaged) by modernity, runs counter to the emergence and awareness of one inter-connected world that would be expected with globalisation.

Within the strategy of superiority it is necessary to consider a sub-category of 'uncritical reversal'.[31] An epistemological strategy of uncritical reversal can be understood as an evasion, a side-stepping that temporarily avoids the deeper forms of awareness of the next stage of relativism. Initially at least, reversal remains internally referential and involves little reorganisation of the dominant intellectual categories. Uncritical reversal takes two forms, neither of which offers a critique of the hierarchical and dualistic construction of the dominant discursive universe: (i) the non-dominant social group rejects its assigned inferior position to identify with the dominant pole of modernity's hierarchically organised dualisms. This kind of 'up-ending of the dualistic structure' (Mies and Shiva, 1993:10) leads not only to the failure to revise false theories, but also to false political strategies based on 'catching up'. Thus in some strands of development theory the Third World, and now the ex-Second World, attempt to 'catch up' with the First World; or, in some strands of liberal feminist theory, women attempt to 'catch up' with men through policies of equalisation, positive discrimination etc. And (ii) the non-dominant group attempts to valorise the inferiorised terms of the hierarchically organised dualisms. This kind of reversal leads to identity politics. Thus, for example, radical feminists have sought to valorise the so-called 'feminine' values; some Third World and indigenous groups have sought to valorise non-modern values.

Although I do not expand upon the issue here, in the longer term uncritical reversal is likely to become critical, and therefore to open into reflexivity, since individuals and social groups are always embedded in an ongoing historical, cultural matrix, aspects of which are 'not loose enough simply to be exchanged' (Cantwell-Smith, 1984:4) without leading to modification of the matrix. As the women's movement in the West, and much postcolonial theorising has shown, uncritical reversal may be an early (optional or perhaps essential) emancipatory step in the passage, through relativism, to reflexivity and transformation. For this reason I have included it in the first stage although it might, alternatively be regarded as an important, if temporary, step towards exogenous reflexivity.

(b) Relativism

The second stage of relativism is based on a deeper understanding and appreciation of the cultural and linguistic mediation of knowledge. Since the charge of cultural relativism is so often levelled at postmodernism,[32] it is clear that at least some strands of postmodern thought (which I refer to hereafter as 'ludic' postmodernism), must be considered within this second stage.[33] Relativism represents a move from a position of cultural superiority which is used to justify hegemony, to a position of cultural relativism that sees all cultures as having their own discursive universes between which it is not possible to evaluate since there is no 'higher' or objective viewpoint. Within the global context, ludic postmodern theory can be understood as the early Western theorisation of the relativisation of cultures and identities that, as discussed above, is characteristic of globalisation. Thus ludic postmodernism involves a (belated masculine, Euro-american) move away from Western culture as normative towards the recognition of the diversity of cultural flows.

Relativism collapses the universal/particular dichotomy by 'splitting' rather than 'absorption'.[34] It particularises all universals and creates barriers of difference. By refusing to acknowledge universality as the opposite and constitutive pole of particularity, relativism avoids the Other by absolutising heterogeneity or difference. Whilst those opposed to relativism rail against it, relativism's positive significance in theorising space for the recognition, emergence and appreciation of 'submerged knowledges' must be acknowledged. Relativism, (whether theorised from the perspective of postmodern or globalisation theory) provides discursive space for the articulation of alternative ways of knowing and being emerging from epistemic communities based not only on cultural difference, but on other signifiers of difference such as gender, religion, politics or lifestyle.

Relativism, however, remains internally referential. As Midgley (1989:161-2) suggests, 'people faced with a painful clash of cultures do tend to take refuge in relativism, subjectivism, and scepticism', as the easy option. Since it fails to contextualise cultural discourse within a broader world-historical or biospherical, context that would provide external points of reference, relativism does not facilitate revision of one's intellectual categories or reassessment of one's political position, privileged or otherwise. Thus ludic postmodernism can be seen as a means of maintaining the privileged status of modernity's elite.[35] In a world where economic, political and military differentials in power skew cultural exchange, the relativism of both postmodern and globalisation theories can seem at best politically naive, at worst perniciously indifferent to the dispossessed of the global system.

The ludic postmodern celebration of difference with its playful collages of particularity can be seen as the luxury of the small elite who, through economic and political privilege, are buffered from the effects of social injustice and environmental degradation that constitute the external, transcultural referents of the shared global reality.[36] This ludic postmodern celebration of difference eclipses universality and generates a distorted view of others consisting of commodified fragments of their lives. It consists of a pseudo-otherness that cannot sustain conversation. The chance of sampling a variety of cultural cuisines, in any of the world's global cities, of choosing an ethnic interior design for one's living space, or consuming cultural displays as a wandering global tourist, needs to be sharply distinguished from the challenge of meeting the globe's multiple others, who coercively or consciously, remain on the margins of the consumerist culture, and who challenge the ethical and political outcomes of our knowledge system.

Whilst relativism introduces a valuable narrative awareness, it provides no means by which we might distinguish between stories. Politically it provides a release from the hegemonic monologue of modernity, but it offers no help in discerning a new configuration of alliances capable of challenging the transnational capitalism of the contemporary global order. Epistemologically, as a strategy for dealing with the globe's diverse others, relativism is inadequate. As Mathews (1994:6) suggests, from the Western point of view 'it perhaps hides within it a residual imperial arrogance, in the form of the assumption that while the belief systems of the West may be no better than those of other cultures, they are at least no worse; they are not simply *wrong*'.

Globalisation theory however calls into question the central and seemingly autonomous position ludic postmodernism accords socio-cultural systems.[37] By recognising that we are involved in an ongoing process of the interpenetration of cultures within the global domain, globalisation theory reveals all socio-cultural systems as hybrids interacting within the tangled economic, political and ecological webs that provide the common context for all cultures. This global context not only relativises cultures but also reveals some as more adequate than others within the contemporary context. Some theoretical streams within both globalisation theory and postmodernism have therefore gone beyond relativism to offer reflexivity as the means of undertaking a critical reassessment of our own culture. I hereafter refer to these streams of postmodern thought as 'critical' postmodernism, which provides the theoretical tools (of deconstruction, decentring, and difference) necessary for taking this step into reflexivity. By turning these tools upon our own subjectivity, critical postmodernism moves us beyond the impasse of relativism into an interior domain, a domain of reflexivity.

(c) Reflexivity

The third stage utilises the increasing awareness of, and cultural sensitivity towards, other knowledge systems to develop critical self-awareness of our own governing forms of identity and knowledge, and to entertain the possibility that (aspects of) these may, as Mathews (1994) contends, simply be wrong. This third stage brings us into the domain of interiority (Lonergan, 1972) which depends, as Greene (1972:282) suggests, 'on the recovery of consciousness – on the individual's awareness of his own . . .-reflective life'. Interiority emerges with the development and practice of reflexive awareness of our own processes of perceiving, reacting, believing, thinking, acting and knowing, *in relation to exogenous referents*.[38] It begins with an understanding of ourselves as historically situated, socially constructed subjectivities, but seeks to go beyond the intellectual deconstructive insight that the subject is a discursive illusion to grapple with the ontological implications of this for us as living fictions. Reflexive postmodernism provides the resources with which epistemes, psyches and societies that have been constituted by modernity, might open to a process of transformation that would move them beyond modernity into new modes of being and knowing.

Epistemologically, reflexivity is concerned with the subjective pole of consciousness which has been accorded less priority and less attention in the Western knowledge system.[39] With this third category of reflexivity we begin to move into ways of knowing that are less familiar and less recognised in the modern Western episteme. When we consider knowledge of this interior domain within the global context, the peculiarity of the Western episteme is revealed. Globalisation, or perhaps reflexive postmodernism, has finally led the Western episteme (once again) to the gateway of interiority, through the recognition that our way of knowing the world, simultaneously constructs our way of being in the world, yet we find that this knowledge is already articulated in much greater depth within non-Western cultures.

The global context reveals the modern West, with its wealth of theoretical knowledge of the 'objective' world and its poverty of 'subjective' knowledge in the interior or transcendent domains, as an exception if not an aberration. In Hindu philosophy, Sankara, in the ninth century, referred to *adhyasa*, or superimposition, as the process by which we construct a world of meaning from the perceived world (Organ, 1988:7). Nagarjuna, in the Buddhist tradition (c.150-250AD), articulated from a different perspective a deconstructive insight. Both of these commentators however surpassed the postmodern deconstructionists by also deconstructing their own position, thus opening the way to a radically different way of knowing, beyond the confines of logocentric knowledge (Spretnak, 1991:52). Far from occupying the normative position, the secular West stands in opposition to an apparent convergence of alternatives which have retained an understanding of the subjective pole of knowing which directs us beyond the third stage of reflexivity, to a fourth stage of transformation.

(d) Transformation

The fourth stage, as Cantwell-Smith (1984:5) suggests, 'subsumes and transcends' the other three. It involves the constructive use of reflexivity to preserve the merits and transform the limitations of our own culture in the face of a multicultural shared global reality, where the very concept of 'the other' is dissolving and our cultural projections are returning home. Globalisation theory points to but cannot articulate this stage.

This fourth stage shares common ground with those Western scholars who understand themselves as engaged in constructive or reconstructive postmodernism.[40] I hope, however, that the path I have taken through the earlier stages of superiority, relativism and reflexivity clarifies my avoidance of terms such as (re)constructive postmodernism. This final stage could only be 'postmodern' from the standpoint of those who, like myself, have been cast in the mould of modernity. Many of the peoples and cultures who now find themselves thrust into the shared global domain have never, or only partially, taken the detour of modernity.[41] For this reason I have adopted the terminology of 'transformative' or 'spiritually-engaged' knowledge as more apt within the global context. It seems likely that any transformative global discourse will include not only postmodern elements but also pre-modern and, indeed, modern elements.[42]

What is being reached for in this fourth category is a discourse that is porous or transparent to universality but which does not obliterate particularity or diversity. This suggests a new genre of discourse that is qualitatively different from the monologic, logocentric, rational Western view of knowledge. It is concerned with transcending the universal/particular dichotomy, not by grasping one end or the other of the spectrum set up by the dualistic categories of discursive knowledge, but by transcending dualistic thought through the recognition of the ultimate non-substantiality and emptiness of all dualisms.

The challenge, as already suggested, is to find a universal way of linking a multiplicity of different discourses 'without', as Grewal and Kaplan (1994:19) suggest, 'requiring either equivalence or a master theory'.[43] One way of doing this is to articulate what might be described as an 'empty set', which defines a universal praxis but leaves open the socio-historical applications of that praxis since they will, of necessity, be diverse. Returning to Sharma's example of 'universal language' which I referred to in chapter one, we can see that the interpretation that language is a 'universal' human praxis constitutes a metalevel of understanding when compared with the interpretation of English as the 'universal' language. The former interpretation identifies a set of human practices for which all human beings have the potential but leaves that set empty of particular socio-cultural content, while the latter interpretation fills the set with a socio-cultural particular, be it English, Swahili or Yiddish, which it universalises. As long as we leave the universal set empty, specifying it as a praxis, a universal physiological human needs *to eat,* for example, without specifying whether it is hamburgers, curry or paella that is eaten, then we have a statement that applies universally.

Now if we turn our attention to the praxis of 'knowing', we may be able to apply the same approach. Lonergan (1972), for example, explores the possibility of a universal noetic praxis grounded in human cognitive potential, that might provide criteria for ascertaining the authenticity of any discourse within the contemporary context where all discursive knowledge systems are relativised. He argues for a 'transcendental method' of knowing (in Lonergan's terminology 'transcendental' signifies 'transcultural'), that is an expression of the unfolding of human attentiveness, intelligence, reasonableness, responsibility and love (Lamb, 1982:83). In this way Lonergan grounds the process of knowing in the universal cognitive capacities of human beings.

Lonergan's work makes an important contribution to the identification of the genre of spiritually-engaged knowledge and I return to it again later. Lonergan's field was theology but his 'transcendental method' clearly has application in the broader domain of the sociology of knowledge. By situating ourselves in the global domain and accepting the relativisation of noematic knowledge that it implies, we are challenged to identify a different kind of knowledge that is noetic and which operates within a transcendental or universal horizon. It is a way of knowing which, to borrow Tarnas' (1991:409) words, is:

> possessed of a certain intrinsic profundity or universality that, while not imposing any a priori limits on the possible range of legitimate interpretations, would yet somehow bring an authentic and fruitful coherence out of the present fragmentation, and also provide a sustaining fertile ground for the generation of unanticipated new perspectives and possibilities in the future.

In this fourth spiritually-engaged or transformative phase cultural particularities are perceived, as Cantwell-Smith (1984:5) notes, as aspects of a 'transcending whole'. In Lonergan's (1972) formulation this macrocosmic wholeness is mirrored by the microcosmic wholeness of a way of knowing that engages not only the rational faculty, but also the ethical, affective and spiritual faculties of the whole person. The exploration of universal values which globalisation engenders is also mirrored in the embodiment of these virtues in persons who reach their full capacity for knowing (Nasr, 1989:312-3). Knowledge becomes an incarnational affair dependent on the full development of the cognitive, ethical, affective and spiritual potential of the knower.[44]

Such knowledge challenges our notions of subjectivity in two ways. Firstly, it challenges our interior development, our reflexive awareness of our own selves. Secondly, it challenges the breadth and scope of our outwardly directed identifications. Globalisation offers the possibility of a move beyond culturally constructed subjectivities to a new horizon of subjectivity constructed within the framework of an inclusive global (imagined) community. As we deconstruct our modern, bounded selves we are confronted with a subjectivity that goes beyond identification with 'humanity', to a subjectivity that includes what might be referred to as 'all creation'. Paradoxically, as subjectivity expands in this way, the ultimate emptiness of identity is discovered and the bounded self is revealed as an illusion. This extended notion of subjectivity requires, as I discussed in the section on global identity above, a degree of self-transcendence that provides a meeting point with the spiritual domain. We are directed towards the world's spiritual traditions because as Webb (1988:302) tells us:

> it has only been in religious thought – even if only on its most critically reflective as well as spiritually sensitive level – that any language at all has been developed for the discussion of the radical contingency of human selfhood and the possibility that selfhood might be transcended.

Indian philosophies have deeply explored subjectivity and transcendent notions of self and identity. I have already mentioned that Indian thinkers such as Nagarjuna or Shankaracharya, centuries ago, deconstructed the discursive self and recognised it, as Derrida (1991:102) far more recently has noted, to be a 'conventional fiction'. And although the respective Buddhist and Hindu spiritual frameworks of Nagarjuna and Shankaracharya differ from the secular interpretations of Derrida, it is clear that the problematisation of identity and the exploration of subjectivity provide common ground for conversation between at least some strands of contemporary Western, and some strands of traditional Indian, philosophy.[45]

However self-transcendence is not the only area which directs us towards a meeting between spirituality and postmodernism. Globalisation theory also points towards a new level of conceptualisation that attempts to leap beyond the sets of binary opposites that have characterised the adversarial mode of Western thought (Moulton, 1983). It seeks to work with the contradictions of the global domain by grasping both poles of the structured pairs of binary opposites with which modern Western discourse has understood the world. This opens the way to stepping beyond the 'A-not A' binary logic of the Western episteme. But such fundamental changes are, as Abu-Lughod (1991:142-3) writes, beyond the capacity of globalisation theory to articulate:

> Our ambition to do equal justice to global and local is limited at the outset by our failure to generate a comparative language beyond the set of tidy binaries which reproduce the global regime in the very attempt to eviscerate it: centre/periphery, core/periphery, western/non-western, developed/developing, etc. .... The long progression of binary oppositions, divorced over time from their colonial and imperial roots, even when deprived of their spatial image, don't seem adequate to the task of providing descriptive or analytic power to fluid and volatile spheres of activity. If we cannot phrase an alternative, if an adequate language eludes us, how can we visualize a comparative theorization of culture(s)?

Again it is in the domain of spirituality, particularly within the Eastern traditions of Hinduism, Buddhism and Taoism,[46] that we can find a language for discussing a nondual mode of awareness and knowledge that seeks to escape the subject/object dualism of modern thought. Certain streams of feminist and postmodern discourse, however, also offer a language for discussing spiritually-engaged knowledge. I explore the feminist contributions later and shortly will consider the relationship between postmodernism and spiritually-engaged knowledge, while in chapter five I discuss some of the surprising convergences between post-deconstructive discourse and spiritual discourse, or what I have referred to as the world of the yogi.

Before moving on, however, let me sum up the characteristics of the new kind of knowledge that is called forth by globalisation. This spiritually-engaged knowledge involves new levels of conceptualisation. It goes beyond the rational domain to include ethical, affective and spiritual aspects both within the interior domain of the subject and in the exterior domain where the other is encountered. Rather than seeking to represent the propositional structure of Truth, spiritually-engaged knowledge is concerned with the praxis of truth construction. It is a post-deconstructive genre that moves beyond the limits of discursivity to point towards the universal, while still remaining open to the multiple particularist expressions of that universal within socio-political realms. Spiritually-engaged knowledge thus seeks to transcend the universal/particular dichotomy, not by absolutising either term, but by transcending dualistic thought. I have proposed that a premodern language for describing this way of knowing can be found in religious traditions, but it also finds expression in the different languages of postmodern ethics, feminism, environmentalism and psychology that are explored in the remainder of this work.

In this chapter I have argued that the contemporary conditions of globalisation create the conditions for the emergence of spiritually-engaged knowledge within the global domain. However, within those parts of the global domain that are emerging from the hegemony of modernity, I suggest that postmodernism plays an important role in creating conditions favourable to the emergence of spiritually-engaged knowledge. In the next section I consider the ways in which postmodernism also, calls forth this genre of knowledge.

The Postmodern Context

It is possible to position postmodernism historically within the global socio-political domain, from which perspective postmodernity can be understood as an historical interlude concerned with the overturning of modernity. As Derrida (1981:41) suggests, this is an unstable 'phase of overturning' – a moment of rupture 'in which a fixed governing form must dare, in its own interests, to destabilize itself en route to its altered global ends' (Mackie 1994:228). In so doing, as Mackie argues, that governing form lays itself open to challenge and to being overthrown by an alternative universe of discourse. There is no certainty that such a revolution will occur for, as Falk (1992:2) suggests, 'modernism is by no means a spent force'. But postmodernity offers the possibility that an alternative, non-modern universe of discourse might yet define the emerging global era. Herein lies the challenge of postmodernity.

Framed thus, postmodernism can be read as the theorisation, from a dominant Western perspective, of the process of globalisation in which the hegemony of modernity is being fractured, and possibly replaced, by an as yet unidentified global culture. This reading understands postmodernism as an evolving universe of discourse that theorises and pursues the destabilisation and rupture of the governing modern discursive universe, while simultaneously defining the conditions for the emergence of a new articulation of knowledge. As critique, postmodernism challenges the discursive representation of the world, incorporating an awareness of both the linguistic construction and the participatory nature of knowledge. Some strands of postmodernism, however, go further to mark out broader ethical and spiritual horizons for the emergence of a new way of knowing.

Following Bertens (1995), two movements can be distinguished within the postmodern universe. The initial movement is the deconstructive postmodernism of the 1970s which is primarily concerned with the crisis of representation. It draws on the work of the (French) post-structuralists, particularly Derrida, and utilises the strategies of deconstruction, decentring and difference. It is textually based, celebrating reflexivity and the deconstruction of the subject and has often been understood, in contrast to the second movement, as apolitical. It is this initial movement that I concentrate on here, since the way the first movement of postmodernism is read largely determines the reading of the second movement.

The historically later second movement occurred in the 1980s and draws more on the work of Foucault. Having concluded that 'representations do not and cannot represent the world' (Bertens 1995:7), this second movement adopts the approach that all representations are therefore political and concerned with the distribution of power and privilege. Knowledge is equated with power and the focus shifts to 'the workings of power and the constitution of the subject' (Bertens 1995:7). This overtly political postmodernism celebrates difference and the Other, and makes possible the links between postmodernism and libratory movements such as feminism, postcolonialism, environmentalism and multiculturalism. Both the deconstructive and the political movements continue to exist side by side within the postmodern discursive universe.

When the initial deconstructive movement is understood solely as a critique of knowledge, then the two movements co-exist in a state of tension, since this critique can be applied with equal efficacy to many of the libratory discourses that have emerged in the discursive universe of political postmodernism. The result is the ludic postmodernism to which I referred in the previous section, which is politically ambiguous. Unable to escape from relativism, ludic postmodernism deconstructs the modern universe and initiates conversation with modernity's others, but offers us no way of distinguishing between the cacophony of incommensurable voices. When, however, the initial movement is understood as going beyond relativism to a reflexivity that defines the horizons of a new articulation of knowledge, then it offers a way of discerning with which voices it may be fruitful to engage in the second conversational movement.[47] As in the previous section, I refer to this stream of postmodernism as critical postmodernism.

My concern here is to trace the development of critical postmodernism and explore the ways in which it creates the conditions for spiritually-engaged knowledge. Critical postmodernism results from turning the deconstructive critique upon ourselves. It can be described as 'a mode of derangement of the accepted [which] brings the chains of that accepted into view *so that we can see how to undo them*' (Mackie, 1985:192 – italics mine). We can then discover what kind of knowing emerges beyond the totalising hegemony of rationality, discursivity and ontotheology that has characterised the modern episteme. Following Derrida, this knowledge is ethically based, for in spite of criticisms of ethical impotence, Derrida (1992:19) is adamant that his own work, and deconstruction more generally, exists within an ethical horizon and does not correspond 'to a quasi-nihilistic abdication before the ethico-politico-juridical question of justice and before the opposition between just and unjust'. Whilst such knowledge is free of moral metanarratives, it offers a new articulation of responsibility that reframes the ethical. It is this promise of a post-deconstructive knowledge grounded in ethical concern that, I argue, is being redeemed with the emergence of spiritually-engaged knowledge and this originary ethical horizon will be investigated further.

Despite the fact that postmodernism is usually framed by secularism if not atheism.[48] I still identify this emerging knowledge as 'spiritually-engaged'. It is possible, I believe, to understand critical postmodernism as opening up a spiritual or transcendent horizon and the nature of this horizon will also be explored. We will first briefly trace its emergence within the domain of philosophy, for this spiritual horizon did not spring unheralded into view with Derrida's work, but arises from the application of the deconstructive approach in the nineteenth century. Whilst this has often been read as the 'death of philosophy', it can also be read as the reframing of the philosophical enterprise within a transcendent horizon. As Berry argues (1992:4), the deconstructive critique has 'subtly and unobtrusively dissolved the clear-cut distinction between secular and religious thinking which Kant and the Kantian tradition had carefully secured'.

In Western philosophy the deconstructive challenge was first launched by Nietzsche whose critique of the subject was, at the time, ignored or reviled (Hans, 1995:2). He sought a new clarity and innocence free of the ontotheological constructions of metaphysical thought. Thus Nietzsche, and his heirs amongst contemporary philosophers, such as Rosset (1993), celebrate *what is* rather than concerning themselves with *what ought to be*. But to celebrate *what is* implies the capacity to perceive *what is*, and as I later contend, this veridical perception calls for an awareness that is free of the projections of the individual, bounded self. Ultimately, as Loy (1988:38-95) argues, such awareness must be nondual, transcending the subject/object distinction fundamental to discursivity. As we have seen, this nondual awareness leads us into a non-discursive domain familiar in Asian traditions of thought, that ruptures the horizon of discursivity and opens to a transcendent or spiritual horizon. Whilst this kind of awareness is untrammelled by moral metanarratives, it rests on a mode of attentiveness that is dependent on virtue, and particularly on love, thus situating it within a horizon that is both ethical and spiritual.

A similar horizon can also be found in Heidegger's philosophy where 'thinking is itself an ethics' and 'ontology becomes indebtedness to what is, a quiet listening vigilant against its own interference, cautious of its own interventions, careful not to disturb. In a word, thinking becomes a lovingkindness' (Cohen, 1985:2). One cares for *what is,* shepherding, or letting be, the giveness, the throwness, of *what is.* By replacing philosophy with the no less difficult task of thinking without recourse to either being or a metaphysics of presence, Heidegger tried to escape the metaphysical closure of ontotheology (Cohen, 1985:2). I suggest that it is possible to read the 'lovingkindness' of thinking as an ethical command that is simultaneously an epistemological praxis establishing an originary ethical horizon that precedes both perception and the articulation of moral metanarratives. A spiritual horizon can also be identified, particularly in Heidegger's later work. Loy (1988:165), for example, argues that 'thinking' for Heidegger 'is designed not to elicit an answer but to effect a transformation' and suggests that the later (post-*Kehre*) Heidegger 'is best understood as nondual thinking' (Loy, 1988:11) which again, is situated beyond discursivity within a spiritual horizon.

If Nietzsche and Heidegger both ruptured the logocentric, discursive horizon of Western philosophy, Derrida might be thought of as causing it to shatter into fragments. By showing that there is no transcendental signified to which language can point (since every signified is only a function of other signifiers), Derrida tries to convince us that our linguistically constructed knowledge is nothing more than 'a general circulation of signs' which cannot point outside of itself (Loy, 1988:259). The propositional truths of philosophy, the absolutes of substance or being which metaphysics has sought, the ontological self, are all merely the play of the system of language (or signifiers) within which they have been sought.

Deconstruction thus confronts us with the limits of the entire structure of Western philosophy and for this reason Cornell (1992a,b) has appropriately described Derrida's philosophy as 'the philosophy of the limit'. Confronted with this limit we have two alternatives. The first is to simply return to the play of signifiers and immerse ourselves in the free play of signs. The second is more radical. It involves stepping beyond the limitations of language into the nondiscursive domain that till now, within the Western tradition, has been consigned to the realm of spirituality. When the first, more common, alternative is chosen, deconstruction is framed by atheism and read as a form of nihilism that confirms the death of both God and philosophy (Hart, 1989). Derrida's own work is often read in this way[49] but an alternative reading is also possible.

As Hart (1989:45-46) suggests, we can frame deconstruction within the context of the Nietzschean madman who cried 'I seek God! I seek God!', rather than that other Nietzschean madman who cried 'God is dead': or within the context of the Heidegger who sought a theology beyond being because the God of Being was not sufficiently divine, rather than the Heidegger who sought simply to deconstruct ontotheology. Deconstruction can then be read, not as a nihilistic *cul de sac*, but as an opening for a new way of knowing that reframes philosophy within a spiritual horizon, leading to a rearticulation of the ethical and 'the attainment of a new capacity for ethical action – whether this is described in terms of love, compassion, altruism or care' (P. Berry *et al*, 1992:5). On this reading, deconstruction is not 'an attack against theology but an answer to the theological demand for a "non-metaphysical theology"' (Hart, 1989:xi).

Commentators with a spiritual perspective have, despite Derrida's disclaimers,[50] read deconstruction as a kind of negative theology[51] which confirms that the 'What is . . . ?' question of Western philosophy cannot be answered by means of (Western) philosophical discursivity. Such a reading points us beyond discursivity and being to something like the mystical 'cloud of unknowing' or the Dionysian 'being beyond Being' of the Western tradition; and to something resembling the Upanishadic understanding of *Brahman* as 'that before which words recoil' or the Buddhist understanding of *sunyata* (the void), in the Eastern traditions.

In arguing that critical postmodernism points us towards a post-discursive spiritually-engaged knowledge I employ the ambiguity in Derrida's (1989) explanation of why deconstruction is not a form of negative theology. Derrida (1989:41) writes, and I quote at some length:

> Between the theological movement that speaks and is inspired by the Good beyond Being or by light and the apophatic path that exceeds the Good, there is necessarily a passage, a transfer, a translation. An experience must guide the apophasis toward excellence, not allow it to say just anything, and prevent it from manipulating its negations like empty and purely mechanical phrases. *This experience is that of prayer.* Here prayer is not a preamble, an accessory mode of access. It constitutes an essential moment, it adjusts discursive asceticism, the passage through the desert of discourse, the apparently referential vacuity which will only avoid empty deliria and prattling, by addressing itself from the start to the other, to you (italics mine).

Derrida then continues ambiguously. On the one hand, he finishes the above paragraph with the phrase: 'But to you as "hyperessential and more than divine Trinity"', thus introducing to the experience of prayer a hyperessentiality of which he has already declared his suspicion. But, on the other hand, he goes on to explore this experience of prayer:

> In every prayer there must be an address to the other as other; *for example* – I will say, at the risk of shocking – God. The act of addressing oneself to the other as other must, of course, mean praying, that is, asking, supplicating, searching out. No matter what, the pure prayer demands only that the other hear it, receive it, be present to it, be the other as such, a gift, call, and even cause of prayer. This . . . characterizes a discourse (an act of language even if prayer is silent) which, as such, is not predicative, theoretical (*theological*), or constative (ibid).

Thus the 'experience of prayer' emerges as a 'differend' – in Derrida's terms 'a new "concept", a concept that can no longer be, and never could be, included in the previous regime' (Derrida, 1981:42) – for it has not and could not be included in the secular regime of modernity. In order to understand this experience of prayer Derrida (1989:42) explains that it:

> implies nothing other than the supplicating address to the other, perhaps beyond all supplication and giving, to give the promise of His presence as other, and finally the transcendence of His otherness itself, even without any other determination.

Prayer is a supplication, an experience of speaking not *of,* but *to* the other (Derrida, 1989:42). And the significance of critical postmodernism is that it enables us to decipher this discourse of prayer without necessarily resorting to a religious discourse of God. This allows us in turn to decipher a spiritually-engaged discourse without resorting to (theocentric) religion. The discourse of this experience of prayer can be recast, as I do in the following chapters, in terms of 'meditation', 'contemplation', 'awareness', or the terms which I employ most frequently, 'attention' or 'attentiveness', directed towards the other as Other.

Attentive love constitutes the epistemological strategy of spiritually-engaged knowledge which is the elaboration of the experience of prayer. In the contemporary context this praxis of attentiveness can in turn be deciphered by means of a plurality of descriptive systems such as post-deconstructive ethics, feminism, environmentalism, spirituality or transpersonal psychology. Although I suggest that this experience of attentiveness, or prayer, is non- or post-discursive, the possibilities of discourse concerning it are not rejected. Ultimately, I argue, it *is* unspeakable because it functions outside the subject/object dualism inherent in language and while this may seem to impose silence, perhaps it also draws forth speech. To quote Derrida (1989:28) again:

> The possible absence of a referent still beckons, if not toward the thing of which one speaks . . . at least toward the other . . . who calls or to whom this speech is addressed – even if it speaks only in order to speak, or to say nothing. This call of the other, having always already preceded the speech to which it has never been present a first time, announces itself in advance as a *recall*. Such a reference to the other will always have taken place. Prior to every proposition and even before all discourse in general – whether a promise, prayer, praise, celebration. The most negative discourse, even beyond all nihilisms and negative dialectics, preserves a trace of the other. A trace of an event older than it or of a 'taking-place' to come, both of them: here there is neither alternative nor a contradiction.

It is this 'call of the other' and the response to this call that lies at the heart of the experience of prayer, the praxis of attentiveness, that emerges out of critical postmodernism and points towards a new articulation of knowledge. Derrida suggests (again ambiguously) that Heidegger's work falls short of this new articulation because in it 'there is never a prayer', there is never an unequivocal acknowledgment of the other (Derrida, 1989:61). Where this unequivocal acknowledgment of the other is present in critical postmodernism, as in the work of Levinas and Bauman, spiritually-engaged knowledge emerges.

Having recognised this prior movement towards the other that precedes discourse and therefore eludes the deconstructive critique, we are now ready to consider the second movement of postmodernism – engagement with the other. If we are to redeem the promise of postmodernity then that engagement needs to articulate a new way of knowing that, in contrast to Foucault's analysis, is not based on the technology of power inherent in modern knowledge. If the discursive universe of modernity is characterised by domination this spiritually-engaged knowledge is non-dominative, based on supplication to the other, which we may call love. Because they have occupied, by choice or social necessity, non-dominative subject positions, the discursive universes of modernity's others contain streams of non-dominative discourse.

Enter the cast of feminists, environmentalists, mystics, social reformers, peoples of colour, Third World peoples, Eastern and traditional philosophers who have finally, under conditions of postmodern globalisation, found their voices. It would be naive to assume that these voices are either unified or innocent; they too have been constructed and colonised over time.[52] But within this multiplicity of discursive universes streams of discourse can be identified that approach the criteria for a new genre of knowledge. We need to listen particularly to discourses that escape the philosophy of the individual bounded subject; that offer an epistemological strategy distinct from the logocentric, rational fundamentalism of modernity; that do not operate from a technology of power; that retain ethical and spiritual horizons; and that exceed the ontotheological approach by asking a different kind of question, an ethical question concerned not with being but with what is *'better than being'* (Cohen, 1985:10).

The ethical question disrupts the 'complacency of being', with 'the compassion of being' (Cohen, 1985:10). And that compassion is drawn forth, according to Levinas, not on the basis of some transcendent principle emerging from a metaphysical ground but on the basis of the encounter with the Other. 'Who are you?' – ontologically, there can be no response – the Other escapes us, overspilling the net of discursive knowledge with which we seek to mediate the being of the Other.[53] But ethically the Other confronts us with the demand for a response that once entered into, calls forth an unlimited responsibility.

As Cohen (1985:11) argues 'the crux of ethics lies in the non-encompassable yet non-indifferent relation between the "better" and "being"'. And this relationship, according to Levinas (cited in Cohen, 1985:11), 'is not a coincidence or a lost union, but signifies all the surplus or all the *goodness* of an original sociality'. This goodness engenders a responsibility that is 'more precious than the fact of being given' (ibid). As Cohen notes, it is also more demanding. With the collapse of ontotheology and the increasing centrality of, and concern with, alterity, this post-deconstructive ethic emerges as the first knowledge based on the response to the meeting with the Other which is the perpetual condition of our existence. It escapes the hold of ethics formulated as universal principles and provides a basis for a human, or plebeian, ethic that both accounts for, and speaks to, the goodness of the 'virtuous peasant' (Murdoch, 1970:74) no less than the goodness of the moral philosopher.

Such philosophising seems a far cry from the woman on the bridge but it is, I think, an essential part of any response to her that seeks to move beyond benevolence in order to grapple with the construction of a just and sustainable world. An authentic response must understand the violence implicit in both the modern project of development and the postmodern project of corporate globalism that it spawns. But it cannot naively assume that violence ends (or begins) there. In India as elsewhere the lower caste and poor communities, as Dass (1994:56) writes, are confronted with 'the failure of the promises of tradition *and* modernity'. Their lives trace out the ambiguities arising from the rupture of traditional frameworks by modernity, but those traditional frameworks are not innocent. They too are implicated in violence, as surely as female infanticide was practised prior to the (violent) intervention of colonialism.

As Derrida (1976:112) argues, 'the structure of violence is complex' and the violence perpetrated by, and against, the woman on the bridge occurs at a tertiary level, dependent already on two prior levels of violence.[54] These two levels Derrida identifies as 'arche-violence and the law'. The originary violence is 'the violence of difference, of classification, and of the system of appellations' (what Derrida (1976:110) refers to as 'arche-writing') in which that which is named is split off from itself in a loss of self-presence. The second level of violence is the law, the concealment of the originary violence of naming through a process of self-occultation that frames difference hierarchically. Only when this discursive violence is in place can the tertiary level of physical violence appear. To truly go beyond violence is to enter the non-discursive domain that exists prior to naming. This domain can be entered by letting go of name and form but such renunciation lies within the domain of the yogi. Only in this domain can violence no longer be thought, and if we would put an end to the violence perpetrated both by and against the woman on the bridge, it is the domain of the yogi, not the philosopher, that we must ultimately approach.

Crowe (1987:8) proposes that 'the more fundamental the level on which we approach a problem, the less relevant is our contribution going to seem to the casual eye, but the more widespread and efficacious is the real impact going to be in the long run'. In order to radically reshape the socially constructed worlds that pre-ordain the woman's place on the bridge, we must understand the process of signification that marks the originary violence. Whilst not denying the necessity for change at political, economic and social levels, attempting this before we have reworked the more fundamental levels may, as history suggests, simply substitute one form of oppression for another.

We are now seeing the emergence of a genre of knowledge which is grounded, not in the totalising principles of a metaphysics of presence, but in the very sea of otherness which constitutes the human condition. This spiritually-engaged knowledge occurs within a transcendent horizon, where 'transcendence' is (re)defined as nonviolent engagement with alterity. Such knowledge precipitates a new meeting between philosophy, spirituality and politics thereby giving rise to what might be described as 'a rational philosophy of love', appropriate to the global domain. This philosophy is grounded in a new kind of empiricism (Derrida, 1978:151) concerned with responding to the shared 'reality' of the world where the crises of injustice and environmental destruction demand a response.

In the optimistic decades of the 70s and 80s there was much millenarian talk of a paradigm shift – a move to a new world view that would be holistic, ecological, libratory, global and, in many accounts, spiritual. From the perspective of early in the new millennium we must recognise that a great deal of this New Age thinking was based on a universalising Western scientistic discourse that attempted to conflate the 'new physics' with mysticism, and particularly with Asian spiritual traditions of knowledge. Little or no account was taken of the profound epistemological differences that differentiate scientific from spiritual discourse. It was assumed that, riding on the authority of science, the new paradigm would usher in a 'New Age'. The claims were excessive and imperialist. During the same decades environmental destruction continued and the gap between the rich and poor grew (UNDP, 1997:9).

The aim of this work is more modest, less optimistic. It is to identify a genre of knowledge that I believe is emerging within the global ecumene. This genre is not backed by the authority of science but seeks, perhaps audaciously, to supplant that authority by making it answerable to a prior knowledge grounded in alterity that simultaneously endeavours to preserve alterity. From the perspective of the modern ecumene, it might be argued that this knowledge has nothing substantive to say. It is, as I explained in the first chapter, 'knowledge under erasure' which delineates a praxis, a way of knowing, that might preserve both existence and otherness. For this knowledge involves a metanoia, a great turning of the consciousness that first shifts, and then dissolves, the whole basis of identification.

Whilst the relativist position argues that all praxes and all 'life worlds' are contextual and culturally embedded so that there seems, at first glance, no way to choose between them, no way to privilege one above the other. I propose, making use of Castoriadis' (1994:142) words, that the spiritually-engaged knowledge I offer here, is 'privileged' both philosophically and politically because it is 'capable of *recognising* and *accepting* this very multiplicity of human worlds, thereby breaking as far as possible the closure of its own world'.

In trying to provide an answer to the question 'Why is this genre emerging?', two primary factors are called forth for those of us situated in 'the West'. Firstly, by the contemporary global crisis in which, as Lyotard suggests, 'it has become impossible to legitimise development by the promise of the emancipation of humanity in its totality' (cited in Bauman, 1995:30).[55] Secondly, it is called forth by the postmodern critique of knowledge which has dispersed the legitimising ethical absolutes and myths that stood between ourselves and the Other. Postmodern globalisation leaves us naked before the Other as it simultaneously confronts us, on a scale never previously known, with the moral demands of Otherness.

Notes

1. Sachs (1992:107).
2. All of these authors have been prolific and I offer here some examples of their seminal works: Immanuel Wallerstein (1984, 1988, 1990, 1991, 1995); John Meyer (1980, 1987; 1989; *et al*, 1975, 1979); Roland Robertson (1977, 1989a, 1989b, 1990a, 1990b, 1991, 1992; *et al*, 1985); Niklas Luhmann (1982a; 1982b; 1987, 1990). As I adopt Robertson's cultural orientation, his work is discussed in more detail in this chapter.
3. Due to the co-option of the term 'globalisation' by economists, the term 'globality' is now gaining currency. I have, however, continued with 'globalisation' throughout this work in an effort to reinforce its broader cultural, social and political meanings.
4. See Dunkley (1997) for a critique of what he describes as *The Free Trade Adventure*. It is, of course, difficult to accurately assess what the 'peoples of the globe' feel about the issue but I am thinking here of the increasingly well-supported demonstrations that are attracted to global events such as the World Economic Forum (see Melbourne newspaper *The Age*, 6 February 1999:19 and 22) and the various United Nations sponsored global summits. Such events not only attract significant numbers of demonstrators but, on occasions, well-organised and well-attended alternative summits. Politically, opposition to global corporatism extends from the extreme right to the extreme left of the political spectrum and includes many new social and religious movements whose political stance and influence is not easily analysed in the traditional terms 'left' and 'right'. The diversity of this opposition has so far made alliances difficult to both form and sustain in any broadly based movement that might offer a viable alternative.
5. See, for example, Coward (1990), Loy (1993, 1996), Berry *et al* (1992).
6. It can, of course, be argued that the poor are with us always, but my concern here is the gap that is steadily widening between the rich and the poor in global terms. The United Nations Development Programme's *Human Development Report 1997* notes that 'the greatest benefits of globalization have been garnered by a fortunate few' (p. 9). The report continues:

   the share of the poorest 20% of the world's people in global income now stands at a miserable 1.1%, down from 1.4% in 1991 and 2.3% in 1960. It continues to

shrink. And the ratio of the income of the top 20% to that of the poorest 20% rose from 30 to 1 in 1960, to 61 to 1 in 1991, and to a startling new high of 78 to 1 in 1994 (ibid).
7. See, for example, Falk (1993b:628-631).
8. There is some debate (Sahliyeh, 1990a,b) as to whether we are seeing an actual *resurgence* of religion or whether we are simply seeing a resurgence in the analysis of religious movements as commentators realise that, contrary to the secularisation predicted by modernisation theory, religious traditions and movements continue to exert considerable influence in a globalising world. Either way, the term 'religious resurgence' is meaningful and I adopt it in this work. Both fundamentalism (Kepel, 1994; Hawley, 1994; Lawrence, 1989) and the so-called 'new religious movements' (Hannigan, 1990, 1991; Griffin, Beardslee and Holland, 1989; Griffin, 1988, 1989, 1990; Needleman, 1970; Anthony, Ecker and Wilber, 1987; Robbins and Anthony, 1978) have emerged as contemporary expressions of this religious impulse.
9. Appadurai (1990), for example, tries to capture the complexity of these global cultural flows by positing five dimensions: (a) ethnoscapes: the shifting landscape of persons around the world – tourists, immigrants, refugees, guestworkers and others; (b) mediascapes: the flow of 'image centred, narrative-based accounts of strips of reality' which are used to constitute, not only our narratives of 'the other', but also to constitute our own proto-narratives, dreams and fantasies, of possible lives; (c) technoscapes: 'the global configuration of technology'; (d) finanscapes: the rapid movement and changing configurations of global capital; (e) ideoscapes: the flow of the various representations of political ideologies, from the ideologies of the state, to counter-ideologies which seek to grasp a portion of state power. They consist of fragments of the Enlightenment master narrative including concepts of 'freedom', 'welfare', 'rights', 'sovereignty', 'representation' and the master-term 'democracy' (Appadurai, 1990:296-300). Appadurai's five 'scapes' are by no means exhaustive but they do convey the idea of the globalisation of culture as a dynamic and fluid process of *exchange*.
10. See Hall (1991:28) for whom the apparent differences of the global domain are symptomatic of the 'peculiar form of homogenization' that is characteristic of mass global American culture. Hall argues that this seeming diversity is only a 'staged' difference that meets the needs of capitalism rather than generating viable alternatives. Compare Kothari (1993), mentioned above.
11. Robertson's example is 'slippery' because of his failure to differentiate between the universal and the Absolute or, in the terminology which I adopted in the previous chapter, between universality and universalism. I argue that his example is notionally correct because Confucianism and Mahayana Buddhism both participate in the 'transcendent' universality of metaphysical traditions which I discuss in chapter five. They both, therefore, represent different expressions of the Absolute, which could be combined and reframed within the Japanese context to give rise to the new and unique expression of the Absolute which constituted Zen Buddhism.
12. See Toubia and Izett (1998); Dorkenoo and Elworthy (1992); Family Law Council (1994); and WHO/UNICEF/UNFPA (1997).
13. A closer consideration of Robertson's example, and of the poignant plight of many indigenous peoples, reveals the political difficulty of a theory that privileges culture. In the global domain the *realpolitik* of power inequities can so skew the exchange between global and local, universal and particular, that the distinction between universality and hegemony blurs with destructive, even genocidal, implications. Whilst some commentators argue that the globalising dynamic

'intrinsically possesses the capacity to generate simultaneously both relativisation and absolutization, secularization and sacralization, instauration and devolution ... from one, albeit complex social process' (Garrett, 1992:302), others would suggest that these alternative outcomes (embodied in the very different political systems that they imply) cannot be freed from their normative or ethical connotations. Despite, or perhaps because of, its attempt to be more 'neutrally descriptive', Robertson's theory (as developed to this point in time) with its privileging of culture, can seem politically naive in a global situation where inequities of power tip the scales in favour of the most powerful locals (be they nation states or transnational corporations) that control the means of cultural reproduction.

14. See Carroll (1992); Hannigan (1990, 1991); Melucci (1989).
15. Again, language is problematic. I use the adjective 'religious' here to include traditional discourses which, from a Western perspective, could not be described as secular. Many of these cultures, however, had no term equivalent to 'religion' since *all* their discourse occurred within a transcendent horizon.
16. See, for example, Smith, W. (1984); Verhelst (1990); Smith, H. (1982, 1984); Guenon (1953).
17. A genre of discourse, Lyotard (1988:xii), advises: 'suppl[ies] the rules for linking together heterogeneous phrases, rules that are proper for attaining certain goals: to know, to teach, to be just, to seduce, to justify, to evaluate, to rouse emotion, to oversee. There is no "language" in general, except as the object of an Idea'. In this sense, one of the 'goals' of spiritually-engaged discourse could be described as inclusivity without hegemony. Spiritually-engaged discourse seeks unity in diversity while simultaneously preserving that diversity.
18. Whilst Robertson and Chiroco (1985) focus on the relativisation of national identity, it is clear that other identity constructs based on different signifiers are also relativised in the global context. Although the nation state has been a characteristic feature of modernity and national identity, a characteristic feature of modernity's dominant elite, many would suggest that national identity has been less central for some peoples than for others. Feminist scholars, for example, suggest that the militaristic and territorial connotations of the nation-state have acted to diminish women's national identification (Grewal and Kaplan, 1994; Jayawardena, 1986; Basu, 1992, 1995; Bhasin *et al*, 1994; Sangari and Vaid, 1993; Mohanty, 1991; Lake *et al*, 1994). Similarly, the construction of many Third World national identities involved tension between existing ethnic or cultural identities and modern geo-political identities marked out by arbitrary colonial borders.
19. See Anderson (1983).
20. Such a formulation of identity is ethical since the reflexive construction of identity clearly has both political and ethical dimensions. I therefore suggest, with Booth (1995), that we need to take into account the significance of this ethical dimension in the process of globalisation and might, therefore, expand Appadurai's (1990) conceptualisation of global flows to include 'ethicoscapes', which could be used to identify and make explicit the changing ethical flows within the global domain. Two of Mazrui's (1995) four ethical revolutions – the green revolution and the revolution of morally accountable economics (which might, as we move into the next century, be revealed as nothing more than a short lived *coup d'etat*!) – could then be conceptualised in terms of changing global ethicoscapes. Overtly or covertly, ethicoscapes and identiscapes are inextricably related.
21. See Ekin (1992).
22. I return to the question of spiritually-engaged politics in chapter six. See also Rothberg (1993a,b); hooks (1993); Kaza (1993); Falk (1988, 1992, 1993a).

23. Whilst the ecological self emerges out of deep ecology, ecofeminism also advocates a self that extends into the natural world. The debate between the relational self proposed by ecofeminism and the ecological self of deep ecology has been of some significance in environmental philosophy (see Plumwood, 1993, ch.7 for a good account from the ecofeminist perspective) but, with due respect to the participants it is, I think, a *fata morgana* that arises from the failure of both ecofeminists and deep ecologists to acknowledge the ultimate emptiness of the (notion of) self. I pursue this more deeply in later chapters, but my argument hinges on the recognition of a nondual subjectivity so inclusive that it cannot entertain an object.

24. Robertson's position has similarities to Giddens (1991), however, Giddens interprets the contemporary condition as 'high modernity' rather than 'globalisation' (see Dass, 1994, for an interesting example of why globalisation needs to be considered as the more inclusive term). Both Giddens and Robertson foreshadow the positive potential of reflexively constructed identities as they see the possibility of people consciously choosing globally benign lifestyles (Giddens' 'life-politics'). There is, however, a problem with this position because it must be asked: Who is this subject that consciously chooses her particular, benign, construct of self? If this subject is socially constructed there can be little sense in the idea of 'consciously choosing'; if this subject is not socially constructed then we are either returned to the 'essential subject', who has been too effectively dismantled by the postmodern critique to be credible, or we must explore the possibility of a different form of subjectivity, one that is so inclusive that it can know no object. My argument for this expanded form of subjectivity unfolds in the following chapters.

25. See Alcoff (1991).

26. See Robertson (1992:170) for a summary of his position.

27. The relationship between globalisation and modernity is a complex one. Robertson (1990a:26-27) maps a five-stage model of globalisation:

> PHASE I in Europe between the fifteenth and mid-eighteenth centuries. During this first phase there was 'an accentuation of concepts of the individual and of ideas about humanity' (p. 26) and the spread of the heliocentric theory of the world and the Gregorian calendar.
>
> PHASE II (mid-eighteenth century to 1870s) – *the incipient phase* – thematisation of nationalism/internationalism issues; problems relating to the admission of 'non-European' societies to the emerging international society.
>
> PHASE III (1870s-mid-1920s) – *the take-off phase* – which saw a rapid increase in ecumenical and global forms e.g. implementation of World Time; First World War; establishment of the League of Nations.
>
> PHASE IV (early-1920s – mid-1960s) – *the struggle-for-hegemony phase* – the Second World War, the Holocaust, Third World independence movements, the atomic bomb, and the formation of the United Nations, all of which brought about a greater awareness of humanity-as-a-whole, and of the potential threats to the survival of this newly recognised entity.
>
> PHASE V (1960s – 1990s) – *the uncertainty phase* – increasing tensions as societies become more multicultural; increasing concern with the survival of humanity-as-a-whole, and with global systems, as awareness of environmental degradation spreads, nuclear weapons proliferate and social injustice increases; consolidation of global media and information networks and of world trade; interests in global systems of civil society and governance. It is in the fifth phase that modernity and globalisation seem to be increasingly at odds with each other. For more concerning this phase, which Robertson suggests is characterised by a 'wilful nostalgia', see Robertson (1990b).

28. Ludic postmodernism (which might also be referred to as 'naïve' or 'relativist' postmodernism) adopts a position of unlimited relativism that emphasises the discursive nature of knowledge. I distinguish this ludic postmodernism from 'reflexive' or 'critical' postmodernism which, as I argue later, leads towards an understanding of knowledge as transformative praxis.
29. Gellner's (1992) somewhat sharply drawn tripartite framework of religious fundamentalism, relativism and rational fundamentalism is helpful in distinguishing different epistemological strategies, although I disagree with Gellner's conclusion that rational fundamentalism offers the best alternative.
30. Although I am referring here to the imposition of Western ways of being and knowing within the global domain, the same strategy is involved in the imposition of a patriarchal or sexist discourse. Some of the most perceptive analyses of the ways in which a dominant discourse is imposed are to be found in feminist and ecofeminist literature. See for example: Harding (1986, 1987, 1991); Plumwood (1993); Shiva (1988, 1991a,b); Mies and Shiva (1993); Sen and Grown (1988); Boserup (1970); Gaard (1993); Warren (1994).
31. Plumwood (1993:31-4) provides a good account of what she refers to as 'the feminism of uncritical reversal'. She deals with this strategy in some detail teasing out the premises involved in the two different forms of uncritical reversal.
32. See Gellner (1992).
33. I distinguish two epistemological strategies at work within postmodernism: (i) relativism which characterises what I call ludic postmodernism, and (ii) reflexivity which characterises what I refer to as critical postmodernism. Other commentators make a similar distinction. See, for example, Griffin (1988, 1989, 1990); Griffin and Smith (1989); Griffin, Beardslee and Holland (1989). Griffin explicitly addresses this issue in his 'Introduction to SUNY Series in Constructive Postmodern Thought' (in all of the above references) where he distinguishes between 'deconstructive' or 'eliminative' postmodernism (which he notes might also be called 'ultramodernism') and 'constructive' or 'revisionary' postmodernism.
34. Rather than 'splitting' and 'absorption' Plumwood (1993:49-52) uses the terms 'radical exclusion (hyperseparation)' and 'incorporation', respectively, in her explanation of the same phenomenon.
35. See Brennan (1993a:vii); Flax (1990:220); Hartstock (1987).
36. As Hall (1991:33) notes, globalisation refers to 'a process of profound unevenness'.
37. See Ryan (1988:559-562) for a summary of the power attributed to culture in postmodern theory.
38. The reflexivity which I am referring to here needs to be distinguished from the internally referential 'reflexivity' that some commentators have ascribed to modernity and postmodernity. Giddens (1991:3), for example, has suggested that 'in the settings of . . . our present day world – the self, like the broader institutional contexts in which it exists, *has to be reflexively made*' (italics mine). He explains this further, asserting that 'the reflexive project of the self . . . consists in the sustaining of coherent, yet continuously revised, biographical narratives' (p. 5). Although his terminology differs from mine, he also recognises the crucial difference between reflexivity within an internally referential framework, such as that of modernity, which is intended to severely 'limit personal engagement with some of the most fundamental issues that human existence poses for us all' (p. 201); and reflexivity that occurs within a framework of external referentiality such as that arising from aspects of the existing world order with its 'degradation of the natural world', its process of globalisation which 'unifies the overall human community'

(p. 225) and its issues of 'biological reproduction' (pp. 224-5), which precipitates an ongoing, and reflexive, confrontation with what it means to 'be human'.

It is interesting that Giddens' three external referents are all described in an impersonal way. I argue that the issue of global social injustice includes but subsumes 'biological reproduction' as an exogenous point of reference and that it is pivotal in understanding reflexivity as dialogue. The exogenous reference points are not *'the facts'* of environmental destruction and social injustice or the growing awareness of a world community, so much as *the others* whom these concerns bring into view. History shows that it is possible for societies to attempt the implementation of 'justice', or the unification of the world, through domination. But the attempt to converse with others must, due to the very nature of the process, begin from a different set of premises. Conversation begins with the acknowledgment that our global context is *shared* and depends on knowing as 'objectively' as possible one's own position, on learning, again as 'objectively' as possible, the position of others and on being willing to change one's position, revise even one's primary intellectual categories, should they be revealed as inadequate.

39. See Organ (1964:11-22; 1987:23-28).
40. See note 33 of this chapter for references to Griffin's work and his edited collections of other authors who make a similar distinction. *Sacred Interconnections: Postmodern Spirituality, Political Economy, and Art* (Griffin, 1990), for example, includes under the heading of constructive postmodernism, the works of well known commentators such as Richard Falk, Joanna Macy, Mathew Fox, Catherine Keller, Joe Holland and John B. Cobb, Jr.
41. Toulmin (1990) provides a useful historical perspective on this 'detour'. He identifies a particular kind of thinking, a particular formulation of knowledge, that began with a historical longing for certainty. Not all peoples have taken this detour. Women of European origin, it can be argued, were less involved in this detour than men. Many non-European peoples, men and women, have never taken the detour, despite the ubiquity of colonisation and the ensuing modernisation.
42. The idea of a 'new start' is, as Toulmin (1990) argues, a modern preoccupation. In the search for alternative ways of knowing and being it seems likely that, as Falk (1992:23) states:

> if we become immersed totally in anti-modernist projects, however valuable, we lose contact with the most powerful set of liberating energies at work in our personal and public lives during this historical epoch we need to develop the practices and nurture the consciousness that simultaneously inhabits premodern, modern, and postmodern realms of actual and potential being.

43. Grewal and Kaplan pursue this with respect to feminisms within the global domain, but I extrapolate from their argument to include all discourse within the global domain.
44. I return to this point in chapter five.
45. See Coward (1990) particularly pp. 8-14 where he explores the potential of Derrida's work as a 'bridge between East and West' (p. 8). Coward includes Buddhist philosophy in Indian philosophy, a usage which I have followed.
46. I mention these three traditions specifically because in them nonduality finds some of its clearest expositions, although it can, of course, be found in other traditions including the Western Christian tradition. But as Loy (1988:3) points out:

> [the seed of nonduality] however often sown, has never found fertile soil [in the West], because it has been too antithetical to those other vigorous sprouts that have grown into modern science and technology. In the Eastern tradition ... we encounter a different situation. There the seeds of seer-seen nonduality not only sprouted but

matured into a variety (some might say a jungle) of impressive philosophical species. By no means do all these [Eastern] systems assert the nonduality of subject and object, but it is significant that three which do – Buddhism, Vedanta and Taoism – have probably been the most influential.

47. The difficulty of effecting this escape from relativism into reflexivity and beyond should not be underestimated. As Derrida (1991:104) suggests, deconstruction appears to have 'left fragile, or recalled the essential ontological fragility of the ethical, juridical, and political foundations of democracy and every discourse that one might oppose' to a destructive or unjust hegemony. In addition, Derrida (ibid) argues, emancipatory discourses as we know them in the Western episteme 'remain essentially sealed within a philosophy of the subject', which implies that the postmodern deconstruction of the subject further undermines library discourses. It is for these reasons that the move beyond relativism implies a move towards nonduality as only this can take us beyond the philosophy of the subject.

48. Gayatri Chakravorty Spivak's translator's preface to *Of Grammatology* offers an example of this atheistic framing. Spivak (1976:lxxviii) says of Derrida's deconstruction:

> Let me add yet once again that this terrifying and exhilarating vertigo is not 'mystical' or 'theological'. The abyss appears when Nietzsche, Freud, Heidegger, Derrida lift the lid of the most familiar and comforting notions about the possibility of knowledge.

Spivak's adamant declaration is very different from Derrida's (1989) own careful response to the question of whether deconstruction amounts to a negative theology in his Jerusalem lecture: 'How to Avoid Speaking: Denials'.

49. See Magliola (1984), or Loy (1988:248-260).

50. Derrida's (1989) Jerusalem lecture addresses the relationship between deconstruction and negative theology. As I show later in this section, it can be read in various ways.

51. See, for example, Williams (1992:72-80), Milbank (1992:30-44) or Klein (1994:114) who cites Paul Ricouer's description of deconstruction as 'a way of addressing religious issues'.

52. I have already quoted Derrida's (1991:104) assertion that many of our library discourses are still tied to the philosophy of the subject (note 45). See for example Fox-Genovese's (1991) book in which she both acknowledges, and tries to tease apart, the influence of the philosophy of individualism on the construction of feminism.

53. See Fowler (1981) in his description of the fifth stage of faith development. Swidler (1990:104-114) draws on this material in a useful discussion of the level of developmental maturity necessary for dialogue.

54. Derrida (1976:101-140) makes this argument in *The Violence of the Letter: From Levi-Strauss to Rousseau*, where he offers a deconstructive reading of Levi-Strauss' account of his work with the Nambikwara people as presented in *Tristes Tropiques* (tr. by-John Russell, New York, 1961). Derrida nowhere offers a systematic philosophy (of violence or anything else), but his reasoning in *The Violence of the Letter* is, I think, applicable more generally in the broader context of globalisation and the interpenetration of cultures which it implies.

55. From Lyotard, 1988, a *Postmoderne explique aux enfants: Correspondance 1982-1985*, Paris, Galilee.

PART III: GENRE ANALYSIS

PART III
ACTOR-BASED ANALYSIS

Chapter 3

Facing the Other: An Ethic of Meeting

> All real living is meeting.
> *Buber*[1]

We now turn to the question: What is this emerging genre of knowledge? I have proposed that spiritually-engaged knowledge is situated within both an ethical and a spiritual horizon, and will now explore this ethical dimension through the discursive systems of post-deconstructive ethics, feminism, developmental and transpersonal psychologies, and environmentalism. In each of these different domains an ethical horizon can be identified which points us beyond the discursive boundary marked out by deconstructive postmodernism into 'the dimension of otherness and transcendence beyond Being' (Levinas, 1995:193). Any ethic, I suggest, which endeavours to relate to the global domain, but also seeks to avoid becoming a metanarrative, ultimately demands a spiritual horizon that offers a way beyond the limits of discursivity.

The ethical horizon of spiritually-engaged knowledge arises out of the moral demand of otherness. 'Ethics', as Wyschogrod (1990:xv) contends, 'is the sphere of transaction between "self" and "Other"'. But if the postmodern deconstruction of the self is taken seriously and we deconstruct our narratives of self, not just intellectually but experientially, then we must release the egoic identifications and obsessions that have maintained the illusion of a separate self thus far and move beyond the bounded self into new, extended forms of subjectivity. Re-presenting our selves in this way also implies re-presenting the other – inventing what Foucault might describe as new 'technologies' of both the self and the other. I refer to these new ways of representation as 'crafts' rather than 'technologies' in order to emphasise that, in the context to which I am referring, they are concerned with creative, skilful and post-rational means of shifting, and ultimately erasing, the self/other boundary.

Such a fundamental reframing of the concepts of self and other clearly unsettles the ethical sphere. It is true that we are witnessing the demise of the universalising discourse of modern humanism with its ethical metanarratives, but we are also participating in the articulation of an alternative universe of discourse in the global domain which reconstitutes the project of knowledge as an inescapably ethical process. As Bauman (1995:43) argues:

> [With] the dispersal of ethical clouds which tightly wrapped and obscured the reality of moral self and moral responsibility – *it is [now] possible, nay inevitable, to face the moral issues point-blank, in all of their naked truth, as they emerge from the life experience of men and women, and as they confront moral selves in all their irreparable and irredeemable ambivalence.*

We will first explore a post-deconstructive ethic, which I refer to as an 'ethic of meeting' because it arises out of the meeting with the Other, and then look at the work of women theorists who have emphasised care, rather than justice, as the primary focus of ethical thought. Their work leads into a consideration of moral development and the possibility that a post-deconstructive ethic may be associated with an expanded form of subjectivity. Since the construction of both self and other are inextricably related, new and expanded forms of subjectivity imply new ways of constructing the other. The third section of this chapter will concern the 'craft of Othering', exploring the ways in which we construct the other. These ways in turn determine the ways that we respond to the other. In the fourth section, we will consider new forms of the ethical emerging in environmental discourse. When these re-articulations of ethical discourse are examined together, the shape of a new ethic can be discerned and a response to some of the concerns raised about so-called 'new ethics' can be mounted.

I present an account of the ethic of meeting which constitutes the 'other-facing', ethical horizon of spiritually-engaged knowledge and refer to it as an *ethic* because it consists of a moral choice, made in the presence of the other, for 'good' rather than 'evil', although the form of either may be uncertain and unknown in the context. The ethic is constituted by this positive orientation towards the other which sometimes, though not always, arises in the encounter with alterity. This ethic of meeting is 'non-discursive' because it is distinct from, and prior to, any formulated system of 'ethics' arising from philosophical or theological theories about universal ethical values or moral attitudes.[2] I use the term 'non-discursive', not to put it beyond discourse, but to mark the threshold of a different way of knowing, speaking and being.[3] The epistemological practice of attention directed towards the other gives rise to that exquisite knowledge to which Basu (1995:20) refers, and generates a way of knowing that bypasses both domination and dependence to discern, honour and preserve the otherness of the Other.

But the ethic of meeting is not simply an ethic of alterity. The risk with the contemporary focus on alterity is that it too becomes a totalising discourse which ensnares and controls the other through difference rather than sameness. In order to balance the emphasis on alterity that defines so much postmodern discourse, we also explore the subjective aspect of the ethical horizon of spiritually-engaged knowledge. It is perhaps best described by terms such as care, love or wonder because it adopts a non-discursive epistemological strategy that renounces mastery in favour of meeting. I previously suggested that this way of knowing is grounded in a primordial experience that Derrida (1989:41) identified as the experience of prayer, an experience of attention directed unreservedly towards the other. Here I argue that the self, in reaching out for the other in true meeting, transcends its own boundaries and enters a post-egoic domain which is most easily discussed in the language of either transpersonal psychology or spirituality. Ultimately this domain is nondual, beyond any separation of self and other.

Before the Face of the Other

A Post-deconstructive Ethic

The works of both Zygmunt Bauman (1993, 1995) and Emmanuel Levinas (1979, 1981, 1985, 1993, 1995) have been particularly significant in the project of articulating a post-deconstructive ethic. Poised somewhere between phenomenology and empiricism, the work of Levinas, particularly, has attracted much attention, including that of Jacques Derrida (1978). Levinas and Bauman offer a way of knowing that emerges from the meeting with the other and is grounded in a primordial ethical encounter. Their work provides an appropriate starting point for my exploration into an alternative ethic of meeting.

Bauman (1995)[4] suggests that in the modern era morality was understood as the *product* of ethics, whereas in the postmodern era we have the opportunity to understand morality as that which *precedes* ethics, since it arises out of each person's 'non-get-riddable, inalienable moral responsibility' (Bauman 1993:37) before the other. Bauman (1995:1) argues that:

> We are so to speak, ineluctably – *existentially* – moral beings: that is, we are faced with the challenge of the Other, which is the challenge of responsibility for the Other, a condition of being-for. Rather than being the outcome of social arrangement and personal training, this 'responsibility for' frames the primal scene from which social arrangements and personal instruction start, to which they refer and which they attempt to reframe and administer.

This primary moral condition is an existential fact of our being-in-the-world. Recognising this is not, as Bauman (1995:1-2) points out, the same as suggesting that all human beings are ethical and will necessarily choose the Good, but simply a recognition of the moral context of our lives. The choice between good and evil seems *always* there, uncomfortably and inescapably defining us as ethically ambivalent, but morally autonomous beings.

Although I have used the term 'ethic' rather than Bauman's term 'morality', the ethic of meeting that I articulate is similarly defined by a decision to move towards an orientation of 'being-for' the other. This ethical orientation always involves uncertainty and ambiguity, for there is no simple, straightforward way of deciding what is an appropriate, or 'good', response to the other. As Bauman (1995:2) says:

> The ambivalence that pertains to the condition of 'being-for' is permanent and incurable; it can be taken away only together with whatever is 'moral' in the moral condition. One is tempted to say that facing the ambivalence of good and evil (and thus, so to speak, 'taking responsibility for one's own responsibility') is the meaning (the sole meaning) of being moral.

To articulate a post-deconstructive ethic of meeting is not therefore to propose a theory of universal or original goodness, nor is it to set down an ethics of righteousness that depends on the correct (or 'right') discursive formulation of good and evil. I agree with Wyschogrod (1990:1) when she suggests that 'the term *postmodern* so [qualifies] the term *ethics* that the idea of ethics, the stipulation of what is to count as lawful conduct, is subverted'. But, when we move beyond discursively formulated ethical systems, we arrive, as I argue, in line with Levinas and Bauman, at a post-deconstructive ethic which acknowledges a responsibility to the Other arising out of a primary moral decision to be-for-the-other. This decision occurs prior to the construction of authoritative social models of good and evil. An ethic of responsibility therefore pushes beyond the socio-linguistic determinism of much postmodernism, to posit the existence of a non-discursive domain from which an ethic emerges. Face to face with the other, who calls us to respond, responsibility may (or may not) emerge. And it is, as Levinas (1993:92) suggests, this primary 'responsibility before the face' that imbues our relation to the other with ethical meaning. Under the gaze of the Other we are called to:

> a responsibility that no experience, no appearance, no knowledge comes to found; a responsibility without guilt, but in which, before the face, I find myself exposed to an accusation that the alibi of my alterity cannot annul.

This meeting with the stranger was not only a historical event that gave rise to human systems of ethics and signification in some past epoch, nor is it only an individual event through which each of us by means of our meeting with the primary (m)other has been drawn into a system of socio-linguistic signification that defines our individuality and our humanity. The meeting with the stranger, with the other, is also the recurring, constitutive event of our daily lives, continuously calling forth the ethical and creative responses through which we renew or reshape the social imaginary that, defining our world, defines our selves. It is the meeting with the stranger which calls forth an ethic that, arising out of the 'secret of the face', 'summons me, claims me, recalls me to a responsibility I incurred in no previous experience' (Levinas, 1993:93-94). It is exactly this responsibility before the other that the face of the woman on the bridge demanded of me. As Levinas (1993:94) writes:

> Strangeness of the other, in that it is precisely by that strangeness that he or she puts me in question by demanding of me with a demand that comes to me I know not whence, or from an unknown God who loves the stranger.

Since that demand arises, at least in part, from the woman's alterity, from her otherness, any ethical response on my part must arise from respect for that very Otherness. It is, as Levinas (1993:94) argues, 'the consciousness of that inassimilable strangeness of the other' that draws me beyond myself into responsibility and 'non-indifference-for-the-other' (ibid) or, more positively, into 'being-for-the-other'. My individual *I* is drawn beyond itself into transcendence. But this is a transcendence that arises out of the ultimate unknowability of the other (Levinas 1993:10) for as Levinas writes: 'The dimension of the divine opens forth from the human face' (Levinas, 1979:78). The face of the other is the icon which leads my gaze beyond the face, to the unknown and unknowable, *which gazes back at me* (Marion 1991:7-24).[5] Since the ethic of meeting is concerned with recognising this divine horizon that opens in the true meeting with the other, I will from now on refer to the capitalised 'Other' as a reminder of this immanence where relevant.

The responsibility before the face of the Other demands a response that preserves the particularity, the alterity and the integrity, of not only the Other, but of myself. It demands a mode of being, an attitude to life, that takes its stand in sociality which arises from non-indifference to the Other. It is this non-indifference to the meeting with the Other that grounds what Levinas (1993:124) refers to as the 'original sociality-goodness', which precedes socially constructed ethical precepts and practices. In 'true' meeting we 'confirm one another as unique and irreplaceable' beings who are inter-related (Levinas 1993:10). The decision to be-for-the-Other is based on desire for the Other that ultimately manifests as sociality which is, according to Levinas, the relationship of conversation. Levinas (1979:51) writes that 'To approach the Other in conversation is to welcome his expression' and, while it may be true that peace and non-violence are essential conditions for that conversation,[6] it is this welcome, this desire for the Other based on a prior openness, that provides the ethical basis of spiritually-engaged knowledge and defines the ethic of meeting. This openness invites conversation which, since it 'brings me more than I contain' (ibid), offers knowledge. It is thus, by radicalising the alterity of the other – what Derrida (1978:151) refers to as 'the theme of the infinite exteriority of the other' – that Levinas reconstitutes the project of knowledge as an ethical process.

This approach opens an unbounded spiritual horizon that is characteristic of the genre of knowledge that I seek to describe. The 'dimension of the divine' is revealed through the face of the Other, where 'face' is understood in Levinas's (1979:50) sense as 'the way in which the other presents himself, exceeding *the idea of the other in me*'. The spiritual horizon opens in the encounter with alterity, rather than through a transcendent horizon of Being. It emerges from a radical empiricism, which affirms the possibility of encountering the world in a way that exceeds my linguistic constructions, allowing me to meet (though not to fully comprehend) the Other in non-violence, peace and openness. Derrida's (1978:151) remarks on empiricism provide further clarification of this way of knowing, enabling us to distinguish between the radical post-deconstructive empiricism that characterises spiritually-engaged knowledge and empiricism as it has been presented in Western philosophy.

> The true name of the inclination of thought to the Other, of this resigned acceptance of ... incoherence inspired by a truth more profound than the logic of philosophical discourse, the true name of this renunciation of the concept, of the a prioris and transcendental horizons of language is empiricism. For [empiricism] has committed ... the fault of presenting itself as a philosophy. And the profundity of the empiricist intention must be recognized beneath the naiveté of certain of its historical expressions. It is the dream of a purely heterological thought at its source. A *pure* thought of *pure* difference.

This radical empiricism is framed by a spiritual, or transcendent, horizon because it relies on the practice of a non-discursive, nondual mode of awareness that exceeds, or breaks through, the bounds of the discursive self in order to encounter the Other. This ethical mode of awareness, or openness, displaces rationality to a secondary domain.

At this point my account of the ethic of meeting begins to diverge from the post-deconstructive ethical account offered by Levinas. Levinas does not claim that the relationship with the Other is non-discursive but that it occurs within language through conversation with the other. This discursive approach, I argue, limits the usefulness of his work. Firstly, it makes it difficult to extend the ethic of the face beyond the inter-human domain to encompass environmental concerns. Secondly, it introduces a contradiction: if we can only meet the other through language then how can we ensure that the encounter is not disrupted or contaminated by socially constructed hierarchies of gender, race or culture that would distort our apperception of, and our responsibility to, the Other? From the perspective of gender,[7] parts of Levinas's *oeuvre* are troubling and have been critiqued from this perspective by Irigaray, Cornell and others.[8] Thirdly, the total supremacy that Levinas accords the other introduces further contradictions unless, as I argue, his work is read within a nondual spiritual horizon.[9]

My alternative approach opens an unexplored possibility, which is alluded to in Levinas's definition of 'face' as that which *exceeds* 'the idea of the other in me'.[10] It is upon this possibility, this realm of excess beyond discursivity, that I will continue to focus. Since this realm is ultimately unspeakable, I refer to it as 'non-discursive', but I reiterate that 'what is at stake . . . [with a negative term such as "non-discursive"] is not the reification of negativity but the recovery of the unspeakable elements in language glossed over by the linguistic turn that dominates twentieth century thought' (Budick and Iser, 1989:xiii). Those unspeakable elements lead us into the realm of nonduality, where the ethical subject is understood neither as an individual, nor as a discursively constructed subject, but as an expanded form of (non-discursive, non-egoic) awareness. This nondual awareness is by no means confined to the mystical or esoteric (which would immediately set up another dualism). The work of two feminists commentators takes us into the fields of human development and transpersonal psychology, and suggests that this nondual awareness is potentially accessible in our daily experience, holding the key not only to an ethic of meeting, but also to our maturation as human beings.

Beyond the Other

An Ethic of Care

Levinas's work is neither alone in contributing to an ethic of meeting, nor definitive of that ethic. Nell Noddings (1984) in her book, *Caring: A Feminine Approach to Ethics and Moral Education*, also articulated an approach to ethics that was 'rooted in receptivity, relatedness, and responsiveness'. Noddings' work was ground-breaking and, like Carol Gilligan's (1982) book, *In a Different Voice*, suggested that there was an ethical domain and, indeed, an ethic which, escaping modern, masculinist, discursive metanarratives, whether philosophical or theological, arose from the day to day experience of women. That Noddings and Gilligan both identified this different ethical voice as 'feminine' laid them open to charges of essentialism as the socially constructed nature of gender has gradually become more apparent. But if we tease apart the essentialist and constructed notions of Woman in their work, it marks an important step in the move away from the discursive formulation of universal ethical metanarratives towards a radical empiricism that apprehends the other by appropriating both the inner and outer experiences (the subjective and objective dimensions) that occur in an encounter with another. Significantly, in these feminist works the encounter with the other is explicitly acknowledged as emerging, not in some esoteric or mystical domain, but in (women's) everyday reality.

I will consider Noddings' approach first since it is formulated as an ethic(s) and offers an accessible, though I believe an incomplete, articulation of an ethic of meeting. Her work is important because it enables us to understand that an ethic of meeting cannot be constituted solely by an ethic of alterity. It must simultaneously be an ethic of care or, since I do not want to limit myself to Noddings' term, an ethic of virtue, where 'virtue' is understood not as a discursive metanarrative but as a praxis or way of being which the ethical subject must embody. I agree with Rose (1993:6) that an adequate alternative or 'new' ethic cannot concentrate only on the other. It must also have a subjective aspect concerned with how the subject encounters the other.

Again, my intention here is not to offer a thorough critique of Noddings' work, but to attempt to draw out the 'rules' involved in constituting an ethically based genre of knowledge. Noddings links the emerging ethical alternative with an empirical approach to (women's) lived experience and to the encounter with others that constitutes our daily lives. Wishing to 'preserve the uniqueness of human encounters' by focussing her attention on 'how we meet the other morally' Noddings locates 'the very wellspring of ethical behaviour in [the] human affective response' and suggests that this response emerges in the meeting with others, where we can 'see their eyes and facial expressions' (Noddings 1984:2-5). Noddings (1984:2) argues that this *ethics of caring* 'begins with the moral attitude or longing for goodness and not with moral reasoning'. The resonances with the Levinasian ethic of the face are evident. A post-deconstructive reading of Noddings' work allows us to enlarge our understanding of the radical empiricism that gives rise to an ethic of meeting, moving beyond the limitations of gender essentialism and identifying it as a potentially universal human response to the Other.

Firstly, we need to bring the distinction between an *ethic* and *ethics* to bear on Noddings' work. Although she uses the two terms interchangeably, I believe her work supports the notion of an *ethic* of responsiveness to the other as necessarily involving the noetic praxes of peace, non-violence, responsibility and openness which Noddings sums up with the term 'care'. I am wary of the essentialism that haunts Noddings', no less than Levinas's, writings. She tells us, for example that 'an ethic built on caring is ... characteristically and essentially feminine an ethic of caring arises ... out of our experience as women' (Noddings, 1984:8). As later feminist analyses show, any ethics of caring that utilises such essentialist gendered constructions may well obliquely authorise the exploitation of women if it is based on a notion of Woman as the (biologically determined) carer.[11]

It can, however, be argued that the construction of Woman, or the feminine, within Western society has been significantly associated with the face-to-face affective relations of the domestic sphere. To the degree that women's enculturation and experiences have been oriented towards caring for others, they have been more heavily influenced by the empirical ethical demands of those encounters and we might expect that more women than men would employ such an ethic in their moral decision-making. This does not necessarily relate the ethic of care to an essentialised femininity but to the realm of face-to-face encounters. Since it is clear that neither all face-to-face encounters, nor all women, are caring, I add the proviso that the ethic of care is related to face-to-face encounters *when these occur in a post-discursive domain*.

If we deconstruct the socio-historical construction of Woman that is implicit in Noddings' work, we can relate the 'ethic of care' to the encounter with the other. Read in this way, Noddings converges with Levinas in grounding an ethic of responsibility or care in the meeting with alterity. We then do not, like Noddings or Gilligan, need to posit the existence of an *essentially* different mode of moral reasoning and development for men and women, but instead need to note how certain constructions of gender, at least in Western society, have defined access to certain kinds of ethical contexts and therefore to certain forms of ethical expression.[12] Caution must be applied, however, to avoid not only unreconstructed notions of all women as caring, but also simplistic notions of all meeting as generating an ethical response. Whilst the potential for an ethical response is there in all meeting since, following Bauman (1995), I argued that we exist in an inescapably moral context, that potential is not always fulfilled. Humanity is not universally ethical. Sometimes the response to the other is unethical and even where it can be described as ethical, it assumes many different forms.

Reframing Subjectivity: Who Cares Anyway?

It is helpful to turn to the work of Carol Gilligan at this point since she offers a more nuanced analysis of the ethical response. In her book *In a Different Voice*, Gilligan (1982) proposed that moral development was gendered. She described two different modes of ethical behaviour. The first, which is predominantly adopted by men, applies universal ethical absolutes to moral dilemmas that are constructed as problems in moral logic. This masculine approach, which can be described as an 'ethics of justice', dominates mainstream modern ethical thought and results in the contemporary emphasis on rights. The second approach, which can be described as an 'ethics of care' is, according to Gilligan, adopted primarily by women. It constructs moral dilemmas as processes of negotiation oriented by a prior feeling of concern within a field of relationships. This feminine approach leads to an emphasis on responsibilities.

Gilligan, like Noddings, argued that the feminine approach to moral dilemmas was based on an ethics of care that arose out of relationship with others. In attempting to construct the two voices as different but equal, she suggested that the 'masculine' ethics of justice was based on 'the premise of equality', while the 'feminine' ethics of care rested 'on the premise of nonviolence' (Gilligan 1982:174). Her assumption was that both are logically constructed from an initial premise within the discursive domain. In her concern to demonstrate that the 'feminine' ethical voice was different to, but not less developed than, the 'masculine' ethical voice Gilligan assumed that both operated within the same domain of logic and rationality. She also assumed that both followed the same developmental sequence, passing through the pre-conventional, conventional and post-conventional stages of Kohlberg's well-known sequential model of moral development, albeit utilising different modes of ethical expression.[13]

Gilligan's suggestion that there was a 'masculine' and a 'feminine' ethics stimulated much discussion. The debate centred around the apparent dichotomy between an ethics of care and an ethics of justice (Benhabib, 1992; Winkler, 1984). Gilligan (1982:6) herself suggested that the two approaches were different but complementary – being different ways of negotiating the six stages of moral development theorised by Kohlberg. In her later work, however, Gilligan (1990)[14] proposed the existence of an additional stage in moral development. She described it as arising 'out of the recognition of the paradoxical interdependence of self and relationship, which then overrides the pure logic of formal reason and replaces it with a more encompassing form of judgement, a polyphonic structure that is able to sustain the different voices of justice and care' (Gilligan 1990:224). Thus Gilligan (1990) argues for a stage beyond Kohlberg's sixth post-conventional stage of moral development. This additional stage in which, for both men and women, care and justice meet, represents a further step towards mature ethical behaviour, but also a step beyond (the primacy given to) the domain of logic and rationality.

Although Gilligan's work is often associated with gendered differences in ethical behaviour, she always approaches ethical difference along two distinct axes – the axis of gender and the axis of moral development. It is this second axis that provides a way of fully utilising the contribution of Noddings. Unlike Gilligan, Noddings asserts the superiority of her 'feminine' ethic(s) of care. Whilst I think that Noddings' intuition of superiority was correct, without the benefit of a sequential model of moral development it could not be developed. 'Care', as Noddings presented it, was undifferentiated along the development axis and included everything from pre-conventional care, to the most mature form of care. Gilligan, however, adopts a maturational approach, arguing that the ethical orientation based on care develops through the six stages (two pre-conventional, two conventional and two post-conventional) of early Kohlberg and also through a more mature seventh stage that integrates care and justice. I suggest that care, or love, provides the key to this mature seventh stage of moral development.

Kohlberg in his later work also concludes that there is a seventh stage of moral development that goes beyond operational moral reasoning. His formulation differs in some respects from the seventh stage proposed by Gilligan because it identifies a domain of knowledge *prior to ethics* that determines the ethical orientation and thus defines an *ethic*, as I have been using the term. At this point in my argument I find Kohlberg's formulation of the later stage more useful and I therefore expand upon it here.[15] Kohlberg and Ryncarz (1990) assert that while the highest level (stage six) of post-conventional moral reasoning could resolve moral problems, it could not 'provide *full* justification for choosing a particular course of action. Thus, not even the highest possible stage of rational "justice" reasoning can adequately answer the question, "Why be moral?"' (Kohlberg and Ryncarz, 1990:206-7). Although they phrase their argument in terms of justice, the same fundamental justification is also required to respond to the question – 'Why be caring in an uncaring world?' I therefore suggest that Kohlberg's seventh stage is applicable equally to the care or the justice approach, since it refers to the prior ethical domain, which has already been identified. I argued that this domain is non-discursive and nondual, whereas Kohlberg and Ryncarz (ibid) argue that it is non-rational, going beyond the rational to depend on nondual experience of self. They describe it as follows:

> the only ethical-ontological orientation that appears capable of generating a fully adequate resolution to ultimate moral questions ('Why be moral? Why be just in a world that is seemingly unjust?') is a cosmic perspective that cannot be structured solely on the basis of formal operational thought. Rather, this orientation appears also to rely upon some type of transcendental or mystical experience – experience of a level at which self and the universe seem unified. Such experience appears to be both necessary in stimulating the shift to a cosmic perspective and instrumental in the structuring of its key features.
>
> Having a cosmic perspective means that one experiences an intimate bond between oneself and the cosmos; one views things not so much from the standpoint of a distinct individual as from the standpoint of the universe as a whole. Some of the great moral philosophers appear to have held such a perspective, and available evidence indicates that it is attainable by those who undergo the appropriate kinds of experience (transcendental and mystical) and reflect upon them in specific ways.

Kohlberg and Ryncarz's description of this mature stage of moral development offers a way of bringing together the various threads that have been developed thus far in this chapter. Kohlberg, Gilligan and numerous transpersonal theorists have by now proposed the existence of (at the very least) an additional stage of moral development that is beyond the rational. This stage is post-rational but not irrational.[16] In proposing this non-rational stage of moral development these commentators are, by implication, proposing the existence of a non-rational genre of knowledge that is ethical. This knowledge is ethical in exactly the sense identified in the post-deconstructive ethic of Bauman and Levinas. Such knowledge is not concerned with the rational discursive formulation of any ethics or ethical system, but is a prior, more fundamental, unifying form of knowledge. It answers the question: 'Why be moral?' with a turning towards the Other and in doing so, defines an ethic of meeting.

This chapter began by articulating the ethic of meeting in the postmodern discourse of alterity and moved on to the expression of a very similar ethic in the discourse of feminism. It is also possible, however, as argued above, to articulate it in psychological discourse. The hierarchical or (holarchical) frameworks of, for example Kohlberg, Wilber (1995, 1997a), Wilber *et al* (1986), and Alexander *et al* (1990),[17] in developmental and transpersonal psychology, allow us to situate the ethic of meeting within a spectrum of developmental stages.

Since, prior to the development of rationality, the human being cannot take the perspective of another, the ethical perspective proposed here must of necessity be located *after* the development of rationality. Such an understanding allows us to move away from describing the ethic of meeting in negative terms as non-rational (non-personal, non-discursive, non-representational etc.) towards understanding and describing this ethic and its associated genre of knowledge as *trans*rational (transpersonal, etc.) because it transcends and includes the rational, or as *post*-rational (post-personal, etc.), since everything is 'post' these days and the prefix indicates the sequential, developmental nature of this perspective.

Subject/object, self/other distinctions are transcended in this nondual, post-discursive domain, which takes us, as Kohlberg and Ryncarz (1990:207) propose, out of the generally accepted domain of human development into the domain of spirituality or mysticism. It is not, however, only the other who is released by this transcendent horizon. In genuine meeting, the self also reaches beyond the discursively constructed boundaries of ego. If we return at this point to the definitions of spirituality that I offered earlier it becomes clear why this kind of knowledge can be described as 'spiritually-engaged'. It emerges when the individual subject breaks through the boundaries of ego to reach out for the Other in a movement of nondual awareness that relinquishes mastery over the other in favour of meeting. The ethic of meeting and the genre of knowledge that it grounds, is thus based on a radical empiricism that challenges the construction of the self/other dualism (and therefore the construction of gender). It postulates a post-discursive, post-individual, and therefore 'post-gendered', experiential domain where the encounter with the Other is *not* defined by any socially constructed relationship (that is, where I care for the Other because she is black, or a woman, or my spouse, child, parent, etc.) but is 'known' or 'experienced' according to the degree to which 'I' can deconstruct the self/other boundary.

By arguing that this primordial ethical relation precedes gender, race or other boundaries of difference, I am positing a domain of experience which is unmediated, transcendent and perhaps transcultural. At first glance this seems to contradict the constructivist model of knowledge by suggesting that it is possible to perceive 'things-in-themselves, percepts as they are, before they have been thought-constructed' (Loy 1988:41). I argue, however, that most of our perception *is* socio-linguistically, discursively constructed because in our own cognitive and ontological functioning we rarely move beyond the stage of rationality. Whilst we can rationally deconstruct our own social constructions (as postmodern theory has so ably demonstrated) we cannot easily move to another mode of perception unless and until we ourselves move to another way of being or another stage of development. To experience a nondual, ethical response we need to 'de-automatise' our perception of the Other by transcending, or deconstructing, the boundaries that delineate self and other. Whilst the rational component of this work of deconstruction is something of which anyone reading this is capable (and indeed which postmodernism is to some extent forcing upon us), the existential component of this deconstruction is more difficult. It is for this reason that so many of our meetings with others do not give rise to a situation of being-for the Other, of caring for the Other, far less of experiencing an unlimited ethical responsibility to the Other.

But how can this 'intimate bond' with the Other required by an ethic of meeting be experienced? How can we 'grow up' enough to escape the ego's hold and enter a genuinely post-modern era of Otherness? Kohlberg (1990:206) suggests that such maturation relies 'upon some type of transcendental or mystical experience'. I find myself in agreement with this answer but anxious that if terms like 'transcendental' and 'mystical' are not carefully interpreted we will rapidly find ourselves back in the spiritual/secular dualism that characterised modernity. It is here that the work of women is particularly important. Whilst Kohlberg (1990:207) argues that 'some of the great moral philosophers' have articulated this post-representational ethic, Noddings' work seems to suggest that many women, who have never had the educational opportunities to be great moral philosophers, may also have reached this stage and that they did so, not through philosophy, but through 'care'.

As I proposed in chapter two, with the contemporary conditions of globalisation the Strangers of the global domain have become our Neighbours. Globalisation confronts us with the choice of maturing into a larger identity capable of being-for our Stranger/Neighbours or regressing into a smaller identity that remains bound to limited and legalistic interpretations of individual justice. The agent of maturation emerges, in Noddings' terminology, as the capacity to care. It is this capacity for care or, as I propose, this skill of 'attentive love', that constitutes the subjective pole of spiritually-engaged knowledge and which finds expression, particularly in the work of women theorists. In the next chapter I explore the development of attentive love as an epistemological strategy within feminist theory but will first discuss the process of Othering and the role that it plays in an ethic of meeting.

The Craft of Othering

Foucault (1988) proposed that human beings develop knowledge about themselves and their world by means of technologies. There are, he wrote, four major types of technologies involved in the construction of knowledge: technologies of sign systems, technologies of production (that allow us to transform and manipulate things), technologies of power and technologies of self (Foucault, 1988:18). As Foucault notes, these technologies do not operate separately but systemically, and Foucault's work has provided many useful insights into the construction of modern knowledge. The critique of the relationship between the technology of power, or domination, and the technology of self is a particularly well-rehearsed part of the critique of modernity.

Feminist commentators[18] have been influential in not only theorising this link between the technologies of domination and of self, but in recognising the gendered nature of the link. Brennan (1993b:52-62), for example, proposes that the modern individual, Lacan's egoic subject, defines himself through 'passifying the other'[19] by fixing the other's identity. Utilising what might be referred to as a 'technology of other', the other is made into an object in order to secure the identity of the egoic self (Brennan, 1993b:65). Plumwood (1993) also explores in detail the construction of modernity's governing form of identity – the master ego – and the simultaneous construction of the bounded identities of modernity's 'others' – women, nature, peoples of colour and the Third World. These analyses offer valuable insights into the construction of the governing form of modern identity, but, I argue, they also point towards the liberating possibilities of acknowledging the other as unlimited, open to the transcendent.[20] Once the other is released from fixity and recognised as unbounded, the identity of the individual ego, which was dependent on the passification of the other, also gives way, so that we can move into a new kind of meeting with the Other and towards a new way of knowing.

The developmental models of human maturation referred to above suggest that it is possible to move beyond the stage of egoic, bounded identity into a more mature 'interdividual', or even nondual identity, with a capacity for 'cosmic concern' that extends to the entire scheme of things. The spiritually-engaged knowledge that arises in these later stages of maturation is dependent on different processes, and also on a different vocabulary, from those identified by Foucault for modernity. 'Technology' is a modern term whose rational and dominating connotations are captured in its dictionary definition.[21] In order to mature beyond the rational domain we require a different kind of process, consciously applied, emerging from a deeper, more creative part of ourselves, and I adopt the word 'craft' to denote this kind of skilled, creative, post-rational process.[22] As we mature Foucault's technology of power is replaced by a 'craft of attentiveness' that defines the epistemological strategy of spiritually-engaged knowledge. I turn to this epistemological strategy in the next chapter, but before doing so, will explore the replacement of another of Foucault's technologies. I suggest that with maturation, not only is the Foucauldian technology of power replaced by a craft of attentiveness, or attentive love, but the Foucauldian technology of self is replaced by a craft of Othering.

It is clear, of course, that the self and the other are simultaneously constructed, although according priority to the individual self is characteristic of the narcissism of the modern era (Lasch, 1978, 1985) and of the dynamic that constructs modernity as the ego's era. In order to emphasise the difference between spiritually-engaged knowledge and the knowledge of modernity I explore the craft of Othering.[23] I have argued that spiritually-engaged knowledge is grounded in an ethic of meeting that comes into effect when we assume a positive orientation towards the Other within a transcendent horizon.

The way that we apperceive, or craft, the Other is therefore fundamental to the ethic of meeting.

It is possible to posit, as do Blaney and Inayatullah (1994), a 'spectrum of otherness' that arises from a range of different epistemological strategies such as I discussed earlier. At one end of the spectrum the strategy of superiority underpins a technology of other that occurs within a discursive horizon and defines a limited other. As we saw, it gives rise to conquest rather than conversation. At the other end of the spectrum a change occurs as technologies of other give way to crafts of Othering. The transformative epistemological strategy discussed in the previous chapter underpins a craft of Othering that recognises the Other as unlimited, and unbounded, within a transcendent horizon. Unlike the technology of other, this craft of Othering does not construct the Other from excluded elements of the self. It is based on recognition of the iconic Other, involving an inclusive process in which the Other is met both within and without. Four different expressions of this craft of Othering will be considered below.

I-Thou Relationship

Buber's classic work *I and Thou* (1994) constitutes one of the significant articulations of the craft of Othering. I consider it here to demonstrate the significance of the craft of Othering in articulating an ethic of meeting. The transcendent horizon in Buber's work is quite explicit. Like Levinas, Buber based himself in the Judaic tradition, while attempting to universalise its wisdom. His emphasis, in contrast to Levinas, is not the face of the Other, but like Noddings, the relationship to the Other. His work, which is concerned with how to bring about a meeting between the self and other, can be read as a description of how the Other must be crafted if 'true' meeting, with its intimation of responsibility, is to occur. According to Buber, the key lies in the 'I' appealing to the Other, not as an object, but as another unique and irreplaceable subject, as a 'Thou'. Yet this appeal does not arise from an individual *I*, addressed to a separate, objective *Thou*, but is the result of a particular kind of subjectivity, or inter-subjectivity, that exists between the *I* and *Thou*.

In a dichotomising approach that is illuminating if perhaps too starkly drawn,[24] Buber distinguishes two primary attitudes to life that are available to human beings. The first is called forth by a technology of other which Buber represents by the primary word *I-It* (where the third person pronouns *he* or *she* can be substituted for *it*). This attitude or word then defines the world of experience, in both the inner and outer realms. The second world is called forth by the primary word *I-Thou* which defines a very different attitude. This word 'establishes the world of relation' (Buber 1994:18), and holds the key to a craft of Othering. According to Buber:

There is no *I* taken in itself, but only the *I* of the primary word *I-Thou* and the *I* of the primary word *I-It*. When a man says *I* he refers to one or other of these. The *I* to which he refers is present when he says *I*. Further, when he says *Thou* or *It*, the *I* of one of the two primary words is present. The existence of *I* and the speaking of *I* are one and the same thing. When a primary word is spoken the speaker enters the word and takes his stand in it. (Buber 1994:16)

The contrast that Buber creates is helpful in clarifying what is involved in a craft of Othering that recognises the other as a Thou, as an Other with no bounds. For Buber the primary word I-Thou implies that I take my 'stand in relation' to a Thou which 'has no bounds', a Thou which is porous to 'the eternal Thou' (Buber 1994:17,19) whom I glimpse in each Thou whom I address. Buber's Thou is not confined to human others, but might be addressed to a tree or an animal (Buber 1994:156-9). He writes that the world of I-Thou calls forth love, which 'is [the] responsibility of an I for a Thou', even to the extreme of loving all beings (Buber 1994:29). Buber makes it clear that the link between the iconic Other, the *I-Thou*, leads back into lived experience through the responsibility entailed in true meeting.

Direct Seeing

The spiritual horizon in Buber's work is quite explicit. Friedman (1986) notes the similarities between Buber's philosophy, which had its roots in Hassidism, and the Eastern spiritual traditions of Tao and Zen. Indeed a similar theme concerned with othering can be found in the thought of the Zen teacher, D.T. Suzuki. The approach is still dichotomising but the terminology is different – *I-Thou-/-I-It* becomes Eastern/Western, contemplative/analytical, (inter)personal/impersonal – but the distinction between different processes of othering is, I think, still apparent. To convey these two different approaches Suzuki (1970) compares two poems,[25] the first written by Tennyson:

> Flower in the crannied wall,
> I pluck you out of the crannies; –
> Hold you here, roof and all, in my hand,
> Little flower – but if I could understand
> What you are, root and all, all in all,
> I should know what God and man is.

And the second, a *haiku* written by Basho, a famous Japanese poet of the seventeenth century:

> When I look carefully
> I see the *nazuna* blooming
> By the hedge!

Both poems describe a similar meeting, an encounter with a small and rather insignificant flower. Basho's meeting involves the craft of Othering which engenders ethical responsibility *to* the flower, a state of being-for the flower, such that it is not interrupted from persevering in its own being. The gaze is attentive and situated within the encounter. Tennyson's meeting, on the other hand, involves a technology of other which, while ostensibly addressing the flower, destroys it. The gaze is impersonal, or transcendental (rather than transcendent), located outside the encounter with an external observer who experiences himself as different from both the flower, God, and nature. Basho's experience is direct, unmediated by ideas, foreknowledge or imagination (Buber 1994:25), whereas Tennyson's is mediated by knowledge and universal laws. The distinction being made here is not between the universal and the particular, but between absolute universals that lead to abstraction, as in Tennyson's case, and the revelation of the Absolute through the particular that leads to ethical wonder and care of the Other, as with Basho.

The difference between the gazes, returns us to Marion's (1991:7-24) distinction between the gaze of the icon and the gaze of the idol as two different ways of being in the world. The gaze with which we perceive an icon is a gaze unbounded by our own conceptions, that is open to the mystery of 'the wholly other'.[26] The gaze with which we perceive an idol is, by contrast, a gaze bounded by our own conceptions, which screen the real strangeness (the transcendent unknowability) of the Other and protect us from any unsettling encounter within an unbounded horizon. Just so, a comparison between a technology of other and a craft of Othering demonstrates that the former binds the other to our own measure, while the latter reveals the iconic Other who unsettles the boundaries of the self.

Despite the dualistic terms in which these commentators have chosen to describe it, this craft of Othering is not the exclusive domain of non-Westerners (Suzuki, 1970; Banuri 1990[27]), nor of those identified with a theistic religious tradition (Buber, 1994; Marion, 1991), nor of women (Noddings 1984; Gilligan 1982). It represents, rather, a post-individual, post-rational, capacity of mature human beings. It would seems, however, that the dominant masculinist, secular world of Western modernity has certainly obscured this capacity, devaluing it and projecting it externally onto the East and internally onto psychical fantasies of the feminine or the spiritual.

Surrendering to the Other

Brennan (1993b), whose work I consider in more detail in the next chapter, offers an analysis of the processes by which modernity blocks the craft of Othering, reinforcing instead the illusion of contained individuals unable to move beyond their egoic identification. Whilst it can be argued that the contained masculine identity has always been formed by objectifying the feminine other, Brennan (1993b:13-17), following Heidegger's critique of technology, goes further to assert that the technological mastery of modernity reinforces the illusion of the contained, controlling identity, making it even more difficult to relinquish (the illusion of) control over the other and thus escape from the bounded self. Sophisticated technologies, large scale production, the decline of religious discourse, and the contemporary Western forms of economic and political organisation, all make it easier to fulfil the individual's desire for instant gratification while refusing to acknowledge any indebtedness, dependence or responsibility towards the other. This technology of other that constructs the modern ego, in contrast to the craft of Othering, involves the domination and objectification of the other. It is 'an attitude in which the seeing of the other is simultaneously a shaping of it' (Brennan, 1993b:73).[28]

The craft of Othering, as described by Buber or Suzuki, is not something that a subject directs at an object, but is something that brings about an integration between the subject and the object, a state of interbeing in which the one participates in the Other. The craft of Othering is based on desire for the Other, but it is the desire to delight in the unbounded difference of the Other, not the desire to shape or dominate her. This mutual delight leads to the recognition of a domain of subjectivity to which, as Buber (1994:85) says, 'no dependent genitive can be attached'. It is a subjective awareness because it is experienced by an 'I', but that 'I' is no longer the separate, individual self.[29] As Klein (1994) suggests in her work on feminine identity, this awareness offers an expanded form of subjectivity that is distinct from either the socially constructed self or the essential (in Klein's case feminine) self. Significantly, this awareness offers a reference point for an 'I' that is not defined through opposition to the fixity of another. It offers an expanded form of identity that does not replicate the dynamics of domination and is no longer dependent on a dynamic of objectification.

The craft of Othering, then, is not a process of domination but of letting go. The self gives in to the wonder and delight of the Other, without seeking to control or determine her. This wonder includes not only a sense of awe and amazement, but also a sense of compassion and even despair that arises out of (connaturality with) the suffering that is also part of an experience of interbeing. It can be argued, as Macy (1993:15-28) does, that our despair at the current environmental destruction offers the best evidence of our inter-subjectivity with non-human others, and that it is this connaturality which, entered into deeply, ultimately offers a way out of that despair. Macy's (1991, 1993) work takes us into the environmental domain which will be considered in the next section. But before considering the application of an ethic of meeting to the environmental domain, I want to consider one more aspect of the craft of Othering which provides a link to aesthetics, as well as to spiritual discourse and practice.

De-automatising Perception

Tacey (1995)[30] formulates a connection between aesthetics, environmentalism and a quotidian Australian spirituality through art, particularly poetry.[31] In language that bridges the discourses of literature and psychology,[32] Tacey (1995:163) writes of the nature poets who 'encounter the soul of the world' or who 'experience the cosmic interiority of nature'. Describing the 'subversive power of our nature poets' to overcome the man/nature dualism, he suggests that the process involves de-automatising 'the old and habitual dualism between self and other' such that 'the "normal" condition of alienation is subverted' (162). This implies that the craft of Othering can be understood to involve the release of fixed and habitual patterns of thought which have sunk beneath the conscious level. This process, I argue, is akin to the de-automatisation that occurs with meditative practices in the spiritual domain. I suggest, and explore further in the next two chapters, that a particular kind of awareness, which has been variously referred to as 'affectionate awareness' (Nisargadatta, 1981:292), 'bare attention' (Goldstein, 1983:19-28; Nyanaponika, 1983:30-45; Kapleau, 1989:10-11); or 'attentive love' (Weil, 1977:333)[33] is crucial to this process of de-automatisation that facilitates the crafting of an unlimited Other. The connection between undoing habitual patterns and attention is confirmed by Deikman (cited in Loy, 1988:85) in his studies of meditation. His findings suggest that de-automatisation involves *reinvesting actions and precepts with attention*.

We might understand this by considering once more Brennan's (1993b) work. She suggests that the maintenance of the contained subject can be understood in terms of an 'economy of energy'.[34] The individual subject is maintained by repressing the knowledge of its inter-dependence, beginning with its dependence on the mother. A continual energetic input is required in order to maintain this self/other boundary and the associated fantasy of separation. The shift to transpersonal stages of development is achieved by relinquishing the fixity of the other, realising inter-being and dissolving the self/other boundary. I believe, although my argument would differ from Brennan's,[35] that this releases energy which can be reinvested, as Deikman proposes, in 'actions and precepts' and that the energy involved takes the form of attention, or a particular kind of directed awareness. Whilst I return to this in the next chapter, my point here is that the craft of Othering takes us into an energetic domain of awareness, a realm of inter-being in which the boundaries of the ego, theoretically and *existentially,* give way.

The craft of Othering is ultimately a nondual practice. This nondualism might be understood as a form of phenomenalism, but it escapes the solipsism of many forms of phenomenalism by deconstructing both the subject *and* the object, both the self *and* the other (Loy 1988:87), to arrive at an unbounded understanding of identity as open to a transcendent or sacred horizon, and constructed through the incarnation of attentive watchfulness or responsibility. Once the craft of Othering has been understood, it is clear that it need not be limited to interactions between people. An animal, a plant, a river, a mountain, a species, even the Earth itself, can all be approached through a craft of Othering that facilitates an ethical encounter. The craft of Othering underpins the ethic of meeting, determining whether we encounter the other with sufficient openness to experience our inter-being and the responsibility which it engenders, or whether we do not. I next consider the application of an ethic of meeting in the environmental domain where the distinction that I have drawn above, between a technology of other and a craft of Othering, is particularly useful in distinguishing between an ethical meeting and a further attempt to master nature.

Earthcraft

Having developed the idea of an ethic of meeting in which responsibility for the other emerges from the encounter with the Other, we now explore this ethic in the non-human, ecological domain. Despite the entrenched anthropomorphism of the modern Western universe of discourse, human others by no means exhaust the diversity of otherness that we encounter within the global domain. At the end of a century which has witnessed unprecedented genocide, Levinas's concern with the face, with the human other, is understandable, but insufficient. The holocaust of non-human species also demands our attention: the destruction and pollution of forests and jungles, waterways and oceans, soil and air, no less than the woman on the bridge, silently cry out for a response.

In order to embrace the environmental domain within an ethic of meeting, the anthropomorphism implicit in Levinas's 'ethic of the face' must be abandoned (or stretched to its absolute limit), as must the priority given to language (at least in the limited sense of conversation or verbal exchange). Here we explore the application of an ethic of meeting to encounters with both other species and the earth itself. I contend that the ethic of meeting, as the objective pole of spiritually-engaged knowledge, correlates with the ethical awareness and the re-articulation of knowledge that is emerging in certain streams of environmental discourse. Spiritually-engaged knowledge allows us to replace the instrumentalism of much resource-based environmentalism with a way of knowing that combines an objective pole in which alterity is paramount, with a subjective pole in which care for that alterity is the overriding responsibility.

There have been many attempts to classify the burgeoning field of environmental discourse (Fox, 1990; Eckersley, 1992), but I want to make use here of a simple division between 'light green' and 'deep green', or 'shallow' and 'deep' ecological thought.[36] Light green environmentalism advocates preservation of the environment for its instrumental value to humankind, while deep green environmentalism advocates preservation of the environment for its own sake, for the sake of its alterity, its Otherness. In light green discourse the 'interpersonal', or 'face-to-face', meeting with other species in nature, or with 'nature herself', goes unacknowledged. Influenced by ecology, which although relational and systemic is still essentially a science, light green discourse adopts an impersonal gaze. Deep green discourse, on the other hand, has its roots in communion with nature. It seeks to know nature through the process of connaturality, and in contemporary environmental philosophy this finds its fullest expression in deep ecology and ecofeminism. Deep ecology proposes complete identity with the environment, suggesting that Nature *is* one's Self. Ecofeminism proposes a relational form of identity in which the self is defined in terms of its relationships to a variety of other forms of being. These approaches are in many ways heirs to the Romantic movement of the eighteenth century, and despite their different conceptions of the self, rest ultimately on a love of Nature in which aesthetic appreciation, nature mysticism and protective moral responsibility are intertwined.

Meeting Earth Others

It is, I think, in response to Nature that many people experience something close to the radical empiricism that I have described. Since my focus in this chapter is to explore the ethic of meeting which constitutes the objective pole of spiritually-engaged knowledge, I begin with an account of a meeting with another species in Nature that leads into an articulation of an ethic of meeting. I explore first an account of a meeting with another species drawn, not from environmental philosophy, but from literature.[37] The account is taken from D.H. Lawrence's poem, *Snake*.[38] It describes a meeting with a non-human other, providing an experiential account of the struggle to escape from a technology of other and adopt a craft of Othering which is associated with the primordial ethical response that constitutes an ethic of meeting.

> A snake came to my water-trough
> On a hot, hot day, and I in pyjamas for the heat,
> To drink there.
>
> In the deep, strange-scented shade of the great dark carob-tree
> I came down the steps with my pitcher
> And must wait, must stand and wait, for there he was at the trough before me.

Initially, Lawrence employs a craft of Othering which is certainly not dependent on the recognition of the snake as ego, but on the priority he accords to the snake as Stranger, as Other. He appears to grant to the snake-as-subject a standing at least equal to his own.

> Someone was before me at my water trough,
> And I, like a second comer, waiting.

Here is neither an egotistical self, nor a relational self, but a self that has averted its gaze from itself to attend to the Other. But it is difficult to maintain the craft of Othering and a struggle ensues:

> The voice of my education said to me
> He must be killed,
> For in Sicily the black, black snakes are innocent, the gold are venomous.
>
> And voices in me said, If you were a man
> You would take a stick and break him now, and finish him off.
>
> But must I confess how I liked him,
> How glad I was he had come like a guest in quiet, to drink at my water trough
> And depart peaceful, pacified, and thankless,
> Into the burning bowels of this earth?
>
> Was it cowardice, that I dared not kill him?
> Was it perversity, that I longed to talk to him?
> Was it humility, to feel so honoured?
> I felt so honoured.
>
> And yet those voices:
> *If you were not afraid, you would kill him!*
>
> And truly I was afraid, I was most afraid,
> But even so, honoured still more
> That he should seek my hospitality
> From out the dark door of the secret earth.

We experience with Lawrence the struggle of maintaining an empty self in the face of the other. We are shown how difficult it is to maintain, through a craft of Othering, an identity that is porous to the snake, particularly when the non-porous, bounded, socially-constructed self dictates an attitude of fear that translates into a dominating technology of other.

From the early glimpse Lawrence offers of the empty self that is totally other-directed and lost in wonder, we are taken through the struggle to maintain a self that remains open to the Other, and finally exposed to the consequences of losing that struggle as culturally automatised perception takes over. The failure to unlearn the 'privilege' of our education, to let go of our socially constructed fear of the snake, is experienced as irremedial loss. As the snake withdraws, the poet 'in a sort of horror' against his leaving, throws a log of wood at him:

> And immediately I regretted it.
> I thought how paltry, how vulgar, what a mean act!
> I despised myself and the voices of my accursed human education.

Even a glimpse of the empty self, a glimpse of the Other mediated only by wonder and undiluted attention, convinces us that something is lost when we return to the bounded self and the dualistic technological gaze.

> And so, I missed my chance with one of the lords
> Of life.
> And I have something to expiate;
> A pettiness.

This description of a meeting with the Other, highlights some of the issues involved with positing a craft of Othering based on a radical, but ethical, empiricism. Firstly, the subject's own state of awareness is a crucial element in such a meeting. Secondly, this awareness must somehow de-automatise, or free itself from, the socially dictated, constructed voices of the phenomenal self that distort the meeting with the Other and blur the responsibility that is engendered. The voices of our education, the voices of society, that construct both the self, the other, and their inter-relation, reduce all three to the paltry dimensions of social convention that prevent true meeting with the Other. Yet Lawrence shows how it might be possible to escape – to struggle with the conventions, to be so captivated, so honoured by the presence of the other as Other, that we can still the insistent social voices of the narrowly defined self to prevent it from intervening between Self and Other. Lawrence's poem, Levinas's ethic of alterity, Buber's *I-Thou*, (a post-deconstructive reading of) Noddings' care, and our own experience, all suggest that it is possible, but difficult, to reach this point of nondual, inter-subjective participation. And, I would suggest, it becomes more difficult as the difference between self and other increases. Lawrence's meeting with a mosquito, for example, ends in a dim dark smudge that is not Lawrence![39] What happens if we explore a situation where the difference between the two parties is very much greater – our meeting, as human beings, with the earth as Other?

The Earth as Other

An ethic of meeting, which is dependent on a particular quality of inter-subjectivity, can be extended to encounters with snakes, and from there to encounters with trees,[40] rivers, or even mountains. But what about 'the whole', 'the environment' that has become the subject (or more accurately object) of so much ecological discourse? What about the globe, the earth as a blue-green ball suspended in space, which Sachs (1992:107) contends has 'irresistibly emerged as the icon of our age'? As Sachs (1994:170-175) points out, it is an uneasily ambiguous icon which, in the terminology invoked above, converts all too easily into an idol created by a technology of other that deflects environmental discourse away from the responsibility engendered in true meeting towards a greater desire for mastery. For the Earth appears as a 'small and fragile ball' only to the distant gaze of the extraterrestrial observer. As Bordo (1992:169) observes:

> Contemporary society has fashioned a technological platform for the transcendental viewpoint. The extraterrestrial technologically secured 'vision' might be better thought of as that later and advanced epoch of the initial Copernican thought experiment when the hypothesis became institutionalized as an administrative gaze.

The gaze of this technology of other directed towards the Earth is impersonal, Copernican, standing somewhere in space from where 'we can see and study the Earth as an organism whose health depends on the health of the parts' (WCED, 1987:1). 'Earth-the-patient' (Bordo, 1992:168), in need of our protective management and care, is constructed by this extraterrestrial, technological gaze that gives rise to the proliferation of technology for the task of monitoring and protecting the planet. State-of-the-art technology becomes the prerequisite for managing nature. Holes in the ozone layer, the proliferation of greenhouse gases, acid rain, desertification, all seem to require global technological and administrative responses in which the organisation of the planet is summoned 'into a unitary techno-administrative system' (Bordo, 1992:169) intended to increase rather than decrease our mastery and control of nature, and of the Earth as other.

The discursive subjects who would manage the Earth, believe that they have a warrant to speak for 'humanity'. But despite their supposedly libratory intent, even such respected bodies as the World Commission on Environment and Development (WCED, 1987) speak from the subject position of the techno-political, modern elite whose activities, ironically, depend upon the very system that is causing massive environmental damage. It is this techno-administrative discourse of responsibility *for* the Earth that sets the parameters of most environmental discourse within the global domain. Such discourse is the result of a technology of other that is difficult to resist because it *seems* to arise from concern for the Earth. This discourse excludes the concept of responsibility *to* the Earth as Other, just as it dismisses the possibility that discourses which do not adopt this impersonal stance might warrant a voice in the environmental debate. Is it possible to apply a craft of Othering to another as extensive as the Earth so that an ethic of meeting and a sense of responsibility *to* the Earth might emerge?

We need a way of knowing the Earth that is dependent, not on the gaze of technological holism that looks down on the Earth from space, but on the gaze of attentive holism that arises out of meeting with the Earth as Other. This gaze is grounded on the Earth and looks with attention and wonder at the particularity of (that part of) the Earth which it encounters. Such a gaze highlights the significance of the iconic understanding of the Other. Without the mediation of technology, no human being can encounter the Earth-as-a-whole. Unaided, we encounter only that part which extends outwards, indefinitely to the human eye, from the place upon which we stand. The Earth unfolds mysteriously before us as we walk upon it, the spotlight of our presence illuminating only a tiny circle within the surrounding mystery that exceeds our reach. Without technology there can be no question of mastering the Earth. If we limit ourselves to the human scale of things, then the iconic mystery of the Earth easily claims us, and the Earth is crafted as Other, as Mother, sustaining and sustainable through the interweaving of wonder, gratitude and responsibility.

Indigenous peoples offer discourses from this perspective. The Iroquois people *(Hau de no sau nee)*, for example, articulated *A Basic Call to Consciousness* in their *Address To the Western World* delivered at the 1977 UN Conference on Indigenous Peoples:

> In the beginning we were told that the human beings who walk about on the Earth have been provided with all the things necessary for life. We were instructed to carry a love for one another, and to show a great respect for all the beings of this Earth. We were shown that our life exists with the tree life, that our well-being depends on the well-being of the Vegetable Life, that we are close relatives of the four-legged beings.[41]

Both voices, that of the Iroquois and that of the WCED, take a universal stand, daring to speak for and about humanity as a whole. But while the WCED report assumes technical responsibility *for* the Earth-as-patient, the Iroquois assume ethical responsibility *to* the Earth-as-mother. Faced with the current destruction of the environment, the difference between the solutions proffered by these two voices is also instructive. The report of the WCED (1987), *Our Common Future*, advocates in an impersonal, though concerned, voice 'the possibility for a new era of economic growth, one that must be based on policies that sustain and expand the environmental resource base'. The Iroquois, on the other hand, issue *A Basic Call to Consciousness* that speaks personally and inclusively of the need for 'we who walk about on Earth . . . to express a great respect, an affection and gratitude towards all the spirits which create and support Life'. The Iroquois warn that 'when people cease to respect and express gratitude for these many things, then all life will be destroyed, and human life on this planet will come to an end' (Mander, 1992:191).

It is the Iroquois who have understood the craft of Othering and managed to fashion from it an ethic of meeting that allowed them to respect and preserve the Earth. Yet it is difficult, and I think unethical, for those of us who are descendants of the European Enlightenment to appropriate the voice of the Iroquois or of other indigenous peoples. What we can do though, is acknowledge that entering into an ethical relationship with the Earth requires a change of consciousness, not a spurt of economic growth. We can then explore how our own tradition of knowledge needs to be re-framed and re-presented in order to acknowledge and foster this change of consciousness.

These changes demand a different and extended sense of who we are and a noetic, rather than noematic, change in our system of knowledge. We need what might be described as a 'vertical' change in consciousness, rather than simply a 'horizontal' expansion of the domain in which dualistic consciousness operates.[42] Just as we can move from talking about a field of wheat, to talking about the entire globe without changing the impersonal, rational, objective, technological structure of the discourse, so we can move from analysing local issues to analysing global issues without necessarily undergoing a shift in noetic structure to another level of conceptualisation. The noetic *structure* can remain the same, even though the noematic *content* may be concerned with global issues. In making this distinction I am not trying to imply that the noetic and noematic aspects of any discourse are independent, certainly they are interrelated in important ways, but the failure to distinguish at all between the two aspects has led to a confusing and perhaps dangerous muddle in environmental discourse. The two different genres of discourse explored above, the discourse of the WCED and the discourse of the Iroquois, are differentiated not simply by the different socio-historical locations of their discursive subjects, but by a difference in noetic structure that implies a different epistemology, a different level of conceptualisation, and a different horizon for the knowledge generated.

Earth Selves, Other Selves, No Selves

This failure to distinguish between the technology of other that sustains modern technological knowledge (albeit environmentally concerned), and the craft of Othering that sustains the relationship of many indigenous peoples with the Earth, reflects the persistent confusion in environmental thought that a new genre of 'holistic' discourse has emerged simply because that discourse is now concerned with bigger things such as the globe, the Earth, the biosphere, or the so-called 'web of life'. A different genre of discourse must be defined by a different noetic structure, and not simply by noematic content that is concerned with a larger domain.

This confusion can be seen in deep ecology, for example, where the original insight of Naess, the founder of deep ecology, involved a noetic change that posited Self-realisation as the key to integrating an environmentally benign world view. But because Naess did not fully acknowledge the spiritual horizon implicit in the notion of Self-realisation, his work remains suspended ambiguously between the realisation of a totally deconstructed 'spiritual', or nondual Self (comparable to the Hindu Atman which inspired Gandhi, from whom Naess borrowed the notion of a capital 'S' Self), and the reconstruction of an ideologically sound, ecological self. Due to this ambiguity, second-generation deep ecologists have for the most part subverted the radical ontological implications of Self-realisation and limited deep ecological discourse to a scientific, cosmological or epistemological praxis, albeit one that attempts to gaze benignly on the biosphere, from the perspective of a constructed ecological self.[43]

It is true that the radical implications of a nondual Self, as Plumwood realises (1993:177), go well beyond the political requirements for an ecologically benign form of identity. They refigure the entire domain of Western philosophy, challenging the ontological and epistemological assumptions that have provided its foundation. Whilst Plumwood (ibid) resists the use of these 'overly powerful tools' that arise from a postulate of non-duality, in order to remain focussed on (the analysis and deconstruction of) the human/nature dualism, I argue that the nondual approach, precisely by tackling dualism *per se*, may be just what is needed in the contemporary situation where multiple forms of oppression operate systemically across the boundaries of multiple dualisms.

Within the domain of environmental philosophy, deep ecological discourse has been challenged by ecofeminists who see in the expanded ecological self of the deep ecologists an attempt to deny difference and absorb particularity (Plumwood, 1993:165-189; Kheel, 1990; Salleh, 1984, 1992). The alternative most commonly offered by ecofeminists is a relational self which is intended to maintain 'the essential tension between self and other' (Plumwood, 1993:175)[44] and thus preserve particularity and difference. This ecofeminism/deep ecology debate is interesting because both approaches, due to their political agendas, move towards, but stop short of, a nondual understanding of self. Both undertake a limited deconstruction of the self and then offer their partial deconstructions – the ecological (deep ecology) or relational (ecofeminist) self – as a way of meeting the needs of environmentally sound praxis.[45]

The radical program of totally deconstructing the self is never undertaken, so that most deep ecological and ecofeminist discourse remains caught in the tension between the partial deconstruction of the ecologically alienated self and the apparently essential self who, by limiting the scope of the deconstruction, effectively reconstructs an environmentally situated self which is vulnerable to further deconstruction. Whilst politically I have every sympathy with these exercises and, indeed, I suggested in the previous chapter that we might think of identity within the global domain as a political strategy, philosophically such exercises gloss over essential questions: Who is it who undertakes this reconstructive exercise? Who is the subject, discursive or otherwise, that sorts through the discourses available to us in order to construct an appropriate form of identity?

As Benhabib *et al* (1995:42) suggest, the process seems to posit a prior, knowing 'I', who 'presides over the positions that have constituted me, shuffling through them instrumentally, casting some aside, incorporating others …'. If the subject is, without remainder, socially constructed then surely this 'I' who would select between the available discursive positions is already constituted by some mix or flux of these very positions. If, however, subjectivity is not fully accounted for by the socio-linguistic construction of identity, then we might posit a non-discursive remainder that persists after the deconstruction of the subject. This subjectivity would be non-personal, an awareness to which no genitive could be attached, such as we saw in Buber's work.

The initial movement of postmodernism deconstructed the subject. It neither limited that deconstruction nor sought to replace it with a 'better' (ecologically or otherwise) subject, because the radical deconstructive insight was that *the subject has never been*, it is a fiction and an illusion. As Derrida (1991:102) writes:

> There has never been The Subject for anyone, that's what I wanted to begin by saying. The subject is a fable, . . . but to concentrate on the elements of speech and *conventional* fiction that such a fable presupposes is not to stop taking it seriously (it is the serious itself).

Derrida is correct, I think, in saying that we will continue to take the subject seriously as long as we concentrate on its constitutive elements of 'speech and conventional fiction'. But what happens if we stop concentrating on these? What happens if, having deeply understood that the subject is a fiction, we decide not to take it seriously any more, to let go of the fable, to cut through the fictions? What occurs *experientially* if the subject-sustaining narratives are dissolved, if the defining discourses of the self are no longer attended to? The nondual Asian traditions of Vedanta, Buddhism and Taoism are predicated on just this possibility which involves 'unlearning' the socio-linguistic construction that is superimposed upon the 'bare' or unmediated attention that precedes the construction of duality. This unmediated perception can be called 'attention' and it is 'bare' when it is 'loving' or empty of self. Bare attention, or attentive love, constitutes the subjective aspect of spiritually-engaged knowledge which I explore in the next two chapters. Before moving on, however, I want to respond briefly to some of the objections that have been raised concerning a post-deconstructive or 'new' ethic that focuses on the Other.

Knowing Other Wise

One of the main objections to a post-deconstructive ethic focussed on the Other is that we cannot meet personally with every being in the larger socio-political, let alone global domain. Nor if we did, could we possibly fulfil the unlimited and conflicting responsibilities to which such meetings would call us. In order to be effective in the socio-political domain, an ethic of meeting must be able to move beyond the domain of particularity and personal encounter, into the domain of multiplicity and politics.[46] This would seem to involve taking up again the ethical and legal systems that operate in the discursive domain, abandoning each person to their own moral sense, or as I suggest here, adopting a judicious mix of the two.

Accepting a developmental model of moral capacity, such as I proposed above, in which the ethic of meeting relates to a post-rational stage of moral development, then there is no need to construct a false opposition between a post-discursive, post-rational ethic and its discursive and rational expressions which will always be partial and imperfect. An understanding of the iconic Other provides the necessary link between the discursive, political domain of the particular other and the post-rational, post-discursive domain of the Other who exceeds the limits of our understanding and discursivity. It is in this way that Levinas, through his stipulation that 'the third party looks at me in the eyes of the Other' (Levinas, 1979:213),[47] provides a passage for moving from the post-discursive ethical domain of the one-to-one encounter, to the discursive political domain of ethics and the law inhabited by a multiplicity of people whom we may never directly encounter.

I argue that it is in order to cope with the ambivalent and unceasing demands of a non-discursive ethic (of meeting) that systems of ethics are constructed. Provided that the process of compromise is not obscured, this is not necessarily problematic. Socio-cultural norms for dealing with strangers are formulated into laws and authorised by religious or civil authorities, giving rise to ethical and juridical systems. The ethics, the laws, the questions of rights and legal obligations, exist within the discursive socio-political domain as particular cultural expressions of the prior ethic of meeting. But these particular discursive expressions are always incomplete. Laws, ethics and rights are *always* a compromise, and must be understood as a retreat from the inescapable and unlimitable responsibility that the singularity of the Other calls forth.

Just as Derrida (1992) argues that the hope of justice lies in the never-ending deconstruction of all systems of justice, so the hope of morality lies in the never-ending deconstruction of all ethical systems. This deconstruction is not based on a nihilistic undermining of all morality but on the recognition of the prior ethic of unlimited, but inexpressible, responsibility to the Other. The discursive, socio-political articulation of ethics must strive to be just but, because it directs itself towards universality (whether within a limited local constituency or a global one), it will always fall short. The ethical foundations of justice originate, not in universality, but in the particularity of the meeting with the Other which is constituted by first person responsibility. From this point of view the ethical has primacy over the political, and an ethic of meeting *has priority* over an ethics of justice.

The challenge of a genre of knowledge that has its origin in the primordial meeting with the Other is to reclaim the non-discursive domain in which this primary ethical orientation originates. This reclamation does not relieve us of 'the unbearable uncertainty of being-for' (Bauman 1995:59) which is the hallmark of postmodern morality. We still face the ambiguity and uncertainty of action in the 'broken middle' (G. Rose:1992). But if the post-discursive domain has been recognised and reclaimed, then our ethical orientation before the face of the Other is secured. We may not, indeed cannot, know with certainty what the right action is, but having secured our ethical orientation of being-for the Other, we can risk the ambiguity of action. To do otherwise is to be left politically impotent or to be returned to modernity's model of moral logic and universal ethics.

I have already explored to some extent the ethical injunctions that, replacing the moral metanarratives of modernity, secure our primary ethical orientation towards the Other: Levinas demands that we be peaceful; Buber, that we love; Noddings, that we care; the nature poets, that we lose our-selves in wonder. Gillian Rose (1992, 1993), however, is critical of what she refers to as 'new ethics' because she interprets these injunctions as ushering in yet another cycle of 'holy universalism' which, despite our best intentions, destroys the Other. Rose reads Levinas, Buber, and Weil[48] (whose work I consider in the next chapter) as evading moral ambiguity and uncertainty. New ethics, she suggests, is an attempt to construct a 'holy middle' – a patched up, beatific, ahistorical 'Between' in which we encounter others who are stripped of the socio-historical particularity which is precisely what makes them 'other'. According to Rose (1993:5-9) new ethics merely repeats in another register the modern diremption of spirit and world, of ethics and law (pp. 37-51). She argues that it is exactly because 'the middle' between ethics and law is irreparably 'broken' that injustice prevails. As soon as we move from the face-to-face meeting with the singularity of the other, to the socio-historical, political domain where there are a multiplicity of others, the holy middle – that posits an ethics of love and unlimited responsibility – becomes not only equivocal but dangerous. As a means of clarifying the position I am taking, I want to respond to Rose's critique in two parts.

The Muddle of the Middle

Firstly, I argue that neither Levinas, Buber, Weil, nor myself, are attempting to construct a 'holy middle', but are pointing towards another domain, distinct from the middle (as conceived by Rose), that escapes the net of discursivity. This is the post-discursive domain of neither ethics nor the law, but of an *ethic* that is an inner, unspoken, unformulated command (Bauman, 1995:58-9). Whilst this inner, unspoken command sounds rather esoteric, it can be understood as the moral voice of conscience that, interestingly, since the Nuremberg trials has been given some recognition within International Law. Following the Nuremberg judgement that it is 'the duty of all persons to act in defiance of state authority and enacted law so as to avoid complicity with official criminality' (Falk, 1993a:139), the Nuremberg Principles were formulated and unanimously endorsed at an early session of the United Nations General Assembly (Falk, 1987:25-6). Moral accountability to attend to the unspoken inner command, which may not be in accordance with prevailing socio-political formulations of ethics and the law, has thus been given *legal* standing in international principles and has been used as a legal defence in actions of resistance against a national government.[49]

No such defence is cut and dried, for the attempt to capture what is unspoken is paradoxical and has failed if it results in a new cycle of 'holy universalism' or in a moral metanarrative that cannot be deconstructed. Yet clearly this is the intent of neither the Nuremberg principles nor the ethic of meeting that I have proposed. What is at stake is an inner direction to which we are accountable and that we must translate as best we can into action in the political domain. Bauman (1995:59) tries to explain this unspoken ethical command:

> The 'unspokenness' means rather that the authority of the command *has not been sought*, that the actor acts without a command and acts as if command was not needed When acting without command and without asking for one, the self accomplishes what Levinas characterized as 'breaking through its form' – breaking through *any socially drawn form*, shedding *any* socially-sewn dress, facing the other as a face, not mask, and facing one's own bare face in the process.

This inner command exceeds both the 'parlance of reason' and the demands of the Freudian super-ego to convey a prior responsibility which issues from a post-discursive domain that cannot be contained within any ethical or legal system.

Access to this domain is not gained through reason but through the noetic injunctions – to be responsible, to love, to care, to wonder, to be at peace – that I mentioned above. Gillian Rose (1992:257) suggests, and I agree with her, that the construction of a 'holy middle', an exercise into which various religious discourses have all too often lapsed, can become an excuse for 'refusing to undertake the labour of discovering how universality and barbarism reproduce each other, and instead to embrace a piety that separates itself from history'. But I hope that by now it is clear that I am not advocating the construction of a 'holy middle'. I am reaching for the post-rational, post-discursive domain that is prior to the middle.

Far from abandoning the labours of deconstruction and reason, I am arguing that a post-deconstructive ethic of meeting provides the essential foundation for ensuring that the labours of reason ultimately bear fruit as responsible praxis, firstly in the discursive domain where the ethic of meeting is articulated, though always imperfectly and incompletely, into a multiplicity of ethics in different socio-historical contexts; and secondly in the political domain where these diverse ethics must be translated into action. In the passage from ethic to articulated systems of ethics, universality is translated into particularity and wholeness *is* broken. But this is not cause for Rose's lamentation – bread must be broken in order to eat. The struggle, which must not be avoided, is to break the bread in such a way that the nourishment is made available to those who most need it within any particular socio-historical context. We must struggle to articulate *both* ethics and laws that preserve and pass on, within our particular contexts, as much of the primordial ethic of responsibility to the Other as can possibly be sustained within that context.

The transcendent or spiritual horizon that I have established only leads to Rose's diremption of spirit and world if we retain the modernist understanding of the spiritual as dualistically opposed to the secular, the transcendent as dualistically opposed to the immanent. The spiritual horizon I have proposed is premised on an understanding of the Other as unbounded, as always overspilling the limits of discursivity and, since I am Other to others, an understanding of my self as similarly free and overspilling the limits of language and discourse. This spiritual horizon *is* a primordial ethical horizon because in meeting the Other in the post-discursive, post-rational space that can be found between us, I shed my 'socially-sewn dress' to break through the boundaries that define my separation from the Other.

Such a meeting depends, I have argued, on a radical empiricism, a mode of knowing that might be described as spiritually-engaged, where this does not imply standing in opposition to the world but circumscribing that world. Radical empiricism is concerned with both the inner and outer poles of experience. By observing closely what occurs subjectively in genuine encounter with the Other, radical empiricism gives rise to injunctions that tell us how we might facilitate true meeting. Radical empiricism is an existential noetic praxis that provides a way of bringing together the various injunctions offered by the commentators studied so far. I interpret the injunction 'Be radically empirical!' – which includes the injunctions to love, to wonder, to care, to be at peace – as a noetic injunction that gives access to a different kind of spiritually-engaged knowledge, rather than as a fundamentalist call to a metanarrative based on 'holy universalism'. Nonetheless the injunction – Be radically empirical! – requires some teasing out if it is to be put into practice and this constitutes the second part of my response to Rose's challenge concerning 'holy universalism'.

The Idea of Injunctions

Injunctions are methodological instructions that determine what kind of data, and therefore what kind of knowledge, any group of practitioners will perceive. A new genre of knowledge involves new and different injunctions, which define new and different methodologies. Such a shift in method occurred at the beginning of the European scientific revolution with the introduction of scientific method of observation and experimentation. New injunctions – to experiment, to observe, to reason – revealed new knowledge which had been inaccessible to those operating on the Aristotelian methodological injunctions that had been accepted since the time of the ancient Greeks. In the same way, the genre of spiritually-engaged knowledge that I am seeking to define involves new methodologies and new injunctions.[50]

In seeking to identify these injunctions the work of Catholic theologian Bernard Lonergan is particularly significant. As the name of his best-known book *Method in Theology* implies, Lonergan's (1972) primary focus was theological, but much of what he wrote is relevant in the broader domain of the sociology of knowledge. Lonergan sought to find a method that would be 'so in conformity with the dynamic thrust of the human spirit that it would be valid for all men and women at all times and in all places' (Johnston, 1995:111). He identified five 'transcendental commands' or injunctions which, he argued, encapsulated the fully mature cycle of human knowing – Be attentive! Be intelligent! Be reasonable! Be responsible! Be in love!

Initially, Lonergan describes the 'method', or noetic praxis, constituted by these injunctions as 'transcendent' (by which he means 'transcultural' or 'universal') because it is grounded in human cognitive and affective capacity, although in his later work he calls it the 'generalized empirical method' (Lamb, 1982:129), which is much closer to the radical empiricism which I have suggested. Since the method is grounded in universal human cognitive capacities it can, like rationality, be universally applied but, unlike rationality, it takes into account the ethical and affective dimensions of human beings. Lonergan attributed the 'success' and global application of the modern scientific method to the way that it deployed the first three transcendental injunctions.[51] The increasingly apparent shortcomings of science however can be attributed to the way that it generally stops short at rationality (Be reasonable!) and does not take into account the ethical (Be responsible!), affective/ spiritual (Be in love!) aspects of human knowing within a participatory cosmos.

For Lonergan this generalised empirical method, like the radical empiricism which I have associated with spiritually-engaged knowledge, excludes neither rationality, nor an understanding of the discursive and socially constructed nature of noematic knowledge. Rather, it includes both of these within broader ethical, affective and transcendent horizons that come into play as the knowing subject matures and becomes capable of functioning on these levels of understanding. For Lonergan, the practice of this empiricism is the practice of attention, or awareness, which in its 'purest' form is synonymous with complete self-emptying or love. Johnston (1995:12) recounts his own meeting with Lonergan in which he 'told him [Lonergan] that his method culminates in mystical experience. Lonergan smiled and said, "Yes, yes . . . !"' Knowing for Lonergan, as for Kohlberg, culminated in a nondual mystical experience. This knowing is virtue-based, defined by the final injunction – Be in love! And what is love but a state of being-for the Other?

In describing his own method, Lonergan (1972:xi) writes that 'Method is not a set of rules to be followed meticulously by a dolt. It is a framework for collaborative creativity.' This suggests that the injunctions are not necessarily to be followed sequentially from 1 to 5, but that each of these injunctions must be present for the emergence of post-rational, or spiritually-engaged, knowledge. Since the injunctions to be intelligent and reasonable apply to the rational and discursive domain of reason, it is the injunctions to be attentive, to be responsible and to be in love that I suggest distinguish this spiritually-engaged knowledge from the knowledge of modernity.

Attentiveness refers to a particular kind of awareness that Lonergan suggests comes into play prior to the discursive functioning of the mind. As I shall suggest in the next chapter, it is a praxis that reveals 'how the world is experienced *without* the superimposition of language' (Loy 1988:88, italics mine). Love as an injunction I almost hesitate to use because of the sentimental baggage that it carries in the modern era. Lonergan's use of the term, however, is not sentimental. The love he refers to is transpersonal and noetic, based on desire for the (good of the) Other. It can be understood, Dunne (1994:121) writes, as 'human wonder, particularly as it illuminates the mysteries of life'. In his account of noetic praxis, Lonergan separated the injunctions relating to attentiveness and love into two 'transcendental commands'. The cycle of knowing begins with the injunction Be attentive! and ends with the injunction to Be in Love! It is important to note that Lonergan directs us, not to love, but to be in love – a curious, almost contradictory, command to which I return later.

In the work of another writer, Simone Weil, these two injunctions are combined into one. Weil advocates the practice of 'attentive love' as a way of knowing and being in the world. In the next chapter, beginning with the work of Simone Weil, I explore in more detail this praxis of attentive love. Weil's work has been taken up and developed by a number of women theorists and their work provides the epistemological key to spiritually-engaged knowledge. We are now in a position to understand the injunction – Be radically empirical! This notion can be thought of in two ways, either as consisting of two injunctions – Be attentive! and Be in love! – or as one injunction that combines these two in the praxis of attentive love.

In this chapter we have explored the ethical aspect of spiritually-engaged knowledge, beginning with a description of an ethic of meeting which grounds spiritually-engaged knowledge. This ethic arises when we encounter the Other in a domain of nondual awareness. It is neither logically nor discursively constructed but emerges from an unmediated experience that is the *essential precursor* of any ethics, whether of justice or of care. However, an ethic of meeting that focuses on the Other is insufficient to sustain an ethically based genre of knowledge. As I have shown, the ethic of meeting requires a subjective component which I describe as radical empiricism or attentive love. This subjective component is also ethical, not because it relies on ethical metanarratives, but because it is founded upon a new set of injunctions. In the next chapter we explore this epistemological strategy of attentive love as it has developed within the discourse of feminism.

Notes

1. Buber (1994:25).
2. This distinction is made by Kung (1993:59-60) in relation to the Global Ethic which he drafted for the 1993 Parliament of World's Religions. It is, I think, useful since it helps to overcome some of the criticisms, to which I refer later, concerning the division between ethics and the law. As I note later, Bauman (1995) makes a similar distinction in his terminology between 'morality' and 'ethics'.
3. Because this genre of spiritually-engaged knowledge has been unspeakable in the language of modernity, I frequently employ negative terms, such as 'non-discursive', to describe it. In this chapter these negative terms multiply to include nondual, non-egoic, non-personal, non-rational, etc. As Budick and Iser (1989: xiii) argue, negativity can function as an agent of dissemination 'allowing the unspeakable to speak for itself'. On occasions I use the prefixes 'trans' or 'post' rather than 'non', to indicate that the term to which I have referred is not a negative or regressive concept, but one which radically exceeds the signifier.
4. Particularly Chapter 1: *Morality Without Ethics* (Bauman, 1995).
5. The reference is to Marion's (1991) two ways of being – the way of the idol and the way of the icon. I offer more explanation of these different ways of seeing/being later in this chapter.
6. Levinas (1993:125) suggests that the desire for peace with the Other is 'the first language', the first ethical demand of meeting, and out of this peace emerges responsibility. As Critchley (1992:223) writes: 'Peace, or responsibility, to the near one, the neighbour, *is* peace to the one far off, the third party, or human plurality. All humanity looks at me in the eyes of the Other'.
7. Clearly gender hierarchy is not the only phenomenological asymmetry that might rupture the ethical relationship, although it has a special place because of the imagery of the feminine that operates in Levinas's work. I will leave aside for the moment the concerns arising from other socially constructed human hierarchies (race, class, ethnicity etc) since, like the gender issue, they also rest on the possibility, or otherwise, of 'pre-subjective' ethical experience. Due to Levinas's use of gendered metaphors in so much of his work, I pursue the issue of gender in more detail later in the chapter. See also note 10.
8. See Cornell (1992b:87-89); also the following essays in Bernasconi and Critchley (1991) *Part Three: Levinas and the Feminine*: L. Irigaray, 'Questions to Emmanuel Levinas: On the Divinity of Love' (pp. 109-118); C. Chalier, 'Ethics and the Feminine' (pp. 119-129); T. Chanter, 'Antigone's Dilemma' (pp. 130-146).
9. Whilst the supremacy that Levinas accords the Other may seem problematic, it concurs with one of the approaches that Loy (1988) identifies in spiritual traditions that attempt to convey nondual (and therefore non-discursive) knowledge. Since any expression of nonduality must be conveyed in language which operates around the subject/object dualism, a common approach to collapsing that dualism is to absorb one pole into the other. As Loy (1988:12) notes, the strategy in advaita Vedanta is to absorb the other into the Self. The strategy in Buddhism, streams of which, it might be argued, are closer to the postmodern approach, is to declare the self non-existent leaving only the other, the world of flux and change. It needs to be noted in spiritual traditions that these moves for collapsing the self/other dichotomy are preliminary moves that are later deconstructed as the understanding (and experience) of the (advaitic) Self or (Buddhist) not-self unfolds. Read within this kind of nondual framework, Levinas's total supremacy of the Other makes sense.

10. The task I have set myself in this chapter is not to provide a full critique of Levinas's work, but, for the sake of completeness, I will outline here Cornell's (1992b:87-89) critique and show how my alternative, nondual reading resolves some of the contradictions in Levinas's work.

The metaphysical ethic of the face, which I have presented above, lies at the centre of Levinas's work. It is free of the gendered metaphors that mar(k) his other work on eros and fecundity (Cohen, 1994:195), but which, nonetheless provide the context for a consideration of his ethic of the face. Despite Cohen's (ibid) defence of Levinas, that metaphor and metaphysics cannot be confused, I agree with feminist critiques that his use of conventional images of Woman as Other is disturbing and too easily reinforces existing gender stereotypes, roles and inequities. This gender essentialism introduces a contradiction into Levinas's ethic of the face which I argue below can most effectively be avoided by explicitly framing an ethic of meeting within a non-discursive, nondual, spiritual horizon.

The ethical asymmetry which is the basis of responsibility before the Other demands, as Cornell (1992b:87-9) argues, phenomenological symmetry. In the gender specific case where the Other is Woman (and the pre-discursive subject is assumed to be Man) the phenomenological symmetry of the situation is destroyed *in the context of Levinas's work* by the 'imaginary fantasy' (Cornell 1992b:88) of Woman that appears in parts of Levinas's *oeuvre*. If Woman is defined by a psychical fantasy of 'mystery', 'hiding' and 'modesty', confined by conventional images such as 'the field of intimacy' or 'the interiority of the Home' (Levinas 1979:155), then there can be no phenomenological symmetry and therefore no ethical asymmetry. The essentialism of the gendered metaphors or fantasies that Levinas uses in parts of his work thus undo his own suppositions in his ethics of the face, that a divine horizon opens through the face of the Other. It is possible, I argue, to excise the gender (and any other) essentialisms of Levinas's work and defend an ethic of meeting in one of two ways.

The first is Cornell's solution which involves the 'specific recognition of the symmetry of woman as ego', in order to provide a measure of universality as the basis of phenomenological symmetry between the ethical subject and the (specific) other (Cornell 1992b:88-89). Whilst this approach does solve the problem of phenomenological asymmetry, it limits the scope of an ethic of meeting. The challenge of the genre of spiritually-engaged knowledge that I am exploring is to offer an alternative to the regime of modernity that Lacan described as 'the ego's era'. One of the merits of Levinas's work, as I understand it, is that it offers a way beyond the ego which is, by definition, individual, discursively constructed and defined by the self/other dualism. Although recognising woman as ego does, as Cornell points out, solve the problem of phenomenological asymmetry, it locks us back into the ego-centred, individualistic approach and excludes the possibility (which is explored later in this chapter) of extending the ethic of meeting beyond the human to the environmental domain.

From my reading of Levinas, it is not necessary to interpret, as Cornell does, Levinas's ethical subject as either an individual ego, or as a discursively constructed subject. Indeed, in order to make sense of Levinas, it seems more appropriate to assume that this ethical subject is somehow non-discursive and non-egoic. This assumption leads to the second way out of the dilemma, which is the approach that I develop here. It involves the explicit recognition of the 'divine horizon' which already exists within Levinas's work, and which can provide a pre-given universality that protects the symmetry of the meeting with the Other. Within this transcendent, non-discursive horizon, essentialism is undone by the recognition that the other, be she woman or man, black or white, plant or animal, ultimately escapes the net of discursivity. The radical exteriority of the other is acknowledged as finally incomprehensible. The Other, the World, the real, always exceed discursive representation. It is important to note that I am arguing that, within a transcendent horizon, the Other is recognised as unknowable and therefore uncontrollable. This Other is transcendent in the sense that our gaze is directed beyond any discursive or socially constructed boundaries.

This transcendent horizon has implications for the subject. Since she is the Other for others, the self or ethical subject, must also be the subject of a reciprocal and no less radical interiority that likewise escapes discursivity. We can therefore distinguish between a discursively constructed self and a non-discursive form of subjectivity. Since in a non-discursive domain any boundaries that might distinguish the Other from the Self are rendered ineffective, the self/other dualism is deconstructed and we are left in a domain of experience which is nondual. This nonduality deconstructs the self/other dualism and therefore offers a pre-given universality that maintains phenomenological symmetry. It is this non-discursive, nondual domain that characterises spiritually-engaged knowledge. It offers a universality that is not posited on an ontotheological Being, but on the 'emptiness' of a non-discursive domain predicated, not on presence, but on absence. It is based on a spirituality of emptiness or kenosis that is not defined by the presence of specific attributes (in self, or human, or divine Other) but rather by their (deconstructed) absence.

11. See, for example, Wood (1994) and Nelson (1992) for critiques of the ethic of care. However, as I shall point out later when considering the work of Teresa Brennan (1993), it may be that the significance of women's maternal role, which makes them the primary other for *all* infants, does indeed introduce a degree of biological asymmetry. It is doubtless true that in some cases the primary *postnatal* carer may be male, and while this may lessen the impact of the prior biological asymmetry, it does not obliterate it. If we go back to the inter-uterine and birth experiences, the primary other has always been the mother/woman.

12. See, for example, Hewlett (1992) who describes 'The Nature and Context of Aka Pygmy Paternal Infant Care', showing how in a different cultural context, gender, and more particularly maternal and paternal roles can be constructed quite differently.

13. Kohlberg's model for moral development consists of three levels and six stages, two at each level. The following brief summary is taken from Kohlberg and Ryncarz (1990:193-5).

    LEVEL A – PRE-CONVENTIONAL LEVEL
      Stage 1 – Punishment and obedience
      Stage 2 – Instrumental purpose and exchange
    LEVEL B – CONVENTIONAL LEVEL
      Stage 3 – Mutual interpersonal expectations, relationships, and conformity
      Stage 4 – Social system and conscience maintenance
    [LEVEL B/C – TRANSITIONAL LEVEL
      Post-conventional but not yet principled: one can make choices, pick and choose socially-constructed obligations, but there are no principles]
    LEVEL C – POST-CONVENTIONAL AND PRINCIPLED
      Stage 5 – Prior rights and social contract or utility
      Stage 6 – Universal ethical principles: the reason for doing right is that, as a *rational* person, one has seen the validity of principles and has become committed to them (italics mine).

14. See also Gilligan (1986a, 1986b, 1987).
15. It seems to me that Gilligan's stage of dialectical reasoning (1990:223) may represent an intermediate, or transitional, step between Kohlberg's stages 6 and 7, although there are real difficulties in trying to bring together within the one framework Gilligan's and Kohlberg's viewpoints. See, for example, Benhabib (1992:148-202). It might be noted that Benhabib's own arguments for an 'enlarged mentality' could be read as an argument for a further stage of moral development, although she herself does not express it in quite those terms.
16. Wilber (1983:201-246) clarifies the difference between these two non-rational possibilities with his formulation of the 'pre/trans fallacy', which he identifies as a common error in contemporary thought. Wilber posits three basic levels of human development. With respect to rationality these are: a pre-rational phase, a rational phase, and a post- or trans-rational phase. The pre/trans fallacy occurs when the pre-rational and the trans-rational are conflated because both are non-rational. I have explained this elsewhere in more detail (Crawford, 1993:26-27).
17. In their book, Alexander and Langer (1990) present views both for and against hierarchical models of human development. However, Alexander *et al*'s paper (1990) 'Growth of Higher Stages of Consciousness' (pp. 286-341) supports the perspective presented here, as does Wilber's work. Wilber's hierarchical, transpersonal model is controversial because it is presented as a universalising metanarrative and, just as I pointed out in chapter two, as a tension exists between globalisation theory and postmodern theory, so a corresponding tension exists between transpersonal psychology and postmodern theory. Within the transpersonal perspective, deconstructive postmodernism would be placed at the upper end of rational development, with the ethic of meeting representing a higher developmental stage. From the perspective of postmodernism, transpersonal psychology is a discursive metanarrative with no privileged correlation to human development. Whilst the dilemma as to which discourse should take precedence is not easily solved, both point us in the direction of a post-rational form of knowledge.
18. There are many books by feminist authors analysing this link which lies at the heart of the feminist critique – see, for example, Chodorow (1979); Code (1991); Griffin (1978); Harding (1991, 1993); Lloyd (1984); Haraway (1989); Flax (1990); Brennan (1992, 1993b); and Plumwood (1993).
19. This term is used by Brennan (1993b:55) and she explains it as follows:

> When 'the subject makes himself an object by displacing himself before the mirror' he constitutes a 'passifying image' (Lacan, 1953:420). In its context, the passive/ passification pun harks back to the discussion of the ego's aggressiveness. In its master-slave struggle to the death, the ego desires to make the other into a thing; and arrogates to itself the right to form or shape it, to objectify it, to make it passive. But it also fears retribution, so wants to pacify the other (or itself). Henceforth I shall use the terms 'passifying' and 'passification' on referring to the process, drama and drives involved here.

20. It should be noted that neither Brennan nor Plumwood acknowledge the other as transcendent, although Brennan (1993b:166-199) certainly toys with the idea of transcendence.
21. '**Technology** *n* 1. The scientific study of mechanical arts and applied sciences (e.g. engineering). 2. these subjects, their practical application in industry etc.' *The Australian Oxford Paperback Dictionary* (1989:834).
22. I am grateful to Werner Pelz for pointing out the negative connotations of the phrase 'technology of Other' which I had employed in earlier drafts.

23. The distinction needs to be made between technologies of self which are concerned with the discursive construction of the individual, and the crafts of Selfing which are concerned with the deconstruction of the individual self, so that the transcendent (Self) might be realised. Ultimately, the craft of Othering becomes indistinguishable from the craft of Selfing, since in the nondual state the Other is experienced as an expression of the Self, just as the Self is an expression of the Other. The interdependent crafts of Othering and Selfing, therefore, culminate in the (mystical) state of recognition of the nonduality of nondual Other/Self.
24. See Cohen (1994:90-111), for example. Some commentators have suggested that Buber's *I-It* is simply a straw person.
25. For a more complete discussion of this example see Crawford (1995).
26. One of Rudolph Otto's (1977) descriptions of the transcendent.
27. Banuri (1990:74) suggests that modernity, or the modern world view, is Western because it is based on the assumption that 'impersonal relations are inherently superior to personal relations'. Banuri calls this assumption 'the impersonality postulate' and identifies it as one of the core assumptions of the Western episteme which introduces a powerful asymmetry into the globalising modern episteme. It is this impersonality postulate that is particularly germane to our consideration of the construction of valid discourse within the global domain. If we take the position that valid global discourse is not simply modernity writ large, then we must ensure that the impersonality postulate does not become the structuring principle of a discourse that seeks universality within the global domain.
28. Brennan's argument is both more subtle and more complex than I have outlined. Brennan (1993b:79-117) proposes the formation of a foundational psychical fantasy in infancy. This occurs prior to the formation of gender identity, as described by Lacan's thesis of a fundamental objectifying fantasy, and it establishes the first boundary of the contained self. In her account, Brennan (1993b:101) describes the foundational fantasy as based on:

> the desire for instant gratification, the preference for visual and object-oriented thinking this entails, the desire to be waited upon, the envious desire to imitate the original, the desire to control the mother, and to devour, poison and dismember her, and to obtain knowledge by this process.

Brennan (l993b:13-4) asserts that while the foundational fantasy is 'an ancient one in the West', the socio-cultural reinforcement of this fantasy is peculiar to the conditions of modernity. She also argues that the foundational fantasy is inextricably intertwined with a psychical fantasy of Woman which stands in causal relation to the contained ego and its dominating aggressive mode of being in the world. At this point it is worth reflecting back to Cornell's argument against Levinas's work (see note 10 in this chapter). Like Brennan, Cornell also perceives the dangers inherent in any psychical fantasy of Woman. Whilst I concur that psychical fantasies of Woman are dangerous, I disagree (as argued in note 10), with the way in which Cornell tries to offset this.
29. This awareness can, with equal validity, be described as objective, although I have adopted the subjective mode in the text at this point. It is objective because it witnesses (and ultimately contains) both the individual self and the multiplicity of phenomenal others. In feminist thought both Brennan (1993b) and Keller (1985) distinguish between two different kinds of objectivity. Since I pick up this distinction again in the next chapter, I will simply comment here that the objectivity of the witnessing consciousness that I am referring to here resonates with Keller's 'dynamic objectivity' that divines 'hidden harmonies and relations' (Keller, 1985:117-8).

The witnessing consciousness marks the first appearance of post-discursive subjectivity. It has been referred to in mystical literature as 'the Witness', an observing consciousness, that provides the basis for an expanded, post-egoic identity. It would seem that this Witness consciousness, which still implies a duality, later gives way to a unified consciousness that transcends even this subtle dualism. In the developmental models of human consciousness it is these states of witness and unity consciousness (although described in a variety of different terminologies) that emerge after the full development of rationality. These states are often described as transpersonal because they are no longer experiences of a contained individual person, but of an expanded subjectivity. Since both self and other are released (deconstructed) into nonduality, some traditions structure their discursive descriptions of method around the objective pole and others around the subjective pole. Thus Vedanta, for example, adopts the subjective pole, while Buddhism adopts the objective pole.

30. See Tacey (1995), particularly chapter 8: *Towards a New Dreaming*.
31. Hans (1993), in his book *The Mysteries of Attention*, offers an interesting account of the role of attention, particularly in the domains of literature and aesthetics. Like Tacey, Hans is a scholar of English literature. He develops the idea of attention very differently to the approach that I am developing here, and I have therefore found Tacey's work more useful, although it does not focus specifically on issues of attention and attentiveness.
32. Tacey was a student of James Hillman and his work is embedded in the discourses of Jungian and post-Jungian psychology.
33. Each of these commentators – Nisargadatta from Vedanta, Goldstein and Nyanaponika from Buddhism, Weil from women's thought – have developed this epistemological strategy, which they variously describe as 'affectionate awareness', 'bare attention' and 'attentive love' throughout their works. The references cited are intended as a starting point only. Particularly in Buddhist literature, there are innumerable references to 'bare attention' or its other equivalent terms.
34. Brennan (1993b:110) writes that 'an intersubjective economy makes itself felt in terms of energetic *attention*'.
35. Brennan's (1993b) account of the formation of an individual self provides an interesting and useful explanatory hypothesis in post-Freudian discourse. She does not, however, attempt to deal with any transpersonal stages of development and for this reason I would tend towards a different account if I were to present in full an argument for the release of energy involved in the shift to transpersonal, and particularly nondual, states of subjectivity. One of my major concerns with Brennan's position is that her foundational fantasy locks us too quickly into a pathological mode of being, from which it is difficult to escape. Wilber (1986a, b and c) offers a transpersonal perspective that is, at the same time, more complex and more comprehensive. Wilber would concur, I think, with Brennan's understanding of attention as a form of energy (an understanding common to the spiritual traditions upon which he draws). His introduction of 'COEX systems', as devised by Stan Grof, seems to offer an explanation as to the way energetic attention can be diverted into 'a dissociated pocket of the self-structure' that has split off (rather than differentiated) from the conscious self-structure (Wilber, 1986c:147-8). This potentially offers a way of explaining how the early failure to differentiate successfully from the mother by a male infant would be carried on through subsequent stages of development leading to the development of patriarchal social structures, and even the penning of patriarchal scriptures, by males, who while they may have reached transpersonal levels of subjectivity, still

carry unresolved COEX structures. Such an explanation falls beyond the scope of this thesis.
36. This distinction was first made by Arne Naess, the founder of deep ecology, in a paper delivered at the '3rd World Future Research Conference' in Bucharest, 1972, and later published in *Inquiry*, 1973.
37. There are of course articulations of this emerging ethic in contemporary environmental philosophy (which I discuss in more detail later in this chapter and in the next) that fully acknowledge the ethical implications of the meeting with other species and with 'Nature herself'. Aldo Leopold's (1966) *A Sand Country Almanac*, in which Leopold begins each chapter with an account of a meeting, is an example of one of the most influential of these. My dilemma in choosing an example of such a meeting is that, according to present disciplinary boundaries, any extended descriptive account lies within the domain of literature, while theoretical analysis of the ethical implications of that account lies within the domain of philosophy.
38. D.H. Lawrence (1964:349-351).
39. D.H. Lawrence (1964:332-4). Poem entitled *The Mosquito*.
40. See Buber's (1994:156-159) postscript in the second edition, where he discusses the possibilities of the *I-Thou* relationship with respect to animals and trees. Whilst Buber affirms that these other kinds of being might participate in the *I-Thou* relationship, the reciprocity that is a component of his work would seem to limit this. It is exactly on this issue of reciprocity that Levinas differs from Buber, with Levinas insisting on the complete asymmetry of responsibility in the ethical relationship.
41. Published by *Akwesasne Notes* cited in Mander (1992:191).
42. See Crawford (1993:23-6) for a more detailed explanation of these (purely symbolic) 'vertical' and 'horizontal' dimensions.
43. I have dealt with this aspect of deep ecology in more detail elsewhere. Crawford (1993), particularly section 5:39-49.
44. See also Warren (1990); Mathews (1989; 1990).
45. Whilst it can be argued that deep ecology and ecofeminism simply offer alternative constructions of self, this is not my argument here. I contend that both the ecological self of deep ecology and the relational self of ecofeminism are more veridical modes of identity than the bounded individual self of modernity. The difficulty is that neither ecofeminism nor deep ecology have taken their deconstruction of the self far enough to the ultimate point where the self/other dualism is collapsed. Considered within a spiritual horizon, the difference between the ecofeminist approach and the deep ecological approach is comparable to the difference between the Buddhist and Vedantic approaches to overcoming duality. As Loy (1988:12) points out: Buddhism collapses the self/other dualism by focussing on the other and emptying the self into a web of inter-connection that leads to the ultimate realisation of no-self; Vedanta takes the opposite approach and focuses on the self while emptying the category of other to the ultimate point of the nondual Self. The work of Thich Nhat Hanh is interesting here. Adopting the Buddhist approach to an inter-connected relational identity, he completes the deconstructive process to realise a state of *inter-being* in which there is neither self nor other i.e. no separation, only a nondual state of *inter-being*, which can be approached from either (discursive) direction.
46. The inability to bridge these two domains – the personal and the political – is the major weakness of Noddings' (1984) work. For Noddings, the other is not transcendent but particular and personal, and her ethics of care has therefore

been criticised for its lack of application in the political domain which is, of necessity, impersonal. Because Noddings' work lacks the universality offered by a transcendent horizon, the primordial ethical response is diminished to a personal, and seemingly ego-centric, concern 'to be in that special relation' of caring with others and to fulfil our own 'longing for caring' (Noddings 1984:5). Caring is then no longer an ethical response towards all others as particular embodiments of the Other whom we encounter within the moral context of the meeting. It becomes limited to those particular others whom we meet in face-to-face encounters (a population of others often heavily circumscribed by socially constructed norms) or with whom we can construct, as Noddings (1984:46-48) suggests, a 'chain of caring'. Nelson (1992:10), for example, argues that the ethics of care that Noddings articulates is too narrow; confined to 'families, friends, and the "proximate stranger", too much of the world is left out: we are too easily tempted to racism, xenophobia, and disregard for future generations'. Although Noddings (1984:14) does acknowledge the ultimate unknowability of the other, for her the other is not recognised as an icon that opens to all humanity, but remains a particular and specific other. Her ethics of caring is thus difficult to extend to the socio-political domain. In her recognition of the existential command 'I must!' as the justification of caring, Noddings opens to, but never explores, the non-discursive domain that could provide the wider horizon her work needs. See also Mathews (1995) who, in distinguishing between a relational and a holistic self, similarly leaves no point of entry into the impersonal, political domain.

47. Cited in Critchley (1992:225).
48. See Rose (1992:247-296) chapter 6: 'New Political Theology – Out of Holocaust and Liberation', and Rose (1993:211-223).
49. See Falk's (1987) essay 'The Spirit of Thoreau in the Age of Trident' where he elaborates on the significance of the Nuremberg judgement, particularly the way that it has been used in the legal defence of anti-war/nuclear demonstrators.
50. Kuhn's (1970) book *The Structure of Scientific Revolutions* provides one of the best descriptions of how revolutions in knowledge occur when injunctions or paradigms are changed. See also Wilber (1995:275).
51. Although it can be argued that Western science applies Lonergan's first injunction – Be attentive! – it generally does so under controlled experimental conditions that have already limited the Other.

Chapter 4

Attentive Love

> It is through a new human love and respect for oceans of difference . . . that we are woven into the neighbourhoods of the earth.
>
> *Bigwood*[1]

This chapter will continue to respond to the question of what defines the emerging genre of spiritually-engaged knowledge. The previous chapter proposed that spiritually-engaged knowledge is inescapably ethical since it is based on an ethic of meeting which emerges from the encounter with the Other. There is, however, also a subjective aspect to this knowledge which I began to identify and which defines the epistemological strategy of such knowledge. I referred to it as radical empiricism or, more descriptively, attentive love. Having explored the ethical dimension of spiritually-engaged knowledge, I now turn to an exploration of the epistemological dimension.

Whilst the ethical impulse, which I described as an ethic of meeting, honours and preserves the alterity of the Other, it is made possible by attentive love that enables us to turn towards others and engage with them as the Other who always and ever exceeds our systems of signification. In the previous chapter, I suggested that attentive love is the capacity that enables us to meet with the Other as an authentic subject. Here I will explore attentive love as an epistemological strategy that facilitates genuine encounter with the Other, rather than with an abstract alterity.

Curiously, in spite of the postmodern concern with the Other, and the contemporary recognition of the construction of Woman as the primordial Other, there has been relatively little attention paid by prominent postmodern male commentators to the perspective of women theorists. I therefore draw on the work of women theorists to explore attentive love as the epistemological strategy that constitutes the subjective component, or 'method', of spiritually-engaged knowledge. I engage less with the work of postmodern feminist theorists than with a stream of women's discourse which began with Simone Weil (1909-1943), in the first half of this century, and which now constitutes a distinctive feminist contribution to the contemporary debate on epistemology and knowledge.

We first examine the construction of attentive love as a feminine praxis, or craft, with which women subversively transform their worlds. I do so by drawing on female commentators from a variety of different fields, not all of whom would identify themselves as feminist.[2] I aim is to build up both a theoretical and phenomenological understanding of attentive love as a feminine praxis – a praxis pertaining to women and their lives. At the same time, I bring to bear on the work of these women theorists the thesis proposed earlier, that the spiritually-engaged knowledge which arises out of an ethic of meeting is a post-rational, post-egoic mode of knowing that becomes available only as the subject matures beyond the cognitive stage of rationality. Whilst most of the commentators whose work I consider have not situated attentive love within this developmental framework, I demonstrate that such a reading does not contradict their work and in some cases might be inferred from it.

Although I have argued that attentive love is a craft associated with a post-discursive domain, this does not mean that it is divorced from the socio-political domain, nor from the discourses that sustain the structures and institutions of that domain. Within the socio-political domain women are frequently assigned a non-dominant position in which their attentiveness and love, or caring, are exploited in both the social and psychic domains. As Julia Wood (1994:168) suggests, 'for caring to be "safe" for women – or anyone – it must be practiced in contexts that neither assume, nor create, the subjugation of those who engage in it'. Our ability, as women, to practise attentive love is often cruelly constrained, as the image of the woman on the bridge so poignantly reminds us.

The second part of the chapter offers a more explicit gender analysis of the way in which the construction of attentive love is linked to the construction of femininity. Neither all women, nor all forms of attention, are loving and positive, and so the distinction between the positive (or loving) and negative deployment of attention will be explored and related to the construction of gendered identities. In order to do this, I introduce Brennan's (1993b) understanding of attention as an interactive form of energy that plays a significant role in the development of the individual identity.

I consider the construction of the governing forms of feminine and masculine identity which have given rise socially, and now globally, to the ego's era. The contemporary global situation provides considerable evidence to support the thesis that we are in the grip of a social psychosis which impacts negatively on much of humanity and on the planet itself. Brennan (1993b), following Lacan, argues that this psychosis is an historical phenomenon that began in the seventeenth century with the onset of the ego's era in the West. Over the ensuing period of time it has gathered momentum as social conditions have coalesced to strengthen rather than weaken the boundaries of a contained, egoic self.

Whilst this contained self is generally constructed as masculine, Brennan (1993b) argues that the governing feminine form of identity is also pathological, since it is constructed at great cost to the feminine subject. Both the psychosis, and the ego structures that underpin it, are social. As Brennan (1993b:80) puts it 'the agency of madness has a locus that is not subject-centred, or more accurately not only dependent on individuals'. Whilst the masculine identity of the contained ego is often thought of as the more destructive, Brennan demonstrates how the masculine and feminine forms are interdependent, and argues that the psychical fantasy of woman that fixes and limits the feminine identity, simultaneously supports the masculine contained ego.

The positive deployment of attention, I argue, offers to the other an open-ended identity that is not bound by these socially constructed forms. This is compared to the negative deployment of attention which fixes the other's identity in a bound form. I suggest, therefore, that the practice of attentive love is a libratory praxis that can free women and men from the bounded, separate selves of modernity. Since attention is used in the construction of identities, it can also be used in their deconstruction. When positive, or loving, attention is turned inwards it can be utilised to 'undo' the bound patterns of energy that have defined a separate, individual self. Loving attention, in other words, can de-automatise our perception of our own self. In the previous chapter, I suggested that meditation also involves the de-automatisation of perception. In the third and final section of this chapter, I therefore consider attentive love as a spiritual practice again through the work of women commentators. This leads into chapter five, where the role of attentiveness in spirituality is explored in greater detail.

A Feminine Craft

Attentiveness as a Way of Looking

I begin this exploration of attentive love with the work of the philosopher and mystic, Simone Weil. Whilst my emphasis is on Weil's theoretical articulation of attentive love, Wyschogrod's (1990) work on postmodernism and saints points us towards another aspect of Weil's contribution, based not on her philosophical writings but on the narrative of her life. In his introduction to Weil's *The Need for Roots* (1952:vi), T.S. Eliot suggested that 'Simone Weil was one who might have become a saint'. Her life, work and death, for all their apparent inconsistencies and excesses, exemplify in some ways Wyschogrod's understanding of saintliness as an excess of desire for the Other. Weil was not just a theoretician of attentive love, but its practitioner. Her life and work operate in a universe of discourse that is distinct from 'the jargon of the market-place' (ibid xii).[3] Weil's life appears to have been motivated by radical concern for others that demanded an emptying of herself, an acceptance of the void.

It is through the kenosis of attentive love that we reach this experience of the void, an experience that is both universal, impersonal and, for Weil, synonymous with God, or the Absolute. Two readings of 'impersonal' are possible in the context of Weil's work and both are useful in enlarging our understanding of attentive love. Based on my argument in the previous chapter, that spiritually-engaged knowledge is associated with a mature post-egoic stage of moral development, I suggest that Weil's term 'impersonal' can be read, first and foremost, as 'transpersonal'. It conveys the understanding of a love that is non-personal, not because it is devoid of any desire or affective component, but because it transcends self-interest and the individually focussed concerns of the egoic self. It is impersonal only in the sense that it has gone *beyond* the personal, by being emptied of self-interest, self-promotion and self-defence. This reading concurs with Weil's understanding that a mother's love for her child is *impersonal* to the degree that it is without self-interest (Finch, 1993:306). Far from being devoid of desire, I argue, following Wyschogrod (1990:150), that this kind of love, which is both altruistic and erotic, arises from an excessive desire for the Other. It is transpersonal because it consumes the self through radical openness to the needs of the Other. The second reading of 'impersonal' as detached or dispassionate is, however, also relevant to our understanding of attentive love, and I return to this second reading shortly.

There are significant points of convergence between the work of Weil and of Levinas, despite their very different readings of the Judaic tradition. Rose (1993:211-223) dubs them 'the angry angels' because she sees both primarily as *ethical* thinkers who 'seek to justify *in philosophical terms* the essentially ethical as opposed to the sacrosanct character of the religious impulse which they elect to represent' (Rose 1993:212). Certainly both Weil and Levinas understand that justice must have its roots in an ethical domain that is distinct from the political domain of rights and jurisprudence. For Weil this ethical domain emerges when we encounter, not the face, but the cry of the Other (Weil 1962:11). And this cry of protest demands a response in terms of first person obligation. Weil understands the concept of rights as existing in the secondary domain of the third person which is the domain of political and social institutions. This certainly does not mean that issues of rights should be ignored. As Weil (1962:30) writes:

> The other cry, which we hear so often: 'Why has somebody got more than I have?' refers to rights. We must learn to distinguish between the two cries and to do all that is possible, as gently as possible, to hush the second one, with the help of a code of justice, regular tribunals, and the police. Minds capable of solving problems of this kind can be formed in a law school.
>
> But the cry 'Why am I being hurt?' raises quite different problems, for which the spirit of truth, justice and love is indispensable.

This cry from the heart demands a different universe of discourse, one that coincides with the post-rational, nondual universe which I have proposed. The political discourse of rights is insufficient, according to Weil, because it depends on 'an inadequate notion of "person", incapable of explaining what it is that is sacred about each human being' (Burns 1993:481). For Weil, it is this sacred horizon that provides the pre-given universality essential for an impartial notion of justice. Again we can see the similarity to Levinas's work. Weil's understanding of 'true' justice sets it in a post-representational domain, beyond any articulations of ethics or laws. This domain is post-egoic and therefore impartial in the sense that it escapes the realm of the individual subject's historical particularity. But the demands of this justice are unlimited and independent of socio-historical differences in gender, race, class, ethnicity and even species. The way that Weil conceives this impartiality of justice is similar to the notions of Derrida and Levinas which I explained in the previous chapter. This contrasts markedly with the 'veil of ignorance' approach to justice proposed by Rawls (1972). As Williams explains:

> For Rawls justice is a negotiated settlement between two or more independently defined sets of interests, in terms commending themselves to a common ground of rationality and prudence; for Weil, it is something more radical. I simply do not have in reality independently definable interests of this kind; if I think I do, I have wholly misconceived the essential character of virtue in human interaction, and perhaps misunderstood the nature of understanding itself. Justice is what occurs when a situation arises in which *unqualified mutual attention* is exchanged between persons; no-one's will is overridden because all understand that the perspective expressed in individual (self-interested) will as such is illusory. The only true 'interest' I can have ... is discoverable through *attention to the reality of others*, to the perspective on the world which they in their distance from me possess. It is not a matter of negotiating terms, but of a universal relinquishing of that idea of rights upon which the practice of negotiation exists (Williams, 1991:156, cited in Burns, 1993:483; italics mine).

Williams' summary of Weil's position clarifies her contribution to the articulation of a genre of knowledge that is ethically grounded. Weil pinpoints the *method* by which we might arrive at a primordial ethical experience through encounter with the other as Other. That method is 'unqualified mutual attention', or attentive love, which is a key theme in Weil's work. She suggests that this 'capacity to give one's attention to a sufferer is a very rare and difficult thing; it is almost a miracle; it *is* a miracle' (1973:75). Weil (1973:75) offers the legend of the Grail as illustration:

> In the first legend of the Grail, it is said that the Grail (the miraculous stone vessel which satisfies all hunger by virtue of the consecrated host) belongs to the first comer who asks the guardian of the vessel, a king three-quarters paralysed by the most painful wound: 'What are you going through?'
>
> The love of our neighbour in all its fullness simply means being able to say to him: 'What are you going through?' It is a recognition that the sufferer exists, not only as a unit in a collection, or a specimen from the social category labelled 'unfortunate', but as a man, exactly like us, who was one day stamped with a special mark of affliction.

Weil (1973:75) goes on to suggest that to truly ask this question we must be able to look at the other in a certain way. She tells us that:

This way of looking is first of all attentive.

For Weil attentive love 'is the basis of justice and not the other way around' (Finch 1993:303). We can understand the transpersonal nature of the subjectivity involved in this attentive love from Williams' explanation, quoted above, that 'the perspective expressed in individual (self-interested) will as such *is illusory*'. When the illusion of the individual self is deconstructed, the subjectivity that remains is the extended, post-egoic or transpersonal consciousness referred to in the previous chapter. It is a non-genitive form of subjectivity which is found only after a shift occurs in the locus of identity from discursive self to transpersonal awareness.

This perspective reveals the sacred through the particular, not by devaluing or absorbing the particular, but by reframing it within an unlimited transcendent horizon. For Weil, the impersonal, or as I would argue, the transpersonal in us *is* the sacred. It is this transpersonal aspect of our own subjectivity that makes us capable of attentive love, which in turn enables us to discern the sacred in the particularity of the Other (Burns 1993:486). When the term transpersonal is understood to refer to the transcendent dimension of particularity and not to an undifferentiated universal, then Weil's work brings clearly into focus the ways in which the transpersonal adds depth to both the personal and particular.

Whilst Weil's work can no doubt be read in ontotheological terms as positing an impersonal Being at the 'true' centre of ourselves and others, I suggest that her work is also consistent with a postmodern reading that is free of presence and universalism. Following Inchausti, for example, we might think of the sacred in post-structural terms as a transcendent which, defying any closure, exists 'as the ultimate trope against the will to power, the will to define, the fascist urge to totality' (Inchausti 1991:124). Such a reading of the sacred in Weil's work allows us to understand more easily the significance of a transcendent horizon in defining a non-dominative, nondual universe of spiritually-engaged knowledge.

Novelist and philosopher Iris Murdoch took the theme of attentive love from Weil's work and developed it in a way that furthers our understanding of attentiveness as a way of looking. Both Murdoch and Weil offer attentive love as a method for moving beyond the ego, beyond the stage of rationality, into a post-rational ethical domain. In this domain, Murdoch (1970:91) suggests that it is 'love which brings the right answer'. She understands attentive love as 'an exercise of justice and realism and really *looking*'. She explains that attentive love 'teaches us how real things can be looked at and loved without being seized and used, without being appropriated into the greedy organism of self'. Attentive love requires the 'unselfing' of ourselves, so that we can 'truly' see the Other who stands before us (Murdoch 1970:84). This unselfing, or deconstruction, of the individual, phenomenological self by means of the *discipline* of attentive love leads us into the extended form of nondual subjectivity that comes after the subject. It is important to note that neither Weil nor Murdoch pursue the construction of alternative forms of identity. They seem to consider that the dissolution of the separate, individual self is all that needs to be done.

Resonating with Kohlberg's description of a seventh stage of moral development, Murdoch (1970:74) writes that 'the background to morals', or to an 'ethic' in the terminology which I am using here, 'is properly some sort of mysticism, if by this is meant a non-dogmatic essentially unformulated faith in the reality of the Good'. It is the Good that denotes the transcendent horizon in Murdoch's work. Murdoch (1970:71) seems to understand the idea of the Good post-discursively, as a 'non-representable blankness', but this does not mean that she sees it as an empty concept. Like the ethical stance of being-for the other, the Good can only be specified in terms of a particular context. The Good is universal but it can only be expressed through particularity.

Murdoch emphasises the inexpressibility and the transcendence that surrounds this primary moral orientation because of the 'inexhaustible variety of the world and the pointlessness of virtue' (Murdoch 1970:99). She understands the acting out of this ethical choice as inextricably connected with the practice and *discipline* of attentive love and she is concerned in her work to explicate what I have called the craft of attentive love. Below I consider her work in conjunction with that of other feminist commentators who have also developed the idea of attentive love. Attentive love emerges from this feminist exploration as a non-dominating praxis, a way of knowing and being in the world, that finds application in the many domains in which women function in the contemporary world. I shall now turn to the praxis of attentive love in one of women's most traditional roles: mothering.

Attentiveness as Maternal Practice

Sara Ruddick (1989) offers an account of mothering in which attentive love plays a central role. Her account helps to bring the notion of attentive love from the domain of theory to that of lived practice. Murdoch (1970:34) describes attentiveness as 'a just and loving gaze directed upon an individual reality', while Sara Ruddick (1989:120), building on Murdoch's work, goes a step further and describes it as 'a kind of knowing that takes truthfulness as its aim but makes truth serve lovingly the person known'. Ruddick (1989:122) is very clear that 'attentive love is a discipline, but not, as Weil would have it, a miracle'.[4] This suggests, in line with my thesis of a post-rational domain of development, that attentive love is an epistemological strategy that can be acquired through disciplined practice, assuming that one is sufficiently mature to have identified its importance and valorised its practice.

Attention, Ruddick (1989:122) writes, is 'a familiar triumph over the allure of fantasy'. It 'lets difference emerge without searching for comforting commonalities, dwells upon the *other*, and lets otherness be' (Ruddick

1989:122). Attentive love fosters the autonomy of the other and in so doing deliberately rejects both domination and dependence. It is this rejection that has significant implications for the form of subjectivity involved in attentive love. This form of subjectivity is defined neither by objectivising another, nor by accepting the object position of another's objectification.[5] Rather, this subjectivity in both male and female, represents a state of being in which the discursive self becomes other to a transpersonal identity or Self that I have described as a non-genitive attentiveness.

On this understanding, not all maternal love is attentive love. According to Lacanian psychology, the masculine ego is secured through the objectification of his (m)other, but the feminine ego is often secured through the objectification of her children. Maternal love can certainly be dominating. It can, as Ruddick warns, also be inauthentic, made monstrous by a socio-cultural context that operates against women's expression of their own values, authority and subjectivity. To be truly authentic, as the woman on the bridge shows, maternal attentiveness must counter more than the 'fantasy' which might arise in the individual mother's mind. It needs to cut through the prevailing socio-cultural constructions, the ideologies, that pervade and define the context of mothering and 'determine the limits of moral reflection' (Ruddick 1989:113).

Male theorists (Lonergan, 1972:58; Solovyov, 1985) have often dismissed maternal love as instinctive and therefore not worth serious consideration in questions concerned with the construction of moral or social issues.[6] One of the reasons that we are shocked by the image of a woman throwing her infant daughter off a bridge is because of the pervasive cultural constructions of maternal love as flowing naturally from the essential biological nature of Woman. But feminist theorists recognise that motherhood is a social institution as well as an intense personal encounter between two beings.

The institution of motherhood is a social construct that interacts with construction of the feminine and with a woman's own personal capacities and development to define, not only the limits of freedom and moral expression of a woman as a mother (Ruddick, 1989:113), but also her sense of self and the form of her subjectivity (Everingham, 1994:3-9). The emphasis in Ruddick's work is on the mother as an agent with varying cognitive and moral capacities. She frames mothering within a moral context that enables us to understand 'good' mothering as an ethical choice, and 'good' mothers as moral agents who have not only developed the (rational) ability to take the perspective of another, but also the post-rational ability to transcend the individual self and meet their child as a 'thou' in the post-representational domain.

I suggested in the previous chapter that transcendence of the individual, egoic subject implies a nondual post-representational domain of ethical experience. The experiences of pregnancy, birth and breast-feeding that initiate natural motherhood, all offer powerful experiences of a fully embodied, but nondual subjectivity. Whilst these are not perhaps the 'mystical' experiences that Kohlberg had in mind when formulating his seventh stage of development, for many women they provide, on deeper reflection, transformative nondual experiences that initiate extended forms of subjectivity. Rabuzzi (1988), for example, writes of the 'binary-unity' of the mother-self as a form of subjectivity that is always, irrevocably, extended beyond the individual.

The capacity for love, care and nurturing, the willingness to accept responsibility for others, and to define oneself in a non-dominative way are understood, by the majority of contemporary feminists, not as biological attributes with which women are born, but as skills and values that define a post-egoic way of being in the world, that has to be learnt. As Rich (1977:19) suggests of mother-love:

> we learn, often through painful self-discipline and self-cauterization, those qualities which are supposed to be 'innate' in us: patience, self-sacrifice, the willingness to repeat endlessly the small, routine chores of socialising a human being.

Attentive love, like rationality, can be learned at a certain stage in the sequential development of a human being. I contend that while the capacity for attentive love is a human universal, representing a post-rational stage in human development that is potentially available to all human beings, its actual practice is not achieved by all. The attainment of this stage is dependent on both the socio-historical context and the (inter-related) 'individual' level of maturity. As I argue later in this chapter, the conditions of modern Western culture militate against the attainment of attentive love. The modern capitalist context which is still very much with us, supports forms of subjectivity that are defined in opposition to the other, and ways of knowing that equate knowledge with power.

Attentiveness as Objectivity

Critiques of Western knowledge as a form of domination are now well-known in both feminist and postcolonial theory.[7] The feminist commentator, Evelyn Fox Keller (1985), in her feminist critique of science, draws out the distinction between knowledge as power, and knowledge as love. She recognises that they belong to different and distinct universes of discourse. Unlike Foucault, who understood knowledge as necessarily linked to a technology of power, Keller (1985:116) interprets 'the equation between knowledge and power [as] a sinister one, . . . [which] allows objectivity to become contaminated with domination'. Keller, like Brennan (1993b), understands that there is both a negative and a positive aspect to objectivity. Their work shows that an epistemological strategy of attentive love does not abandon objectivity but reframes it by reconnecting it to the ethical and affective aspects of knowledge.

Keller's critique of objectivity provides an opportunity for considering the second reading of Weil's description of attentive love as 'impersonal' which I referred to earlier. In this reading 'impersonal' is understood as detached or dispassionate – in other words, objective – and it is my contention that attentive love must be objective. In many of the recent critiques of modernity and particularly science, objectivity has suffered from a 'bad press', but what is required, I think, is a way of distinguishing between the negative and positive aspects of objectivity. Brennan (1993b:72) describes the positive aspect of objectivity as the dispassionate attitude that, when directed inwards 'is the vehicle for self-criticism of desires and feelings which otherwise strive to legitimate themselves simply because they are "*our* feelings" (*our* feelings matter, and the other can go hang)'. The negative aspect of objectivity she describes as 'sadodispassionate', summing it up as 'the refusal of empathy in a dry attitude [that] can also be an aggressive act towards the one who is refused' (Brennan, 1993b:72). It is, of course, the positive aspect of objectivity which I argue applies to an epistemology of attentive love.

Keller, in her reconstruction of knowledge based on a non-dominative technology of love, elaborates on this positive aspect, which she refers to as 'dynamic objectivity'. For Keller (1985:117-118) dynamic objectivity is:

> premised on continuity it recognizes difference between self and other as an opportunity for a deeper and more articulated kinship. The struggle to disentangle self from other is a potential source of insight – potentially into the nature of both self and other. It is a principal means for divining what Poincare calls 'hidden harmonies and relations'. To this end the scientist employs a form of attention to the natural world that is like one's ideal attention to the human world: it is a form of love. The capacity for such attention, like the capacity for love and empathy, requires a sense of self secure enough to tolerate both difference and continuity; it presupposes the development of dynamic autonomy.

Keller presents the paradox that is characteristic of a craft of attentive love. The more that we struggle to disentangle our selves from the other in order to see her justly, the more we perceive the hidden relations and responsibilities that irrevocably bind us to the Other. Dynamic objectivity, in other words, reveals interconnection – not necessarily an interconnected or relational *self* – but an interconnected reality. Nonetheless, getting our individual discursive selves out of the way is, as we have seen, essential to the practice of attentive love. As Murdoch (1970:91) writes:

The difficulty is to keep the attention fixed upon the real situation and to prevent it from returning surreptitiously to the self with consolations of self-pity, resentment, fantasy and despair.

Murdoch (1970:89) also understands attention as objective, for, as she advises, 'attention is rewarded by a knowledge of reality'. It is, returning to the terminology of the previous chapter, a kind of radical empiricism that results, not simply from 'opening one's eyes' or encountering a stranger, but from a 'kind of moral discipline' (Murdoch 1970:38) that involves unlearning our ideological projections. Every 'true' meeting with another, is a meeting with a Stranger whom we perceive totally free from the contamination of our self-absorbed projections. In the previous chapter I suggested that the ethical aspect of spiritually-engaged knowledge could be applied within the environmental domain, and I turn next to the work of ecofeminist commentators who take us into that domain.

Attentiveness as Interconnection

Mathews (1993) follows Keller in exploring an epistemology of attentive love in science, but she also develops a different direction by taking the praxis of attentive love into the environmental domain. Mathews (1989) develops the theme of inter-connectedness and her paper on attentive love as an ecofeminist epistemology explores the connection between environmental and feminist discourse. Using object relations theory, particularly Chodorow (1979), Mathews (1989, 1993), like Keller, proposes a connection between the masculine formation of an individual self and a tendency to deny dependency and connection. The result is a masculine, contained subject that is split off from the object. Both Keller and Mathews explore the connections between the masculine contained subject and the detached, objective, rational mode of knowing that is characteristic of Western science.

Mathews, however, also develops the connections between this contained, individualistic mode of being and environmental destruction. She proposes that it is the failure to acknowledge our dependency on, and inter-connection with, Nature that leads to environmental destruction and, conversely, argues that it is the acknowledgment of our inter-connectedness which will give rise to 'the right moral attitude to Nature' (1989:16). Chodorow's work, I think, provides an ambiguous foundation for this ecofeminist argument.[8] Chodorow (1979) argues that the feminine self, which is not forced to renounce its connections with its primary carer in order to form a sexual identity, offers a more inter-connected form of self. If we adopt this conventional feminine self as the model for an inter-connected form of ecological self then we run the risk of overlooking the costs to women of the construction of femininity in patriarchal or sexist cultural contexts.

Salleh (1984) also argues that the feminine self provides a model for an inter-connected ecological self. This would seem to imply that the feminine self constructed under conditions of modernity is basically healthy, a position with which I disagree. Salleh (1984:340) argues that 'if women's lived experience were recognized as meaningful and were given legitimation in our culture, it could provide an immediate "living" social basis for the alternative consciousness which the deep ecologist is trying to formulate and introduce as an abstract ethical construct'. Salleh is not advocating essentialising ahistorical theories of female identity. She clarifies her position in a later article where she states clearly that: 'It is nonsense to assume that women are closer to nature than men' (Salleh, 1992:208). She does, however, go on to assert that: 'Although men and women both wear historically manufactured identities, in times of ecological devastation, the feminine one is clearly the more wholesome human attitude' (Salleh, 1992:209). Whilst I think that Salleh is correct in asserting that the 'historically manufactured' feminine identity is more environmentally friendly, I disagree that it is 'more wholesome'.

I argue that a 'healthy' feminine self must be constructed. It does not simply fall into place as a result of being born female and adopting the governing form of feminine identity. Brennan (1992, 1993b), whose work I will explore shortly, offers a psychological approach that may be more fruitful than Chodorow's for grounding a non-dominative form of identity. Brennan sees the dominant modern forms of the feminine and masculine self as pathological – symptoms of the social psychoses that affect us all. Brennan offers a way of theorising the connection, which several theorists have pointed out, between the construction of femininity and attentive love. Before considering Brennan's work, however, I want to complete my exploration of attentive love in feminist theory and therefore return to Mathews' ideas.

The significance of Mathews' work lies, I think, in her suggestion of attentive love as the epistemological strategy that will enable us (both men and women) to fully recognise our inter-connectedness.[9] Mathews' exploration of attentive love as both an epistemological strategy and 'a daily spiritual discipline' seeks to integrate feminist, environmental and spiritual discourses while defining an ethically-based knowledge. She suggests that 'attentive love is a discipline which integrates the proper epistemic, ethical and spiritual responses to a metaphysics of interconnectedness' (1989:26).[10] Echoing very closely the work of Buber, whom I referred to in the previous chapter, Mathews (1989:12) writes that:

> To know the object fully, then, we have to be prepared to lose ourselves in it – we have to be prepared to merge with it temporarily. But such a merger with the object involves an at least temporary feeling of kinship or affinity with it – love. And to experience this feeling of kinship with the object is to address it – for the duration of the contemplative act – as a 'thou' rather than as an 'it', as a responsive other with a 'viewpoint' which its behaviour could in principle communicate, rather than as a fully externalised object.

Mathews (1989:14), referring to the work of both Ruddick and Keller, describes the required epistemic stance as 'a contemplative one which involves a surrendering of ordinary self-consciousness'. She suggests that what may be involved is a contemplative state in which 'conceptual thought is switched off altogether' (Mathews, 1989:15), a state which seems to approach very closely the post-rational state to which I referred in the previous chapter. Mathews goes on to suggest that 'there do exist meditative disciplines which claim to teach the art of such "direct seeing"' (ibid). It is this suggestion that I want to develop next as I explore attentiveness as both meditative awareness and as spiritual practice within feminist discourse. These approaches foreshadow the next chapter, where I focus on attentive love as a meditative, spiritual practice within the discourse of religious traditions.

Attentiveness as Meditative Awareness

The work of Josephine Donovan in the literary domain is helpful in enlarging our understanding of the sacramental or spiritually-engaged nature of this genre of knowledge. Donovan (1996), independently of Mathews, develops an ecofeminist approach that relies on an epistemology of attentiveness. Her work is particularly useful in clarifying what I have referred to as the post-discursive nature of attentive love. Donovan (1996:176) adopts a sacramental theme to suggest an ecofeminist approach to literary criticism that rests upon 'meditative attentiveness'. Such an approach is quite different from the post-structuralist acceptance of the limitations of language because it understands language or texts, as 'vehicles for the disclosure of being ... thereby helping to reconstitute the "objects" of discourse as "subjects"' (Donovan 1996:162). Whilst I have argued that language cannot *fully* describe or communicate our lived experience, I certainly do not wish to assert that discourse plays *no* role in shaping that experience. Clearly discourse is not an optional extra in human knowledge and experience. Donovan's work demonstrates the way that discourse, employing a craft of attentive love, can point beyond the signified to the unbounded referent. Her explanation of attentiveness refers us back to the possibility of a radical empiricism that is not ideologically mediated.

Drawing her examples from women writers such as Virginia Woolf, Adrienne Rich, Dorothy Wordsworth, Sarah Jewett, Helene Cixous and Clarice Lispector, Donovan suggests there is a feminine literary tradition in which 'images [are] not killed into meaning' (Homans, 1986:51[11]). Rather, words are used to convey 'the thing itself' (Lispector cited in Donovan 1996:163), and are a means of capturing 'reality before it is transformed into an object by signifying texts' (Donovan 1996:167). The words still name, but this naming through meditative attentiveness does not dominate the object or imprison it within the net of discursivity, rather it attempts to address the object in a pre-symbolic mode that imposes no limitations. Donovan (1996) discloses to us the possibility of a universe of discourse that 'restore[s] the absent referent as a "thou" to the text' (Donovan 1996:162).

In a very similar vein, Cixous (1990:99) suggests the existence of a feminine mode of writing (*écriture féminine*) that, while it is 'prelogical, prediscursive' (Cixous 1990:23[12]) is nonetheless expressed in discourse. Cixous (1990:12[13]), referring to Clarice Lispector's work as an example of *écriture feminine,* suggests that she 'names through love' in such a way that the quotidian becomes sacramental. The spiritual horizon is named, and yet remains unnamed, because it lies in the non-discursive domain before which all names recoil. Lispector calls this non-discursive domain 'God', but as Cixous (ibid) suggests:

> Clarice does not imprison [God]. She gives [her] a name, but she does not take [her] by the name. She does not give [her] a name in order to take [her]. She gives [her] . . . a name that does not belong to any language, and . . . is not going to capture [her].

It is at this point that I take a different direction from Donovan (and Cixous) in suggesting that the universe of discourse to which they refer is not *pre-*logical or *pre-*discursive, but *post-*logical and *post-*discursive. Whilst I think that children, depending on their age and stage of cognitive development, do approach the world in a pre-logical, pre-discursive way, this approach is closed to adults whose capability for rational discursive thought is already developed. The domain of attentive love is a post-egoic, post-discursive domain in which the seat of consciousness is no longer the physical body, as is the case with the child, but a transpersonal awareness which transcends but includes the body. In this domain the boundaries of the contained individual ego are breached so that the repressed connections that exist between the subject and object, the mutual interdependencies that sustain all of life, are once again experienced. If, with Ricoeur, we understand childhood as the time of the 'first naivety', then this post-representational domain emerges *after* the development of language and rationality as a second or 'willed' naivety (Fowler 1981:187). Whilst the postmodern critiques of rationality and discursivity can open this domain to us, it is only attentive love, I suggest, that allows us to enter and experience this way of knowing.

In Donovan's work we find again the intimate connection that exists between love and reality, suggesting that it is the former which reveals the latter. The universe of discourse that Donovan refers to as ecofeminist (to which I apply the term 'spiritually-engaged') is concerned with apprehending rather than comprehending reality. It is a non-dominative universe of discourse that does not want to confine the other within the bounds of meaning, but wishes to encounter the Other within the transcendent horizon of love. Such discourse uses words, but continuously points beyond the words, since words are inadequate to the experience itself.

This is very close to Murdoch (1970:67) when she defines that which cuts through the socially constructed representations: 'What counters the system is attention to reality inspired by, consisting of, love.' Murdoch (1970:42) relates the virtue of love to both the real and the good.

> 'Good': 'Real': 'Love'. These words are closely connected. And here we retrieve the deep sense of the indefinability of good Good is indefinable ... because of the infinite difficulty of the task of apprehending a magnetic but inexhaustible reality.

We see appearing in both Donovan's and Murdoch's work a transcendent horizon that in this case opens, through neither the face nor the cry, but through the 'ordinary' context of our lives. When we see reality in the light of this uncontainable Otherness, we perceive it justly without the distortion of our own projections. And when we do perceive the Real, the World, the Other in that way then we understand it through a connaturality that arises from our inextricable inter-being.

For Murdoch love is inseparable from justice, just as the humility essential for patient attention is inseparable from accurate seeing. Murdoch's work offers an understanding of the essential, noetic function of virtues. She argues that value concepts or virtues, are 'stretched as it were between the truth-seeking mind and the world', and it is by means of these virtues that 'patient attention transforms accuracy without interval into just discernment' (Murdoch 1970:90-91). The just discernment that Murdoch seeks to explain (which I refer to as spiritually-engaged knowledge) is ethical because it is virtue-based, not because it either includes, or generates, moral precepts or ethical commands.

Like the post-deconstructive ethic proposed in the previous chapter, this feminine understanding of ethical is unrelated to any universal set of moral precepts. Indeed as other feminist commentators[14] have pointed out, moral precepts, or ethics, have often been employed in a dominative mode since they have been formulated by the powerful to separate the 'good' people from the 'bad' and enforce the will of the former upon the latter. A non-dominative ethic is noetic rather than noematic. The exploration of 'attentive love' as a feminine praxis leads us to the recognition that this kind of radically empirical knowing is irrevocably related to virtue. Our capacity for love, humility and the other virtues is directly related to our ability to apprehend reality. I return to this point in the next chapter, for in the spiritual domain, virtue has always been regarded as the prerequisite for spiritual or sapiential knowledge.

I argued in the previous chapter that a transcendent or sacred horizon is also essential to the apprehension of reality. The transcendence to which I referred was, I stressed, not defined in either its pre-modern or modern sense of opposition to the physical world, but in a post-deconstructive sense of recognising the already existing (w)hol(i)ness of that world. I suggest that it is just this sense of transcendence that also emerges from feminist theory. In Western culture, the feminine has been defined by exclusion from certain categories. Tracing the construction of the feminine in Western philosophy, Lloyd (1984) found that transcendence was one of those categories.

'"Transcendence" in its origins, is a transcendence *of* the feminine ... the ideal of transcendence is, in a more fundamental way than de Beauvoir allows, a male ideal; ... it feeds on the exclusion of the feminine' (Lloyd 1984:101). As Lloyd (1984:102) understood: 'Male transcendence ... is different from what female transcendence would have to be. It is the breaking away from a zone which, for the male, remains intact – from what is for him the realm of particularity and merely natural feelings. For the female, in contrast, there is no such realm which she can both leave and leave intact.'[15] Lloyd (1984:104) therefore concludes that: 'Women cannot easily be accommodated into a cultural ideal which has defined itself in opposition to the feminine.' And yet emerging in feminist discourse is a new understanding of transcendence as the domain beyond the violence of language and rationality.

Drawing on examples from a diversity of fields I have shown, in this first part of the chapter, some of the ways in which attentive love has been constructed as a feminine epistemological strategy that offers the Other an open-ended imprint. The women commentators, whose work I have considered, describe this craft of attentive love as an objective way of knowing that gives access to reality, unimpeded by fantasy or other projections of the mind and ego. Their work reveals attentive love as a praxis that is not related to thought or the functioning of the rational mind. Rather, it occurs when the mind is transcended and thought is brought to a standstill. Weil's term – 'attentive love' – effectively captures the epistemological strategy involved, clarifying that this universe of spiritually-engaged discourse is not the outcome of the rational operations of the mind.

Attentive love both results in, and is the result of, a different level of consciousness or awareness. It is the outcome of a disciplined practice of attentiveness and offers a way of knowing that is both ethical and spiritual. As such, attentive love facilitates 'otherness' by releasing the other from the fixity of egoic or social constructions and offering the other an open-ended affirmation of her reality. Attentive love is the essential epistemological strategy for radical empiricism, enabling us to approach an ideologically unfiltered way of knowing. Following the argument outlined in the previous chapter, I propose that this unmediated knowledge is the prerogative of a nondual subjectivity that is post-egoic or spiritually-engaged. Returning again to the work of Carol Gilligan, I propose that, just as rational thought is the hallmark of a particular stage of human development, so attentive love is the hallmark of a post-rational stage of development. As might be expected if this were so, attentive love appears as an epistemological strategy adopted by some but not all women across a variety of domains from mothering to scientific research. But the concept of attentive love has not been accepted uncritically by all feminist theorists. I next look at the work of some feminist commentators whose work helps to clarify the difference between positive or loving attentiveness and attentiveness that is negatively deployed.

An Interactive Energy

Positive and Negative Attention

In many ways the virtue-based injunctions to love, to be humble, to be caring and nurturing sound all too familiar to women, echoing the cultural constructions of femininity, and particularly of motherhood, that have led to their exploitation and exclusion from the public sphere. According to Weil, the mother-child relationship based on the need for care and 'the expectation that good will be done to us', provides the model for all relationship to the Other (Finch 1993:303). The attentive love of a mother represents the original gift, the incarnation of responsibility to the Stranger who is not a stranger. It is in the maternal response that Weil discerns both the promise and the pattern of justice for the social domain. What we receive in the early months and years of life is not earned, bartered or traded, but freely given. This gift, however, is not without a cost and under conditions of traditional patriarchy or contemporary capitalism, much of that cost is borne by women.

Fox (1992:112-113) expresses this concern in response to a passage in which Weil (1973:74) utilises the metaphor of a slave to convey the attitude of watchfulness and waiting that characterises attentiveness. Fox writes:

> It is fairly clear why no contemporary feminist should be willing to accept Weil's notion of attention without some important modifications. The posture of the attentive slave might work when directed toward God, or the truth, but when directed toward other human beings, it is a recipe for disaster. Particularly when practiced by women toward men, it has not, historically, produced the reversal described by Weil in which the master serves the slave with meat. Thus, though Weil's development of and emphasis on the notion of attention and attentive seeing are powerful and evocative, the notion needs to be reworked for secular use.

Weil's metaphor of the slave is unfortunate I think, since it is readily misinterpreted. Taken in the context of Weil's life and writings, which contain little to suggest that women should be the watchful and attentive slaves of men, it points towards the necessity of a clearer understanding of the praxis of attentiveness. As I read this passage, Weil is arguing that both men and women should become slaves to their own 'higher' faculties, to the expanded sense of identity and knowledge that are the result of post-egoic development.

Fox (1992), by contrast, is wary of suggestions of self-transcendence because, she argues, 'self-transcendence is too much like self-abnegation, a process that is profoundly dangerous for women' (Fox, 1992:112). I argue however that, correctly understood, attentive love and the self-transcendence that it implies can be libratory for women and men, but it is necessary to distinguish carefully between the various ways that attention can be deployed, not all of which are loving, as well as between the different things towards which we can direct our attention. Unless this is carefully done then the praxis of attentiveness can become distorted and a gift freely offered can be turned into an instrument of psychological and economic exploitation.

Fox (1992) provides a useful summary of some of the ways that feminist theorists have understood attentiveness allowing us to distinguish between loving and exploitative modes of attentiveness. She outlines how for Weil and Murdoch, the failure to attend lovingly disadvantages the would-be-knowing subject, blurring her perception of Reality. She contrasts this with Marilyn Frye's perspective that unloving or 'arrogant' perception can actively harm the person or object beheld. This arrogant, exploitative form of attention involves 'grafting the substance of the other' to ourselves (Frye cited in Fox, 1992:113), so that attention becomes an instrument of 'metaphysical cannibalism' by which the self of one is consumed by the other (Fox, 1992:114). Frye suggests that this 'cannibalistic' deployment of attention characterises the dominant pattern of attentive exchange that operates between men and women in patriarchal societies. Men's attention, according to Frye, is negatively deployed to limit and define the identity of women, while the attention of women facilitates the development and expansion of men's identity.

It is at this point that the argument presented by both Fox and Frye falters. Whilst I agree that men's attention is often negatively deployed to limit the identity of women to a restricted feminine form of subjectivity, the attention that such feminine subjects direct towards men, I argue, cannot facilitate the development of an expanded subjectivity in men, but rather limits the men, in a reciprocal fashion, to a bound and limited subjectivity – the dominating, master identity[16] that has been described as 'masculine'. This master identity no doubt has greater access to wealth and power in the socio-political domain, but it cannot, unless we have no criteria other than material gain by which to assess developmental maturity, be described as an expanded or mature form of subjectivity. It is rather the outcome of a subjectivity that, through the denial and rejection of its emotional and physical inter-connections, has failed to expand. The dominator (masculine) and dominated (feminine) identities are co-dependent because a subjectivity that is itself limited and bound cannot easily offer an unlimited, open-ended imprint to another.

Frye's work, nonetheless, makes an important contribution to our understanding of attentiveness. She offers an active rather than a passive model of attention, which is consistent with an understanding that we do not simply submit to reality but are involved in constructing it. Perception, for Frye, relies on an exchange of attention and, as she correctly notes, the ways that attention is exchanged influence the patterns of power and privilege in the socio-political domain of the 'outer' world. It will also affect, I argue, the subjective patterns of identity in our 'inner' world. Frye (1989) tries to capture the dynamic involved in sexist or patriarchal cultures with the metaphor of a dramatic production on stage in which the actors are men and the stagehands women. She argues that 'the maintenance of phallocratic reality requires that the attention of women be focused on men and men's projects – the play; and that attention not be focused on women – the stagehands' (Frye, 1989:92).

This argument falls short in two respects: firstly, the assumption that women always direct loving rather than negative or binding attention towards men; and secondly, that positive or loving attention is limited and defined by social context. I have already addressed the latter point above, where I argued that loving attention is a way of *overcoming* rather than re-enforcing, socially constructed, limiting images of the other since it de-automatises perception. The former point is simply addressed by considering studies of women who deploy attention negatively in order to adopt an epistemological strategy of superiority with respect to certain others. Women who support fundamentalist religious movements, women in the Klu Klux Klan, or women in the role of colonisers in the colonial era,[17] are just some of the examples of women who utilise their attention in a dominating mode to limit the identity of other women and men.

Maria Lugones, for example, explores attentiveness in the context of racism between women (Fox, 1992). Lugones' (1989) work dispels the illusion that all women, simply because they are women, will deploy their attention in non-dominative, loving ways. Whilst supporting Frye's notion that attention operates between people in an inter-psychic domain, Lugones, by exploring the relationship between white and coloured American women, offers a more nuanced account of the praxis of attentiveness, one which avoids a simplistic division into loving and arrogant along either gendered or racial lines. Lugones (1989:279) writes that 'there is a complex failure of love in the failure to identify with another woman, the failure to see oneself in other women who are quite different from oneself' – through metaphors of 'playfulness' and 'world travelling', she relates this lack of loving perception or attentiveness to imperialism and the destruction of other people's worlds.

Teresa Brennan (1992, 1993b) moves beyond metaphor in considering the role which attentiveness plays in the construction of self and others within the discourse of Western psychology. Brennan's work marks a significant shift from an understanding of attentiveness as an epistemological strategy to an understanding of attentiveness as a form of psycho-physical energy that operates within the psychic domain. Brennan thus offers a way of understanding the pivotal role of attention in breaking through the bounded selves of modernity. Not all attention however is loving or freeing, and we need to understand the ways in which attentiveness has been manipulated to construct the ego's era, as well as the ways in which attentiveness can be positively deployed to deconstruct that era. It is therefore helpful to further explore Brennan's understanding of attentiveness as a form of energy.

An Economy of Energy

Brennan (1992, 1993b) offers a detailed analysis of the role of attention in the inter-psychic domain and its impact on the formation of masculine and feminine identities. Starting from Freud's work, she develops the concept of attention as a form of energy that generates both psychic and physical effects. She explores how this attention or energy operates between people as well as within the individual psyche. Brennan, following Lacan, suggests that the ego, the contained self, is an illusion created by the fixing, or binding of attentive energy. This brings us close to the position of Eastern traditions in which the ego is also understood as an illusion, but one which can be deconstructed through meditative praxes that control attention.

Brennan develops 'an interactive economy of energy' that offers, within the discourse of Lacanian/post-Freudian psychology, insights into the praxis of attentiveness, the construction of subjectivities and the link between the two. As with other commentators whose work I have considered, my aim is not to articulate a critique of Brennan's work, although aspects of post-Freudian psychology certainly raise important questions, but to highlight her understanding of attentiveness and its significance in both the construction, and later deconstruction, of our notions of self. I concentrate on conveying her understanding of attentiveness, in both its negative and its positive aspects, in the construction of subjectivity.

Brennan's work is of particular interest because she frames attentiveness not simply as a way of knowing, but as a form of energy which is intimately bound up in our construction of our selves and which, with sufficient awareness, we might consciously and positively direct. She thus shifts the emphasis from subject/object knowing to knowing/being our selves. Attentive love emerges as a means of knowing/recognising subjectivity. Brennan's work offers an alternative to the linguistic mode of postmodern discourse, and allows us to think of the Other in terms of energy flows. Discourse is, of course, one of the most powerful human means of directing and controlling attention, but attention is also directed by various non-discursive, bodily and psychological means.

Brennan distinguishes between the negative and positive deployment of attention: negative attention is understood as energy that fixes or binds, while positive attention can be understood as facilitating the free flow of energy. Thus in the dynamics of the inter-psychic domain, the negative deployment of attentiveness fixes the identity of the other, confirming social or personal habits of identification and limitation which are understood as fixed pathways of energy utilisation. Conversely the positive deployment of attentive energy, which I refer to as attentive love, enables the other to break through fixed patterns of energy utilisation (personal and/or social conditioning) into an open-ended expression of subjectivity and action in the world.

Like Lacan, Brennan is concerned with an analysis of 'the ego's era', which she understands as a social psychosis that has its starting point in the West. But her work escapes the sexism of both Freud's and Lacan's accounts since the perspective she offers sees the contemporary forms of *both* masculinity and femininity as pathological, albeit in different ways. Brennan's account builds on the object-relations account of identity formation in which the mother is central, but she openly acknowledges the social and psychic costs to women of the governing forms of feminine and maternal identity.[18] Brennan builds on Freud's understanding of femininity as pathological. According to Brennan (1992:6) it is 'a psychical state that restricts and inhibits both men and women', although in patriarchal or sexist societies it is more likely to afflict women.

Femininity, as understood by Brennan (and Freud), is a particular pattern of identity construction that results from the operation of *both* intra-psychic patterns of energy use and extra-psychic patterns of power. The inequitable ways in which socio-political (i.e. extra-psychic) power is distributed in patriarchal or sexist societies, impacts on the intra-psychic structures of the governing forms of identity in such a way as to maintain the existing imbalance of power. Under these conditions the feminine form of identity maps more frequently onto women than men. Whilst the feminine self is more relational and less dominating than the masculine self (Salleh's ecologically desirable attributes mentioned above), it is also, according to Brennan's account, more rigid, less active, more subject to repression and depression, masochistic, envious and less concerned with justice.[19]

In the modern context the masculine ego takes the form of a psychically contained, individual self which, by denying its ineradicable connection with others, must ultimately be regarded as psychotic since it persistently engages in projects of (environmental and ultimately global) destruction and self-annihilation. Like the feminine self, this contained masculine self is ultimately an illusion that is given the semblance of reality because of the attentive energy that it binds. The masculine self is contained, dominating, lacking in affect, sadistic and active. In conditions of patriarchy or sexism it maps more frequently onto men than women, but should not be thought of as exclusively male. These governing masculine and feminine forms of identity are still very much with us. According to Brennan they are interdependent, both having their origin in the psychical fantasy of woman that offers a fixed point of either opposition or identity for the subject-to-be.

Brennan's (1992, 1993b) understanding of attentiveness demonstrates how attention can be both positively (lovingly) and negatively deployed in the construction of self and others. It also offers a way of theorising the link that exists between the physical, psychic and social domains in identity formation. Brennan's work is complex and not easily summarised. Its significance for my argument lies mainly in her understanding of attentiveness as an energetic exchange, and in the way that she distinguishes negative from positive attentiveness, relating these respectively to psychoses and well-being. In the next part I examine three aspects of her work which are relevant to the perspective I am developing.

Firstly, the formation of the contained ego; the role of attention in this; and the asymmetry of the process with respect to gender. Secondly, (aspects of) Brennan's interactive economy of energy/attention; the continuing gender asymmetry; and, albeit briefly, her thesis that the psychical fantasy of Woman in the West stands in causal relationship to the contained ego and its destructive social manifestation. Thirdly, I explore the deconstruction of the contained self, which I describe as 'cutting the ties that bind'.[20]

Constructing the Ego's Boundaries

In order to understand the construction of the bounded modern identity, Brennan (1993b:79-117) posits the formation of a foundational psychical fantasy based on the desire for instant gratification and the desire to control the mother.[21] In reality of course the infant has recourse to neither instant gratification, nor control of the mother (or the breast), since s/he is totally dependent, and the fantasy must be repressed in order for the infant to respond more appropriately to the felt need for food.

According to Brennan's account, this repression forms the first boundary of the contained subject. It begins the process of differentiation of the infant from the mother and it also marks the beginning of psychical reality (as opposed to material reality) for the infant. *The force which represses the fantasy 'consists of nothing less than attention'* (Brennan, 1992:113).[22] Following Freud, the infant subject-to-be is understood as conceived within a sea of freely mobile psychical energy. The repression of the foundational fantasy constitutes a fixed point of bound energy which gradually becomes the focus of the multiple pathways of bound energy that will constitute the contained ego. The term 'ego' is here understood in Brennan's (1993b:30) terms as:

> a 'carapace': a rigid construction harbouring the resistances to self-understanding, the defences against what the subject wants to conceal from itself.

The ego can thus be described in energetic terms as inertia or as a binding or deflecting of energy that is initially free, mobile and uncontained. The ego is a psychic habit, a conditioned pattern of energy that becomes more and more difficult to release with each successive reinforcement of the bound energy pathways. Since this binding is based on a fantasy, it can accurately be said that the ego is also an illusion, but one that is given 'reality' through the energetic processes involved.[23]

Brennan's work provides a link to the work of another woman commentator, Caroline Myss. Drawing on the Judaic, Christian, Hindu and Buddhist traditions, Myss (1996), like Brennan and Freud, proposes an 'energy anatomy' that deals with 'the human body's inborn energetic system'. Myss, unlike Brennan, adopts the Hindu/Buddhist-based chakra system to describe the flow of energy through the human system. However, both seem to agree that there is a free, uncontained, unlimited sea of energy, and that the 'individual' may limit this energy and deflect its free flow by directing attentive energy to particular desires, or their repression.[24] This again brings us very close to the position of Asian traditions which postulate the existence of an unlimited life force, or energy *(prana*, in India; *chi*, in China). Illness, both physical and psychological, is related to 'blockages' in the flow of energy within the body. The body itself is understood as a 'desire-body', which is given individual existence through the concentration of energy or attentiveness around a particular nexus of desires. Thus the illusion of the ego is founded upon desire.

But this is jumping ahead a little, and I still need to clarify the role of attentiveness that Brennan proposes in the early stages of identity formation. The foundational fantasy is hallucinated by both female and male infants. The female infant generally goes on to identify with (some aspect of) the mother (or become a mother herself), thus withdrawing energetic attention from both the fantasy of controlling the mother and the illusion of the contained ego. But for the male infant, who identifies with the father, the fantasy may be energetically reinforced either by the father's own behaviour or by existing social conditions which act out the control of women. According to Brennan (1993b:173) 'the power of a psychical fantasy depends on the extent to which it is reinforced or negated by social practice and the language of the times', and she explains the ways in which both traditional patriarchal and contemporary, sexist capitalist societies reinforce certain aspects of the foundational fantasy.

Clearly, patriarchy reinforces the fantasy of passification[25] and control of women. Dependency on the mother is denied in traditional patriarchies, but since other kinds of dependencies and connections are recognised (dependency on the father, on God, on Nature), the foundational fantasy is still partially repressed and the contained ego is countered. In modern, sexist, capitalist society however the fantasy is dangerously reinforced because the counter forces of recognising connection and dependency through the father, Nature or religion have been weakened.[26] More significantly, however, the technological revolution of production has led to the availability of commodities which feed the fantasy for instant gratification in a way that has never before been possible.[27]

Those aspects of the foundational fantasy concerned with instant gratification are reinforced in both men and women by a technologically advanced society. Since other aspects of the fantasy are concerned with the control of women and the denial of the maternal origin, the fantasy is more easily countered by women than men. The foundational fantasy does not, however, exist as an isolated event in the psychic domain of either Western adults or society. It emerges in the earliest stages of development of the child and is to some extent replayed at all later stages of development, particularly, according to Brennan's account, at the oedipal stage where it is again likely to be reinforced for men and countered, to some extent, for women. It is also at the oedipal stage that the associated psychical fantasy of woman is reinforced and the gendered dynamic of the interactive economy of attentive energy becomes more apparent.

Gendered Identities

For a boy, identity formation in the oedipal phase is relatively straightforward. He grounds his self-image by passifying or objectifying the mother (although it could be any other) and then identifies with the father who, since he is a shaper and a namer, provides entry into the symbolic domain. The objectification of the mother is effected through the 'psychical fantasy of woman' which is created by splitting the mother/woman into an idealised, but asexual, figure on the one hand, and a denigrated image of projected aggression on the other. This fantasy is imaginary but because of the energy exchanges involved is 'real' in the sense that it is acted out in the social domain and allows the boy to secure his self-image.

In terms of energetic exchange the boy takes more than he gives 'in the ego's currency of recognition' (Brennan, 1993b:63) because he secures his own self image by withholding recognition of the feminine subject, replacing it with the psychical fantasy of woman. This inequitable energetic exchange can be understood in terms of attention which is the psycho-physical currency of recognition. The attentive energy that the boy gives the mother is bound (arrogant or exploitative), since it fixes her identity within the limits of the psychical fantasy of woman. In a patriarchal or sexist society that also objectifies women, it is difficult for the mother to resist this pacification, since to do so she must also overcome the energetic pattern of the conventional, societal imprint.

Brennan argues, inconsistently I think, that the attentive energy that the mother gives the boy in exchange is living (or loving) attention that is unbound and secures for him a masculine identity as a namer in the symbolic domain. This unequal exchange confers upon the boy entry into the symbolic domain, but it objectifies the mother, confining her to a pacified identity as an 'it'. For the boy, the process interlocks with the foundational fantasy, reinforcing again both the denial of maternal origin, dependency and connection, as well as the illusion of a separate individual ego. The resolution of the oedipal complex for the boy thus creates a second boundary around the contained masculine self.

Brennan, it seems to me, falls into Lacan's error of assuming that entry into the symbolic is the acme of subjectivity. Entry into the symbolic domain as a namer implies an identity bound by rationality and discursivity – this offers neither an open-ended image nor a post-egoic subjectivity. There are other inconsistencies which Brennan's argument glosses over, particularly the fact that maternal attention is not always open-ended and loving. I argue that if the mother has accepted the passified, feminine identity, then she is unable to offer the son an open-ended identity imprint. She offers him the dominator image, which reinforces the societal image of the masculine in a patriarchal or sexist society. Alternatively, if the mother is still seeking to resolve her own identity, she may attempt to objectify her son and offer a dominated, feminine, bound image to the boy, although this strategy may be countered by the societal imprint of masculinity. I argue that it is only if the mother herself has managed to ground her identity in a non-dominative way (i.e. mature to a post-rational, post-egoic, *post-gendered* subjectivity) that she can offer the boy genuinely loving attention and the open-ended identity imprint that goes with it. This mature, loving attentiveness is not a personal possession, and even an inequitable exchange of such attentiveness can neither exploit nor diminish the one who has seen through her own individuality.

Resolution of the oedipal stage is more complex for a girl, as it is more difficult for her to ground her self-image by passifying or objectifying her father. If he is securing his own self-image through the passification of the feminine, the father will resist passification himself by refusing the bound energy that the girl projects. This resistance is further reinforced by the social structures of a patriarchal or sexist society that confirm the male prerogative on power and prestige.[28] If the father and dominant social structure fail to give the girl the unbound, loving attention necessary for subject recognition, the girl may either (a) accept the passive, shaped (denigrated or idealised) fantasmic feminine identity,[29] (b) attempt to ground an authentic self-image through the passification of a 'not-father' other,[30] or (c) *adopt an alternative way of grounding her subjectivity that does not involve domination.* It is clearly this last alternative that is of the greatest interest because, if the girl/woman can find a way of grounding a nondominative and unbound identity, then she holds the key to unravelling the psychosis of the ego's era.

It seems likely that this third option will not occur till later in life. The girl may linger in the oedipal phase with an unresolved identity (as Freud suggested) or adopt one of the pathological (masculine or feminine) forms as an interim identity until she can free herself from it. But how can she attain this freedom? Klein suggests that 'creative labour' may offer a path to a non-dominative identity for both men and women. If this is to be a solution then outlets for creative labour must be available to women, and this has not always been the case. Mathews (1995) suggests that small eco-communities, tied to place, might facilitate the formation of non-dominative identities. Brennan (1993b:189) suggests that solidarity may provide another alternative[31] that offers a means of grounding a subjectivity that is not based on the passification of another. These alternatives all operate within the socio-political domain, suggesting helpful, but not sufficient, conditions for the formation of non-dominative identities. I suggest that it is the disciplined praxis of attentive love in the psychological domain that provides the sufficient condition which underpins each of these mutually supportive, socio-political alternatives.

Cutting the Ties that Bind

Attentive love then, can be thought of as a form of psycho-physical energy. It is energy that is unbound, that is not conveyed in the form of a fixed imprint, but as 'free' or 'loving' energy. Within the inter-psychic domain that exists between people, this positive energy can be exchanged. It can be given to another and, since the energy is unbound and the associated imprint unfixed, the transfer is the gift of 'Thou-ness', the gift of a transcendent, open-ended subjectivity that neither defines, limits, nor attempts to control the other. Since it effects a transfer of free energy to the energetic system of the other, it can be put to various uses. The other may direct it outwards into activities and projects, or she may direct it inwards.

But what becomes of attentive love that we direct into ourselves? There is no doubt that inward-turning attention can be utilised negatively. Brennan (1992:105) connects it with daydreaming, hysteria, and hallucination, in all of which the energy is 'fixed', trapped within more or less well-defined pathways or patterns of thought that have at best an indirect relationship to reality. However inward-turning attention is not necessarily fixed or harmful and, as Brennan (1992:103) also observes, inward-turning energy which is detached can facilitate self-awareness, described as 'an attempt to grasp a reality that is not (necessarily) self-serving'.

Although Brennan does not develop this point, I argue that inward-turning attention, if it is 'unfixed' or loving, can be a means, in both the intra-psychic and inter-psychic domains, not only of perceiving reality but of releasing fixed patterns of energy that limit and bind the self. As we have seen above, Murdoch argues that attentive love is a way of looking and, directed inwards it can enable the subject to 'see' negative fixed patterns. Seeing these patterns is the first step in eliminating them. In psychoanalysis, for example, the subject verbalises these insights in order to objectify them and withdraw the energy from the fixed, habitual pathways that define them. We are reminded here of the commentators cited in the previous chapter who understood attentive love as a tool for de-automatising perception. It would seem that it may also be understood as a means for de-automatising the habitual psychic pathways that distort subjectivity and limit our perceptions of our own subjectivity. As I discuss in the next chapter, this process of turning loving energy inward, and utilising it to 'undo' fixed psychic patterns, is generally referred to as meditation.[32]

Contemplative or inward-turning attention, if used constructively or lovingly, can free the subject from fixity. This suggests that attentive love offers a means of establishing a subjectivity that is not based on either domination or dependence, but on refusing both of these options in favour of a subjectivity that is simultaneously particular (in the sense that it is unique) but post-egoic. This brings us back to the topic of contemplation or meditation which was foreshadowed at the beginning of this chapter. Brennan refers to briefly, but does not develop, the possibility of an alliance with spirituality. She notes that the 'counter-cultural stress on spiritual connection' (Brennan, 1993b:194) is aligned with other movements that counter the ego's era. It is this potential we now explore from the standpoint of women commentators, while considering attentive love as a way of knowing/being in the spiritual domain.

Here I try to convey an understanding of attentive love in the psychological domain. Although my focus and terminology differ from Brennan's, I believe that the notion of living attention that Brennan posits closely parallels the notion of loving attention or attentive love that I have been developing. Brennan's work offers a way of distinguishing between the negative and positive deployment of attention, so that the former can be thought of as fixing or binding energy, while the latter, which I have called attentive love, can be understood as facilitating the free flow of energy.

The negative deployment of attentive energy, when directed towards the other, fixes her identity, locking her into certain fixed pathways of energy utilisation, and similarly when directed towards the self, locks the self into a fixed, closed pattern of identity. Conversely attentive love, or the positive deployment of attentive energy, when directed towards either the other or the self, facilitates the breaking of fixed patterns of energy utilisation thus enabling an open-ended expression of subjectivity and action in the world. This energetic understanding reframes attentive love as a particular way of deploying energy in the physical and psychological domains, which in turn makes clear that the transcendent domain to which I have been referring is not in any way opposed to either the physical or the psychological but is totally engaged with them in such a way that it can exert a profound influence on events within both of these domains.

A Spiritual Practice

As we have seen, both Mathews and Keller describe attentive love as a contemplative practice, while Donovan refers to it as 'meditative attentiveness'. Contemplation and meditation have usually been constructed as practices within the domain of spirituality and I now want to pursue attentive love as a feminine construction into that domain. To approach the transcendent from a feminine standpoint, demands the dissolution of the secular/sacred dualism that has defined spirituality. The feminine leads into a nondual spirituality that is concerned with the face of the divine as it is reflected in the quotidian and mundane. It is a non-dominative spirituality that has been preserved, at least in part in the contemplative aspects of religious traditions. Although it is not absent from the Christian tradition, this contemplative aspect has been given greater emphasis in the sacred texts of Asian traditions of spirituality. The commentators whose work I have considered above were all women and, although sometimes having spiritual connotations, their theories of attentiveness were mainly concerned with the secular, quotidian domain. Before finishing this exploration of attentive love as a feminine praxis I want to point briefly to the work of four more women commentators – Miriam-Rose Ungunmerr and Deborah Bird-Rose, who comment on Australian Aboriginal practices of contemplative awareness; Ann Klein who introduces a Buddhist perspective on attentiveness or mindfulness; and Gangaji who offers an advaitic point of view.

In different ways the work of these women offers a bridge between the understanding of attentive love as a feminine epistemological and psychological praxis, and the appreciation of it as a spiritual praxis. The work of these women is located in the cross-cultural currents that are characteristic of the contemporary global era where many people's lives are deeply influenced by more than one cultural stream. Ungunmerr's interpretation of her birth tradition of Aboriginal spirituality, for example, has been influenced by Christianity.[33] Klein, Rose and Gangaji all offer interpretations of traditions into which they were not born but which, through study or practice they have, to varying degrees, made their own. Yet these intermingling influences and traditions that constitute their work do not, I believe, render that work inauthentic, but place upon it the imprimatur of the global context.

Dadirri – An Indigenous Australian Gift

Interestingly Miriam-Rose Ungunmerr (1988) offers her way of knowing (*dadirri*) as a gift that is needed by the white (European immigrant) population of Australia. She suggests that the quality of *dadirri* is 'the gift that Australia is thirsting for' (1988) and she describes it as 'an inner, deep listening and quiet still awareness' (Ungunmerr 1988). It is this insight upon which Stockton (1995) draws in his work on Australian spirituality.[34] Ungunmerr suggests that *dadirri* is 'something like what you call "contemplation"' and that it is bound up with receptivity and waiting. She tells us that, like the other descriptions of attentiveness which I have explored, the practice of *dadirri* is not the outcome of the rational mind's activity: 'there is no need to reflect too much and to do a lot of thinking. *It is just being aware*' (Ungunmerr, 1988; italics mine).

If Ungunmerr's work is considered alongside the work of another woman, Deborah Rose (1985, 1992), a (white) American anthropologist who worked with the Yarralin people, an interesting parallel emerges with the genre of spiritually-engaged knowledge that I have been describing. Two components are again present: an objective one based on the face-to-face lifestyle of the Aboriginal peoples (Stockton, 1995:102), and a subjective one, which Ungunmerr refers to as *dadirri*, concerned with a particular type of awareness or consciousness. Rose (1985) suggests that in Yarralin spirituality the intimate face-to-face lifestyle of the people in both family and community is extended to the experienced cosmos, so that 'All parts of the cosmos act responsibly and engage in a mystical union with the cosmic whole' (Rose 1985:14). This sense of harmony and wholeness seemingly arises out of the 'mutual attentiveness' that constitutes Aboriginal mysticism (Stockton 1995:102). It brings about an integration, not just of the environmental and the spiritual, but of the feminine.

Rose identifies Yarralin spirituality as a religion of immanence, suggesting that:

> religions of immanence are based on a fundamental wholeness of which each singular entity is a manifestation. *There is no Other*, there are no 'usual barriers' to be transcended. I understand Yarralin people to be saying that *there is only Us*: this world, these manifestations of life. Spirit moves through us all; to be at One is to be powerfully at Home. Mysticism in this tradition is an apprehension of the world in an intensely heightened awareness of intersubjectivity. *Self is not incorporated into the Other, but is totally engaged with others* (D. Rose, 1992:232; italics mine).

Rose's work makes a significant contribution in the field of anthropology, but her interpretation of Aboriginal spirituality as a 'religion of immanence' is, I think, questionable.[35] Stockton (1995:102-104) takes issue with it, suggesting that perhaps what is at work is not immanence but a 'horizontal', as opposed to a 'vertical', transcendence. Stockton (1995:104) offers 'sacramentality' as an alternative, arguing that in it 'the transcendent is made immanent' in a way which offers 'a balance between divine immanence and transcendence'. This position is close to the iconic understanding that I have already discussed in chapter three, which also transcends the dualistic, immanent vs transcendent, categorisation that has characterised much Western scholarship on religion.

Iconic understanding is nondual and requires what Zimmerman (1988) refers to as a 'radical shift of experience' away from the individual, egocentric subject. Exactly this shift occurs with the praxis of attentive love I have been describing. *Dadirri*, as described by Ungunmerr, seems to closely parallel the praxis of attentive love. It is a praxis that facilitates an expanded subjectivity, as it simultaneously facilitates a 'mystical union with the cosmic whole' (Rose, 1985:14). Zimmerman (1988) uses the term 'panentheism' to describe this position which reconciles divine immanence with divine transcendence.[36] This term, I suggest, more accurately describes Aboriginal 'religions' which, as Cowan (1989) argues, are metaphysical in their teaching, method and intent.

Altering the Tone of Consciousness

Klein, drawing on Buddhist sources for her formulation of attentive practice, uses the term 'mindfulness', which she likens to 'evenly hovering attention' (Klein

1994:118). She suggests that mindfulness is a state of mental concentration capable of focussing on the Other without interference from the constructed self (Klein 1994:114). The practice of mindfulness seems capable of incorporating both essentialist and constructionist theoretical orientations. It allows us to see the contingent, constructed nature of the individual, discursive self, while simultaneously 'lending coherence to the subject' by grounding it in 'present experience' (Klein 1994:118,114). Mindfulness is not concerned with the (noematic) contents of the mind, but with the (noetic) state of mind. It is an attentive state that is alert, receptive, concentrated and aware.

One becomes mindful, Klein (1994:119) writes, not by reformulating the contents of the mind, but by 'altering the tone of consciousness'. Although Klein is writing from a Buddhist perspective, her description of mindfulness concurs with the descriptions of attentiveness offered by the women commentators whose work I considered earlier in this chapter. All of these women have drawn on the work of Simone Weil and there is little doubt from Weil's work that she understood attentiveness as different from thought, concerned with a different level of consciousness. In her own words:

> Attention consists of suspending our thought, leaving it detached, empty and ready to be penetrated by the object, it means holding our minds, within reach of this thought, but on a lower level and not in contact with it (Weil, 1973:72).

Dietz (1988:97), commenting on Weil's work, describes attention as 'waiting', as receptivity, or a kind of negative effort that holds us in openness, so that the object of our attention might reveal itself to us. For Weil, attention was primarily an act of knowing, but this capacity for attention was an essential part of the spiritual quest for God. Not surprisingly, therefore, attentive love provides a bridge between contemporary feminist theories across a diversity of fields and a variety of writings in the spiritual domain.

The Unfixed Imprint

I have already alluded to Brennan's suggestion that in a patriarchal society religion might counter (the foundational fantasy and therefore) the bounded, egoic self by continuing to affirm connection through the acknowledgment of a fundamental dependence on the Absolute. In chapter one, I made a distinction between religion and spirituality, and it is the spiritual domain rather than the institution of religion to which Brennan, I think, refers. The two, as I have already elaborated, have a close connection, and certainly the traditional Christian injunctions to love and be charitable offer a means of challenging the egoic self, and therefore articulate an oppositional way of being that might counter the ego's era.[37] In the next chapter I explore the spiritual domain in more detail, but here I want to show how the notion of attentive love as a particular form of psycho-physical energy allows us to link the psychological and spiritual domains.

To do this I want to refer back to my earlier discussion concerning the positive and negative deployment of energetic attention. I have already described the difference between these as the difference between living or loving attention and bound or fixed attention. However, the difference can also be articulated by considering the *direction* of these different flows of attention. The direction indicates that towards which attention is directed. As Fox (1992), whom I quoted above, suggested, attentiveness directed towards an ill-chosen goal 'is a recipe for disaster'.

What is it then to which we should direct our attention in order for that attention to be positive or loving? I have argued that for attention to be loving it must not be fixed or bound. As soon as we direct a fixed imprint towards either our self or the other we are involved in binding and objectifying. We need an imprint that is unbound, which implies, as I argued in the previous chapter, an imprint that is non-discursive and transcendent. For Murdoch (1970:71) the correct direction of attention was 'the Good', understood as a 'non-representable blankness'. For Weil it was God. And provided that we understand 'God' in something like Inchausti's (1991:124) sense 'as the ultimate trope against the will to power, the will to define', then we can understand the necessity of having a notion of the spiritual or the transcendent as an unfixed imprint, an open-ended gift of energy that does not bind.

To be denied a transcendent imprint is to be denied the open-ended gift of subjectivity. Irigaray makes this point clear from the perspective of women:

> The only diabolical thing about women is their lack of God and the fact that, deprived of God, they are forced to comply with models that do not match them, that exile, double, mask them, cut them off from themselves and from one another, stripping away their ability to move forward into love, art, thought, toward their ideal and divine fulfilment (cited in Deutscher, 1994:88).

Irigaray (cited in Brennan, 1993b:194[38]), Kristeva (cited in Brennan, 1993b:172, 6n[39]) and a number of feminist theologians, have argued strongly for a 'feminine divine', and particularly for a 'maternal divine'.[40] Whatever form she may take, however, the significance of a feminine divine ultimately lies in the transcendent imprint which she can offer women. Paradoxically this transcendent imprint must go beyond any gendered conceptions of masculine or feminine. The feminine divine re-sacralises the feminine and the female, and makes possible the understanding that women as well as men are icons, and that in their undistorted nature women, as well as men, are unbounded, unlimited potentiality.

The unfixed imprint of the divine marks a transcendent domain in which connection makes ultimate sense. It was Gregory Bateson *et al* (1987) who observed that the sacred is 'the pattern that connects' and once the illusion of the contained self is dissolved, and the bound energy that maintained it released, then we ourselves are released into the freely mobile energy which we tried to bind. Another name for that energy might be love, or, as Kovel (1991:1) suggests, spirit, which is the domain we enter when the boundaries of the ego give way and subjectivity is no longer contained within a personal boundary. As Gangaji (1995:2), a contemporary woman commentator and American-born Indian guru, expresses it:

> You are already free. You are pure, uninterrupted consciousness. Somehow in the play of yourself, of consciousness itself, there has been a veiling of the inherent truth of freedom. Who you imagine yourself to be is annihilated by the revelation of freedom. You, as you have known yourself to be, are no more. You, as you have imagined yourself to be, are revealed to be non-existent. There remains only that.

Initially we must, as Brennan does, delineate attentiveness from 'consciousness' or awareness. Brennan (1992:96) describes attention as 'an active deployment of psycho-physical energy, or rather as an act of deployment of that energy'. She contrasts this with consciousness which she understands as psycho-physical energy that is 'neither active nor passive in its connotations' (1992:96). And yet it seems as though ultimately attentiveness is a tool with which we deconstruct all self-definitions to finally discover our own consciousness. Equating 'vigilance' with 'attention', Gangaji (1995:156) writes:

> Vigilance is attention. Attention gets its attentiveness from pure awareness which you are. Self-definition only keeps you fixated on waves while yearning for the deep. The ocean has no problem with waves. Never for a moment does the ocean imagine the waves as separate from itself. Never for a moment does the ocean imagine its depths as separate from itself. Never for a moment does the ocean imagine there is any separation between wave and depth.
> Be the ocean. This is vigilance.

By maintaining vigilance, by being unswervingly attentive, we reach a state of nonduality in which the conflict of the mind ends and love engulfs us. Only then can we fulfil Lonergan's final injunction – Be in love!

But this is jumping ahead into the spiritual domain, and for that we require, as Lonergan suggested, a conversion, a metanoia. Brennan (1993b:172) acknowledges the difficulties involved in making this change. We live, she suggests, in socio-historical conditions 'which make atheism less of an intellectual decision than a position based on affectual resistance to its alternative'. Brennan acknowledges in herself the conflict between her intellectual convictions and 'the idea of an easy way out', by which she seems to be referring to God, religion, or spirituality, though what form these take she does not say. Referring to Irigaray's and Kristeva's work on divinity, Brennan revealingly acknowledges that 'the difficulty with these writings is less with the writings as such than with the commentators' attempts to deal with the embarrassment of having an otherwise admired thinker apparently endorsing God' (Brennan, 1993b:172, 6n).

I recognise a similar struggle in myself to acknowledge and integrate the undeniable experience of love and expanded consciousness offered by the yogi in the turban and his 'con-spiritors' in India. In the academic domain, I have felt torn between two stances: one, the allure of acceptable and, indeed, elegant, discursive constructions that employ spirituality in an instrumental way to bolster rational arguments for environmental or emancipatory goals. The other, is a less acceptable alternative that acknowledges the existence of a genre of knowledge based on virtue and transcendence, and which seeks to articulate that knowledge within the framework of rational, academic discourse. For Western subjects caught in our cultural over-identification with discourse, spiritually-engaged knowledge produces great resistance because it reframes both modern and postmodern intellectual endeavours within an ethical, affective and ultimately transcendent horizon that diminishes the authority of discursive knowledge and calls into question the authority of both intellectuals and the academy as the producers and guardians of knowledge. Strange to think that it might be our limited construction of knowledge as rational and discursive which keeps us from truly knowing.

It is always possible, of course, to retreat into rationality and to suggest, as Whitford (1990), Grosz (1986) and perhaps Brennan (1993b) do, that the call for the return of divinity and the reintroduction of a transcendent horizon, are merely intellectual strategies for undermining the existing symbolic of modernity. It is true, provided we confine our understanding of knowledge to a discursive construction wrought by a technology of power, that they can be read this way. But the yogi in the turban was offering a gift of love, not power. If we let go of the technology of power, which is the tool of the contained ego, and reach for a craft of attentive love, then the transcendent returns, not as a political strategy, but as I have argued, as a psychological and spiritual reality of unlimited, living, radically free energy that might be called consciousness, or love, or perhaps even God!

In this chapter I have explored the construction of attentiveness in feminist discourse. I have situated it within three different frameworks – as a feminine craft, as an unbounded, free form of psychic energy that can be exchanged both within and between psyches, and as a spiritual practice. Within each of these frameworks the constructive practice of attentiveness frees the bounded subject from its limitations and opens into an expanded form of subjectivity that simultaneously constructs the Other within an open-ended, transcendent horizon.

Whilst women developed the practice of attentiveness in the domain assigned to them, I suggest that it was in the contemplative and devotional strands of religious traditions that (some) men kept alive for themselves the non-dominative praxis of attentive love. There has been much theologically oriented obfuscation surrounding the praxis of attentiveness in the various religious traditions. But the contemporary global era challenges this by drawing the world's religious traditions into dialogue with each other. The relativising effect of globalisation cuts through the socio-cultural overlays that obscure the core transformative praxes of different traditions, revealing much common ground. Attentiveness, as I will later assert, is part of that common ground.

The instrument of this kind of knowing which brings together visceral, emotional and cognitive experience is the heart, where the meaning of 'heart' is released from its modern exile and returned to its earlier understanding as the seat of the divine, the seat of transforming wisdom or gnosis. The spiritual heart then is the source of wisdom which connects knowing and loving, and in the next chapter we explore this spirituality of the heart.

Notes

1. Bigwood (1993:207).
2. Some of the commentators to whom I refer, particularly Weil and, to a lesser extent, the early Murdoch, wrote in an era before the present flowering of feminist theory. Their work, however, provides the basis of certain streams of thought within contemporary feminist discourse (Donovan 1993a:171-186) and resonates with new lines of thought currently being developed by women in feminism. Contemporary feminism has many voices, but most include a specific element of gender analysis that is lacking in the work of Weil and Murdoch.
3. Eliot (1952) suggests that her books need to be read by the young, before they become 'committed to the jargon of the market-place' (xii); before, in other words, their perception is automatised by the contemporary capitalist context.
4. This idea is, of course, not new. An earlier and very accessible explanation of it is found in Erich Fromm's (1975) book *The Art of Loving* first published in 1957.
5. The former is a Lacanian description of masculine identity, the latter a Lacanian understanding of feminine identity.
6. Everingham (1994) offers an excellent account of mothering and of the way in which it has been theorised. See particularly her Part 1.
7. See Harding (1991) for a feminist perspective, and Harding (1993) for both feminist and postcolonial perspectives. A comparison with traditional sciences is useful in relativising the Western perspective – Burckhardt (1987) offers a traditional viewpoint on science. Griffin (1988), Tamil Nadu Science Forum and Pondicherry Science Forum (both 1989), also offer alternative perspectives from the Western and postcolonial viewpoint respectively.
8. In Mathews' (1995) later article, which explores the construction of relational, 'eco-communitarian' selfhood, she argues 'that relationality rests on various forms of community, or identity-formation in community' (Mathews, 1999, personal communication). Thus Mathews moves away from Chodorow's explanation in the psychological domain, to a constructivist explanation in the socio-political domain that is similar to Noddings' (1984) ethic of care. Face-to-face relationships in small eco-communities which are tied to place, will enable us to recognise the

subjectivity of non-human others (and hopefully of human others too!). This, in turn, will allow us to take non-human interests seriously, both within our own particular eco-community and in the broader global domain (Mathews, 1995:79-80). Mathews recognises, however, that only certain kinds of relationships could facilitate this outcome. These relationships, she says, would be based on the kind of communication that emerges from epistemologies of attentiveness. We are thus returned to the psychological domain where, I argue, it is necessary to take into account both the developmental perspective that I explained in the previous chapter, and an account of gendered identity formation that is more complex than that offered by Chodorow. I offer Brennan's (1992, 1993b) account later in this chapter as one possible alternative.

9. Another ecofeminist commentator, Warren (1990:134-138), also introduces loving perception into ecofeminist discourse. Mathews' (1989) approach is more comprehensive, however, so I have taken it as the basis of my discussion.
10. I argue that a metaphysics of interconnectedness is not radical enough, we have to go beyond inter-connectedness to nonduality. Attentive love requires a nondual metaphysics that exceeds the eco-centric, inter-connected metaphysics for which Mathews argues. See Crawford (1993).
11. Cited in Donovan (1996:164).
12. Cited in Donovan (1996:170).
13. Cited in Donovan (1996:171).
14. See Frye (1992) and Hoagland (1988), both of whom seem to be making the distinction (albeit in very different contexts and language) that I have already made between ethics, which implies bringing something in line with a pro-established rule and an ethic, which is about a particular orientation or relationship to the other, that involves a process of creating value or manifesting virtue. Thus ethics involves an element of regimentation, a process of getting it right, and therefore being able to identify those who get it wrong. An ethic, on the other hand, involves incarnating value or 'rightness' (as opposed to righteousness!) within a particular situation or context.
15. See, for example, Kishwar (1989:5) on women devotional poets in India. She notes that *bhakti* (the spiritual path associated with devotion rather than knowledge in Hinduism) inevitably meant different things to women and men. One significant difference was that male *bhaktas* could follow their chosen path while remaining householders, but this was not possible for most women practitioners.
16. The term is Plumwood's (1993).
17. See Dietrich (1994) and Bacchetta (1994) on women in fundamentalist movements in India; Blee (1991) on women in the Klu Klux Klan; George (1993) on the colonising role of British women in India.
18. Object relations theory devolved from the work of Melanie Klein (1985), Dinnerstein (1976) and Chodorow (1979). It shifted the focus of psychic development from the oedipal to the pre-oedipal phase and therefore from the father to the mother. Object relations theory makes the mother the most important factor in the psychical life of the child since the mother is the primary other from whom the infant has to differentiate her, or him, self.
19. As I already mentioned in part (iv) of section I above, Chodorow's (1979) account, since it is less critical of feminine patterns of identity and their relational structure, runs the risk of falling into what Plumwood (1993:9-10) ironically refers to as 'the angel in the ecosystem' or 'the angel in the household' trap – the uncritical notion that the existing 'historically manufactured' form of feminine identity is

non-dominating, relational and therefore just what 'we' need in times of ecological and social crisis.
20. This phrase is taken from Phyllis Krystal's (1982) book of the same name. The book is sub-titled *How to Achieve Liberation from False Security and Freedom from Negative Conditioning*. It gives an account of various techniques for breaking through fixed, bound patterns of energy.
21. While I am drawing on Brennan's account here, similar ideas have been proposed by feminist commentators in a variety of fields. As Brennan (1993b:23) writes:

> The central idea in the foundational fantasy, that an objectifying projection is a condition of subjectivity, evidently overlaps with the work of Irigaray, Kristeva, and that stream of feminist critiques of science (largely American based: Chodorow, Gilligan, Fox Keller, Jessica Benjamin) which situate the subject-object distinction in infancy.

22. The repression of the psychical hallucination of containment and control requires an expenditure of energy and it is the mother herself, by means of selective attention directed towards the infant (i.e. judging when and when not to respond to the infant's cries), who provides much of the energy necessary to repress this fantasy of separation that marks the first boundary of the contained separate self. The attentive love of the mother is crucial in repressing the foundational fantasy of containment and separation. It is, to borrow Jessica Benjamin's phrase (1990), 'the bonds of love' between the mother and the infant that prevent the infant subject-to-be from 'splitting off' from the mother into a hyper-separated identity. The energetic attention of the bond of love provides the tension that allows the infant to differentiate from the mother without separating off from her in a denial of connection.
23. Paradoxically it would seem, according to this account, the fixing of energy that marks the first boundary of the contained self, comes into being precisely because the infant subject-to-be is *not* contained and can utilise energetic attention from the mother to bind the foundational fantasy of control and instant gratification. The subject is thus founded, as Weil intuited, on the basis of a gift (or an inequitable exchange) of attentive energy (Brennan's term is 'living attention') from the mother.
24. It is important to note that Brennan's work has a gender dimension which Myss' work lacks, and which is given little emphasis in the Asian traditions. Brennan (1993b:93-5), following Klein, proposes that this foundational fantasy contains an element of aggression which the infant projects outwards, with the result that the infant splits the breast/mother into two – the 'good' and the 'bad' breast/mother – thus simultaneously splitting the ego and constructing a (split) *psychical fantasy of woman*. This pattern of projecting unwanted or aggressive desires outwards is repeated at later stages of development, recurring again, for example, at the oedipal stage, where it reinforces this psychical fantasy of woman that has its origins in the foundational fantasy. Whenever it occurs, the projection of aggression initiates a 'spiral of aggression', since it leads to anxiety that the other may retaliate and therefore the projection of still more aggression is needed in order to counter the anxiety of possible attack (Brennan, 1993b:62). While aggression can be projected onto various others, Brennan (1993b:62-3) argues that:

> the spiral of aggression has a possible point of departure in the psychical fantasy of woman. More specifically, it has points of departure: (a) in the way in which 'man' makes the 'woman' the negative, the other, both to secure his recognition and simultaneously be pacified, making him the victor in the master-slave dialectic,

and (b) in the way in which the ideal woman fantasy takes over from the God or Truth that concerned him hitherto.
25. Brennan's term (1993b:55). See note 19, chapter 3.
26. Many men have themselves been objectified through the (un)employment and alienation of their labour, as modern capitalist society has become increasingly urban and technologically insulated from nature and religion has declined as a social institution.
27. As religious injunctions to exercise moderation in consumption weaken and socialist, or leftist, political restraints on individual accumulation of wealth diminish, the only limit on instant gratification is the economic one. This is a pseudo-limit at best, since it simultaneously entices people into the capitalist mode of profit-making in order to acquire the money to overcome the limit and feed the fantasy of the contained, controlling ego, free of connection and dependency, that demands instant gratification.
28. Whilst Brennan (1992:209) writes of 'imprints' which children receive from their parents, she does not develop this in connection with the images or imprints that are received from society. If, as Brennan suggests, the parental images are energetic imprints, one might suppose that the social imprints would also take an energetic form. The work of biologist, Rupert Sheldrake (1988), on morphogenetic forms and of Caroline Myss (1996, 1997) on archetypes, both offer energetic ways of conceiving how this might occur.

For the girl we can see that if the bond of love with the father is sufficiently powerful (and the father sufficiently mature) at the oedipal phase, then his energetic gift of an open-ended, or transcendent, imprint can enable the girl to ground a self-image in a non-dominative way. However, in a patriarchal/sexist society, the cultural imprint of femininity will be fixed. This means that the father's energetic gift must be sufficient to counteract the fixity of the cultural imprint.
29. If the girl adopts alternative (a), then she accepts the shaped feminine image (through projection from her father and identification with her mother); the cost is a doubly fixed identity. According to Lacan this forever denies her a subject position in the symbolic order, although not surprisingly feminist theorists offer a different interpretation! As I have already argued, the shaped feminine identity is not grounded in the objectivication of another, and is therefore, as feminist theorists have noted, a non-dominant, more relational and more dependent identity. Nonetheless, it is a bound identity, and it is possible that when the chance arises the girl/woman who has accepted a shaped identity will try to break free of it, either by seeking to identify with the masculine form of identity (b), or by seeking a method of grounding her identity that does not involve domination (c).
30. If the girl adopts alternative (b), she seeks release from domination by herself becoming a dominator. She identifies with the dominant masculine form of identity and finds an alternative other whom she *can* passify (her mother, her children, a man other than her father, persons of another race, class or colour) thus acquiring a 'masculine' identity that is contained, dominating and denies connection to other women. Maria Lugones' work on racism between women, mentioned above, provides an example of this solution to identity formation in which white women adopt the role of dominator with women of colour. But this identity also has its pathological side associated with the denial of affect and connection, so that the girl/woman may eventually try to break out of it and seek (c), a means of grounding identity that does not involve domination.

31. Compare this with Nerfin's (1987) 'mobilising themes', referred to in chapter two, which are essentially forms of solidarity that facilitate the construction of a porous, non-dominating, global identity – a Citizen in Nerfin's terminology.
32. In *Vedanta* these psychic or mental habits are referred to as *vasanas*, often translated into English as 'desires'. It is taught that, while *vasanas* can be overcome through meditation, the strongest *vasanas* may have to be 'lived out', or experienced, during the course of one's life.
33. This comes through in her writing, for example:
    The sound of Deep calling to Deep.
    The sound is the Word of God – Jesus (Ungunmerr, 1988).
34. I am indebted to Eugene Stockton for his material on Aboriginal spirituality. Whilst Stockton's Christian emphasis is not my own, I have benefited both from the analysis offered in his book *The Aboriginal Gift* (1995) and from personal discussion with him.
35. See, for example, Cowan (1989) for a quite different point of view.
36. See Crawford (1993:23-27, 46) for a more detailed discussion of the issues involved in the immanence/pantheism vs transcendence debate.
37. This countering of the autonomous ego has to be balanced against the negative symbolisation of women that runs through many scriptural texts.
38. Irigaray (1984).
39. Kristeva (1983).
40. Whilst agreeing that a feminine image of the divine is important to counteract the predominance of masculine symbols and imagery in the discourse of the major religions, the construction of a feminine divine is fraught with ambiguity, for only a fine line separates any such construction from a psychical fantasy of woman. This point returns us to Cornell's criticism of Levinas's work which I referred to in the previous chapter. Levinas's construction of woman can be read at least two different ways. Cornell interprets his construction negatively as a psychical fantasy, hence her criticism. Levinas might alternatively be read as reaching for the feminine divine, but it is the very fact that both of these readings are possible that reveals the dangerous ambiguity inherent in constructing a feminine divine. Bacchetta's (1994) work on Hindu nationalism provides an example, within a different cultural setting, of the ways that symbols of the feminine divine can be co-opted to the anti-Other causes of communalism, fundamentalism and nationalism.

Chapter 5

The Spiritual Heart

> We must close our eyes
> and invoke a new manner of seeing ...
> a wakefulness that is the birthright of us all,
> though few put it to use
>
> *Plotinus*[1]

In the two previous chapters I have tried to define the emerging genre of what I call spiritually-engaged knowledge. I argue that it is ethically based, arising from the encounter with the Other that defines an 'ethic of meeting'. This spiritually-engaged knowledge marks out a transcendent domain that is non-rational, non-discursive and non-personal. It demands an epistemological modality based, not on power, but on attentive love, and it points to an ontological modality that is subjective but not personal or individual. I have referred to this alternative genre of knowledge as 'spiritually-engaged' because it seems to require a mode of subjectivity that is non-egoic, that might be said to arise after the bounds of ego have given way. In this chapter I want to engage with the domain of spirituality, since it is there that this alternative way of knowing has been most fully explored.

Historically, spiritual and religious discourses have been inextricably intertwined. There is no doubt that as social institutions the major religions have often fallen into the dominative ways of knowing that have characterised the cultures from which they grew. But, I would argue, within the religious traditions there can also be found accumulated streams of spiritual, or sapiential, knowledge concerned with methods of transformation. These methods, in all traditions, have included the practice of both virtue and attentiveness (variously referred to as prayer, meditation, or contemplation), as essential means of experiencing a non-dominative way of knowing and being in the world.

Webb (1988:302) argues that spiritual discourse (which constitutes an essential part of religious discourse) deals with the transpersonal, and that it is only in religious traditions that the transpersonal has been fully explored. Although in the previous chapter I undertook an exploration of attentiveness in feminist discourse, this led to the realm of spirituality because the dedicated practice of attentiveness eventually deconstructs the self/other dualism (which sustains all dualisms, gendered or otherwise) and leads into a nondual domain that finds expression in spiritual discourse. The contribution of feminist discourse is significant, however, if the gender bias that permeates the domain of religious language and symbolism is to be avoided.

Following my method in previous chapters, I will begin by briefly pointing to examples of attentiveness or mindfulness in various spiritual discourses. I offer examples from Christianity, Buddhism and Hinduism, in order to show that this spiritually-engaged genre of knowledge can be found in religious discourses from different cultures and eras. The glimpses that I hold out in this first section can in no way do justice to the practice of attentiveness in these traditions, but I hope that they are sufficient to suggest that this way of knowing has been practised by (some) men and (some) women, across a wide variety of traditions, cultures and historical periods.

With globalisation, the diversity of religious traditions has become accessible across cultural boundaries and the possibility of a more universal, spiritual discourse has emerged. Both the means for, and the possibilities of, consciousness transformation (*theosis, moksha, nirvana*) can now be teased apart from their specific religio-cultural settings to explore the apparently universal potential of human consciousness. Nasr (1989:310) describes such an exploration as being to 'attain that knowledge which is beyond time and becoming, which, rather than engrossing us ever further in that accumulation of details and facts, elevates man to the level of that illimitable Being which is the source of all existents yet beyond them'. Whilst this involves comparisons across traditions of practices and doctrines, such an exercise must be carefully distinguished from the epistemological violence of syncretism, and of certain forms of 'new age' ecumenicism, which glibly assert that all religions are one. Although I am seeking to identify an epistemological modality that is common to the three traditions briefly considered here, it is not my intention to imply that the disciplined practice of this modality can be easily achieved without the help of the specific and distinct forms (doctrinal and symbolic) of each of the traditions involved.[2]

After offering a glimpse of the practice of attentiveness in three major traditions, I then look at the possibilities of a post-representational psychology that takes seriously the claims of spiritual practitioners to have experienced a way of knowing beyond all frames of reference. Both Brennan and Lonergan point towards the possibility of a metapsychology, an understanding of human knowing that is universal because it is dependent on the psycho-physiological structures of human cognition. Universal metanarratives are, of course, amongst the primary targets of postmodernism, and any attempt to resurrect the issue of universality runs counter to the current orthodoxy concerning the socio-linguistic construction of knowledge. Whilst the linguistic turn of postmodern theory offers many insights, I suggest that the issue as to whether *all* experience is socially mediated remains open to debate. In contemporary religious studies this debate has centred around the phenomenon of mystical experience in spiritual traditions. Mysticism has often been associated, not only with claims of unmediated knowledge, but with claims of universality. Mystical writings from various traditions contain references to nondual, non-discursive, non-egoic states of knowing/being that, if taken seriously, certainly challenge the constructivist model of understanding (Rothberg, 1990). I turn to this debate later in the chapter to consider its implications for the radical empiricist approach that I am arguing is characteristic of spiritually-engaged knowledge.

The transdisciplinary formation which has emerged from the meeting of Western psychology and traditional spiritual discourse in the global domain is known as transpersonal psychology. By expanding the spectrum of human consciousness studied in modern psychology, transpersonal psychology offers a non-religious framework within which post-rational, post-discursive states of awareness might be understood and cultivated. I will also look at transpersonal psychology which has much to offer in understanding post-egoic states within a developmental framework exploring, however, a more conservative thesis that considers different epistemological modalities within a less complex frame of reference.

Finally, I will return to an exploration of attentiveness as a spiritual epistemological modality, suggesting that it plays a crucial role in the transformation from ordinary, everyday consciousness, to a nondual state. Understanding attentiveness as a meditative technique offers the possibility of a unified theory of meditation that can be situated within both psychological and traditional religious discourses. Such a shifting of boundaries brings into view something which may be referred to as postmodern spirituality, which I explore in the final part of the chapter, where I return to my definition of spirituality, showing how it is reframed by the global postmodern context. I suggest this postmodern understanding of spirituality offers an alternative, indeed superior way of knowing, that can be referred to as spiritually-engaged, or (at its fullest potential) sapiential. This sapiential knowledge reframes in its turn the project of knowledge, drawing us away from mastery and the technology of power associated with modern knowledge into a way of knowing that is non-dominative. I conclude the chapter by looking at the relationship between knowledge and tradition, acknowledging that while the religious traditions, at their best, offer a disciplined path to transformation, part of the postmodern experiment seems to be the exploration of spirituality beyond the boundaries of those traditions.

Glimpses of Mindfulness

Even a brief glance across the traditions of Christianity, Hinduism and Buddhism such as I offer here, suggests that there is nothing new about an epistemological strategy of radical empiricism or attentiveness that claims to be a non-rational, non-discursive, nondualistic mode of awareness. Unlike modern psychological theories of human cognition, these religious traditions have for centuries mapped pathways of cognition that go beyond the domains of rationality and language.

Particularly in the Eastern traditions, where attentiveness or mindfulness were associated with contemplative, meditative praxes, or with particular kinds of prayer, nondual states of awareness were highly valued and sought after.

In the domain of religion, these attentive praxes were specifically linked with knowledge, but with a kind of knowledge and a state of being variously referred to as wisdom, gnosis, *jnana* or *prajnana*, that the traditions suggest exceeds discursivity. Here the humility or hesitancy of feminism to declare this way of knowing superior is lacking. Religious practitioners generally had little doubt that the knowledge gained by the practice of attentiveness was superior to the discursive knowledge generated by the rational mind. Indeed, the traditional religious systems (including Christianity and Judaism in the West) can be read as alternative understandings of human consciousness that take into account expanded or altered states of self-transcending consciousness. Modern psychology, with its emphasis on childhood development and adult pathology, largely ignores these altered states and has, to that extent, limited our understandings of the possibilities of human consciousness.

I offer glimpses from Christianity, Hinduism and Buddhism in order to demonstrate the similarity of attentiveness practised in these traditions to the examples of attentive love described in the previous chapter. I find that although the religio-cultural contexts within which attentiveness has been practised vary enormously, the actual practice of attentiveness as an epistemological strategy is common across religious traditions. The capacity for attentiveness is, I argue, a universal human characteristic which leads eventually to a kind of knowledge that can be thought of as transcultural or universal.

Christian Contemplation

In the previous chapter, the affinity between attentive love and contemplative practices was alluded to. It is therefore not surprising to find in religious/spiritual discourse that there is a similarity between the phenomenological descriptions of contemplative and meditative praxes and the descriptions of attentive love as a feminine praxis, although the terminology involved may sometimes differ. As previously noted with Klein's (1994) work on Buddhism and feminism, the terminology of 'mindfulness', 'awareness' or 'attentiveness' is common in the spiritual domain, particularly with reference to Asian traditions. Thus, for example, when Dom Aelred Graham (1963) suggests that 'the West has something to learn from the East on the importance of "mindfulness"', his phenomenological description of this attitude of mindfulness seems very close to the practice of attentive love described in the work of Weil, Murdoch, and other women theorists considered in the previous chapter:

> What is called for is not intense concentration, with a knitting of the brows, but, rather, the opposite, an awakening of the mind without fixing it anywhere, the quietness of pure attention (Graham, 1963:143-4).

Graham, however, links this attentiveness, not with mothering or quotidian secular activities, but with religion and, indeed, with a specifically Christian understanding of a creator God.

> What we may need to learn is that merely to look at things as they are, with bare attention, can be a religious act. We are thus enabled to apprehend God's creation as it is, our minds unclouded by egoistical emotions, and so made more aware of God Himself (ibid).

Despite Graham's eastward gaze, the practice of attentiveness was certainly known in the early Christian church and, history would suggest, was always retained in the Eastern church. Needleman (1982a) writes that the practice was present in Christianity in earlier eras but was 'lost' or marginalised, particularly in the Protestant churches, due to a combination of historical factors.[3] For Needleman, the practice of mindfulness or attention represents a recessive aspect of Christianity that is essential both to make sense of, and to put into practice, the teaching of love. To support this contention Needleman turns to the *Philokalia* (Kadloubovsky *et al*, 1951) which is described as 'a collection of the writings of the [Christian] Fathers from the earliest times after the Declaration of Constantine the Great'. The foreword of the *Philokalia* advises that the purpose of this collection is to show 'the way to awaken attention and consciousness, and to develop them' (Kadloubovsky *et al*, 1951:5).

I suggested previously that 'the heart' is the instrument of attentive love, and in the writings of these early Christian practitioners this terminology is used. According to the Church Fathers, attention is of the heart not the mind, and throughout their writings repeated references are made to 'attention', to the 'heart' and to various combinations of the two that seem to revolve around a practice of 'taking the mind into the heart'. This practice is concerned with establishing a state of consciousness or awareness that is devoid of concepts, of thoughts, or of language. Nicephorus the Solitary, amongst others, was quite explicit about this: 'Attention means cutting off thoughts' (Kadloubovsky *et al*, 1951:32).

By way of explanation, Needleman, drawing us more deeply into the discourse of Christian theology, suggests that:

> The power or function of the soul is *attention*; the development of attention is therefore approximately equivalent to the development and growth of the soul.... The principal power of the soul, which defines its real nature, is a gathered attention that is directed simultaneously toward the Spirit and the body. This is 'attention of the heart' (Needleman, 1982a: 162).

This 'attention of the heart' is a puzzling phrase, as is 'gathered attention'. In the latter phrase there are echoes of Brennan's understanding of attention as a directed form of consciousness that is energetic and therefore able to be 'gathered', or accumulated, and indeed, as we will see later in the chapter, there is some suggestion that concentrative meditative practices aim to increase the intensity of attention.

The *Philokalia* refers to 'the active method of the prayer of mind-in-heart' and links it with contemplation. Nicephorus counsels his readers to 'enter into the place of the heart' and to 'force the mind to descend into the heart' (p. 33), while St. Simeon discourses on the 'three methods of attention and prayer' (pp. 152-161). However as Needleman (1982a:157) notes, we in the contemporary West no longer know where to find this 'place of the heart'. With the exception of transpersonal psychology, which I explore in the later part of this chapter, our theories of human development have been concerned with the development of the mind, and the rational faculties *of the individual*. Heart and soul as the non-rational and inter-subjective faculties of attention have been excluded from the modern understanding of human development. Eastern spiritual practices and doctrines seem to have retained, in accessible form, the exercise and understanding of these non-rational, inter-subjective faculties and there are signs that these are now being reclaimed in Western traditions as a result of the global encounter between traditions.

This reclamation involves the revivification of earlier aspects of Christianity, and particularly of the contemplative practices which were either lost or confined to the cloisters of monasteries and nunneries. The Christian Meditation Network provides an interesting example of a contemporary Christian movement that is reclaiming the contemplative praxes of the earlier desert Fathers. The Network was founded by John Main who, having learnt to meditate from a (Hindu) Ramakrishna Swami in Malaysia, sought to reclaim the practice within his own Christian tradition. He identified the same meditative practice in the writings of the early Church Fathers (as already mentioned in the *Philokalia*), particularly John Cassian, and went on to found the rapidly growing ecumenical global network of 'Christian' meditators. The Network exemplifies the process of reclamation, or *anamnesis*, as Nasr (1976:14) calls it. First, there is the recognition of a valuable teaching or practice in a non-Western tradition. This is followed by research which reveals, or rediscovers, that same teaching or praxis in an earlier phase of the Western tradition. Finally, there is the reframing of the praxis or doctrine within a 'new' form or discourse that is more appropriate to the contemporary context. Within a global era, this implies acknowledging the universality of the doctrine or praxis, while nonetheless working to reframe its particularity.

Main's observations on meditation resonate with the radical empiricism that I believe is associated with attentive love, but they also echo the ideas of the previous chapter, that this epistemological modality is a disciplined practice that can be described as 'easy' in the sense that it is simple and devoid of cognitive content.

> Meditation is not about making something happen. What it is about, and this is the basic aim of meditation, is to become fully aware of, fully inserted into, fully grounded in *what is* The way to realize this reality is the way of discipline and seriousness of purpose, of daily return to the discipline. It is the way of simplicity, of fidelity and, as you will find, it is the way of love (Main, 1989:28 and 31).

Main's writings fall within the discourse of mainstream Christianity. Yet when we consider from a phenomenological viewpoint the contemplative epistemological strategy that he is both recommending and describing, it is interesting, firstly, that he experienced it initially within a Hindu context, and secondly, that it is difficult to distinguish it from the feminine *praxis* of attentive love described in the previous chapter. Main (1989:38) understands meditation as a de-automatising of perception:

> Learning to meditate is learning to unlearn. The big problem that faces anyone who starts to meditate is the simplicity of it. God is One. And Christian prayer has been described as the way of one-ing, becoming one, becoming one with the One who is One Meditation is the way of rediscovering our innate, childlike sense of wonder.

The particular meditative technique which Main advocates is a *mantra* technique. This involves the internal repetition of a single word (or phrase), initially during periods of silent sitting and, as the practice matures, unceasingly with every breath. The technique is common to many religious traditions, since it replaces distracted and unfocussed patterns of thought with the attentive, focussed repetition of one word, and this gradually stills the thinking mind, so that we can 'learn to be silent, to be still and to *be attentive* to the presence in our hearts' (Main, 1989:53 – italics mine).

Whilst Main linked his meditative technique particularly to Cassian and other early Christian Fathers, its similarity to the Hesychast tradition in Orthodox Christianity is apparent. This tradition offers another rich stream of Christian teaching and experience concerning the practice of attentiveness. The Christian Meditation Network focuses on a mantra technique for attaining a state of attentiveness and discursive silence, while Main's emphasis on 'unlearning' and 'unknowing' also reclaims the apophatic aspect of the Christian tradition that has been recessive in the modern era. This *via negativa* originated with the Cappodocian Fathers in the fourth century and found perhaps its fullest exposition in the fifth century with *The Mystical Theology* of Pseudo-Dionysius (Stockton, 1998:22). Nicholas of Cusa, one of the great Christian metaphysicians of the fifteenth century, also expounded this way of knowing. He formulated it as a 'doctrine of ignorance' and emphasised the need to 'dissolve', or 'undo', the rationalistic categories of medieval theology in order to realise a spiritually-engaged, or sapiential, knowledge. This knowledge was understood as the *coincidentia oppositorum,* a knowledge that transcended the dualistic categories of thought. Nicholas expounded his doctrine of ignorance just as humanism and its attendant tide of rationality were emerging. Nicholas's doctrine of ignorance was submerged and Christianity, along with the entire Western episteme, was dominated by humanism and rationality right up to the contemporary era.[4] As I discuss again later in this chapter, the apophatic tradition, the way of not-knowing, the path of deconstruction, now seems ripe for reclamation.

Advaitic Awareness

If spiritually-engaged knowledge, with its praxis of attentiveness, has become a recessive way of knowing within the Western episteme that needs to be 'rediscovered' from the East, or the historical past, this is not the case with Hinduism, despite the inroads of modernity. Advaitic Vedanta, arguably the most significant and influential school of Hindu philosophy (Sharma, 1993a, 1993b), is so named because it is concerned with the realisation of a state of nonduality that goes beyond the subject/object distinction that grounds all other dualisms. Although mantra meditation is recommended in advaitic teachings only as a preliminary exercise, the practice of attentiveness is strongly recommended.

Sri Nisargadatta Maharaj (1981), a respected contemporary practitioner of advaita, repeatedly advised seekers that what is needed to attain *jnana*, or wisdom, is attention: 'alert immobility, quiet attention' (Nisargadatta, 1981:217). It is this attention or 'affectionate awareness' that 'is the crucial factor that brings Reality into focus' (Nisargadatta 1981:292). Nisargadatta (1981:439) is explicit that this is *not* a task for the mind. 'Put your awareness to work, not your mind. The mind is not the right instrument for this task'. Nor should we get lost in the endless play of signifiers: 'too much analysis leads you nowhere . . . . The legitimate function of the mind is to tell you what is not. But if you want positive knowledge you must go beyond the mind' (Nisargadatta 1981:341). Echoes of both Nicholas of Cusa and poststructural philosophy here – the only legitimate function of rationality is to *deconstruct*. The rational mind cannot construct a system of truth; it can, however, deconstruct that which obscures the truth.

By means of cognition, it is difficult to grasp what this means, but the explanation of Nisargadatta Maharaj (1981:268-9) links such a state to attention, love and wisdom:

> Look, my thumb touches my forefinger. Both touch and are touched. When my attention is on the thumb, the thumb is the feeler and the forefinger – the Self. Shift the focus of attention and the relationship is reversed. I find that somehow, by shifting the focus of attention, I become the very thing I look at and experience the kind of consciousness it has; I become the inner witness of the thing. I call this capacity of entering other focal

points of consciousness – love; you may give it any name you like. Love says: 'I am everything'. Wisdom says: 'I am nothing'. Between the two my life flows. Since at any point of time and space I can be both the subject and the object of experience, I express it by saying that I am both, and neither, and beyond both.

In response to further questions Nisargadatta (p. 269) continues to describe the experience of this altered mode of knowing/being:

> The main change was in the mind; it became motionless and silent, responding quickly but not perpetuating the response. Spontaneity became a way of life, the real became natural and the natural became real. And above all, infinite affection, love, dark and quiet, radiating in all directions, embracing all, making all interesting and beautiful significant and auspicious.

Also situated within the advaitic tradition, the Indian sage Sri Ramana Maharshi (1879-1950) used slightly different terminology to refer to an apparently similar state of knowing/being. In a remarkable parallel to the Christian description of taking the mind into the heart, he advised his followers to: 'Enter into the heart with questing mind or by diving deep within or through control of breath and abide in the Atman' (in Mudaliar, 1977:11). Interestingly, Sri Ramana used the terms Heart, *Atman*, and Self interchangeably, making explicit that attention is related to a changed understanding of Self or subjectivity that is to be distinguished from the 'I-thought'. Whilst the Self is understood by Ramana as nondual and beyond discourse, it is not correctly described as post-egoic, or trans-personal, because from the advaitic perspective the ego or discursively constructed self is an illusion that results from ignorance.

> You must distinguish between the 'I', pure in itself, and the 'I'-thought. The latter, being merely a thought, sees subject and object, sleeps, wakes up, eats and thinks. But the pure 'I' is the pure being, eternal existence, free from ignorance and thought-illusion. If you stay as the 'I', your being alone, without thought, the 'I'-thought will disappear and the delusion will vanish for ever (in Godman, 1985:52).

Attention must be unremittingly directed towards this pure 'I' so that there is no room for any thought, even the thought 'I am meditating' (cited in Cohen, 1980:78). In this state of awareness the distinction between epistemology and ontology breaks down. The Self (as distinct from the constructed individual ego) is, according to Sri Ramana (in Mudaliar 1977:224), awareness:

> You are awareness. Awareness is another name for you. Since you are awareness there is no need to attain or cultivate it. All that you have to do is to give up being aware of other things, that is of the not-Self. If one gives up being aware of them then pure awareness alone remains, and that is the Self.

But this awareness is neither an awareness of something objective, nor an identification with the subjective pole of experience. It is a nondual awareness that Merrell-Wolff (1973) describes as 'consciousness without an object'. It encompasses not only the subjective but also the objective pole of experience, as Ramana (in Godman 1985:7) makes clear:

> That in which all these worlds seem to exist steadily, that of which all these worlds are a possession, that from which all these worlds rise, that for which all these exist, that by which all these worlds come into existence and that which is indeed all these – that alone is the existing reality. Let us cherish that Self, which is the reality, in the Heart.

Ramana's exposition of the Self is generally regarded as describing the fullest possible attainment of spiritually-engaged knowledge within the Advaitic tradition. His terminology is that of advaita Vedanta and his use of the terms *Atma* and Self seems, exoterically at least, to stand in contradiction to the Buddhist teaching of *anatma* or no-self, but from a phenomenological viewpoint descriptions of awareness within the two traditions bear a remarkable similarity.[5]

Buddhist Mindfulness

It is within the Buddhist tradition that the most detailed exposition of the practice of attentiveness or mindfulness is to be found. I have already mentioned Klein's (1994) work in this area but will explore again, briefly, the Buddhist understanding. As described by Nyanaponika Thera (1983:7) of the Sri Lankan Theravadan tradition:

> The teachings of the Buddha offer a great variety of methods of mental training and subjects of meditation, suited to the various individual needs, temperaments and capacities. Yet all of these methods ultimately converge in the 'Way of Mindfulness' called by the Master himself 'the Only Way' (or the Sole Way, *ekayano maggo*). The Way of Mindfulness may therefore rightly be called 'the heart of Buddhist meditation' or even 'the heart of the entire doctrine' (*dhamma-hadaya*). This great Heart is in fact the centre of all the blood-streams pulsating through the entire body of the doctrine (*dhamma kaya*).

The *Satipatthana Sutta*, which is the Buddha's discourse on the Foundations of Mindfulness, appears twice in the (Hinayana) Buddhist scriptures,[6] and is considered a central text of the canon, particularly in the Hinayana tradition. The Mahayana traditions of Zen, Dzog Chen and Ch'an retain much of the centrality of mindfulness, combining it in varying degrees with the Bodhisattva Ideal (Nyanaponika 1983:13-14). In the Kagyu lineage of Tibetan Buddhism, for example, mindfulness or awareness is regarded as the 'body of meditation'.

Thus in the *Supplication to the Gurus of the Kagyu Lineage*[7] we find that the 'foot of meditation' is described as renunciation; the 'head of meditation' is understood as devotion. The prayer then continues:

> Awareness is the body of meditation, as is said. Whatever thought arises, its nature is nowness. To the meditator who rests there without effort, grant your blessing, so that the subject of meditation is free from conceptions.
>
> The nature of thoughts is *dharmakaya*, as is said. Nothing whatever, but everything arises from it. To the meditator who sees the unobstructed play of the mind, grant your blessing, so that he realises the identity of *nirvana* and *samsara*.

From the perspective of the Buddhist tradition, Nyanaponika (1983:8) argues, mindfulness is a 'timeless and universal' component of enlightenment or wisdom. Goldstein (1983), in his guide to Buddhist meditation, uses the term 'bare attention' rather than 'mindfulness'.[8] Despite the different terminology involved, I suggest that the practice of mindfulness, or bare attention, has much in common with the practice of attentive love explored in the previous chapter. Goldstein (1983:20) offers a Japanese haiku as an example of this 'powerfully penetrating quality of mind':

> The old pond.
> A frog jumps in.
> Plop!

The example closely parallels Donovan's (1996) account of an ecofeminist, meditative awareness discussed in chapter four, which does not sacrifice images for the sake of meaning, but remains true to the thing itself. Goldstein (1983:20) suggests that bare attention is 'learning to see and observe, with simplicity and directness. Nothing extraneous.' Nyanaponika (1983:35) offers a more detailed explanation:

> Bare Attention, first allows things to speak for themselves, without interruption by final verdicts pronounced too hastily. Bare Attention gives them a chance to finish their speaking, and one will thus get to learn that, in fact, they have much to say about themselves, which formerly was mostly ignored by rashness or was drowned in the inner and outer noise in which ordinary man normally lives. Because Bare Attention sees things without the narrowing and levelling effect of habitual judgements, it sees them ever anew, as if for the first time; therefore it will happen with progressive frequency that things will have something new and worthwhile to reveal. Patient pausing in such an attitude of Bare Attention will open wide horizons to one's understanding, obtaining thus, in a seemingly effortless way, results which were denied to the strained efforts of an impatient intellect.

Nyanaponika (1983:35) makes it clear that this attentiveness does not replace either the rational or synthetic functions of the mind, but is the essential precursor to both. If analytical knowing is not preceded by a sufficiently long period of bare attention, then it is likely to overlook significant elements of the object of knowledge. Similarly, Nyanaponika suggests that integrative or systemic knowing is also likely to be deficient, missing certain aspects of the relationship and connections between the object of knowledge and other things that exist in interaction with it, if it is not preceded by a sufficient period of bare attention.

The Buddhist teaching thus distinguishes different components that constitute perception. The first is bare attention, a non-discursive phase that apprehends the bare sense data prior to the superimposition of the socially constructed attitudes or interpretations that constitute the second stage. The third stage of judgement comes later with the application of rational thought. This understanding of perception does not deny the significance of rational thought but identifies it as a secondary function of knowledge. In Buddhist understanding it is possible to cultivate the primary function of perception through the cultivation of non-discursive mindfulness. This is done by purifying perception, removing not only the personally constructed barriers of aversion and liking, but also the socially constructed barriers that automatise our perception and cast over reality the shadow of discursively constituted, socially constructed concepts. Thus, mindfulness, like attentive love, represents a post-discursive, post-rational achievement, not a regression to an earlier, or simpler, stage of cognitive development.

It is important to note here that for the Buddhist practitioner both the material outer world of objects and living beings *and* the inner world of thoughts, emotions and bodily sensations are to be brought under the scrutiny of bare attention. When the perception is purified the practitioner is able to see clearly that 'the mind is nothing beyond its cognitive function' (Nyanaponika 1983:38), that all perception is impermanent, involved in a constant state of flux and change, and that there is no permanent individual subject of perception. The self/other dualism is thus deconstructed. In the resulting nonduality 'there's no self, there is a unity, a communion. And without the thought of "I'm loving someone", love becomes the natural expression of that oneness' (Goldstein 1983:38), and indeed the final stage of perception.

Sapiential Knowledge

This Buddhist understanding of perception as a sequence of acts having its source in bare attention parallels the work of Catholic theologian, Bernard Lonergan, on a transcultural 'method' of knowing. As I mentioned in chapter three, Lonergan also suggested that perception occurred in a sequence of acts, each governed by a transcendental command or injunction. These commands were transcendental, not in the sense of having been shouted from a mountain top by a vocal if faceless deity, but in the sense of transcending cultural boundaries *because they emerged from the universal structure of the human cognitive faculty* (mind/heart/brain). Lonergan's commands find common ground with the Buddhist understanding of the stages of perception: Be attentive! Be intelligent! Be reasonable! Be responsible! Be in love!

Similarly, the advaitic understanding distinguishes attentiveness from love, which is the *result* of the practice of attentiveness. As Adamson (1998), a contemporary advaitin, writes:

> Look at all things with your eyes and all your senses fully awake, but without a single thought in your mind, without naming. Then you will know what it means to be without separation. Looking at all things without a single thought, without a single word, you will know what it means to have no space between you and the other. To look without the movement of the machinery of thought, you will know what love is. You look without the look of the observer, you look without the value of the word and the measurement of yesterday. The look of love is different from the look of thought. The one leads in a direction where thought cannot follow, and the other leads to separation, conflict and sorrow. From this sorrow you cannot go to the other. The distance between the two is made by thought and thought cannot by any stride reach the other.

Despite the similarities demonstrated in these brief glimpses of different traditions of thought, there are also disjunctions. If I were to explore in more detail the texts from which I have drawn my quotes, significant differences in terminology would emerge. John Main, for example, writes in terms of God and Christ, while in advaitic or Buddhist texts these terms are (almost[9]) completely absent. Similarly, the Buddhist way of describing attention as a 'quality of mind' (Goldstein 1983:20) seems to differ from the Christian way (and feminist way mentioned in the previous chapter) of understanding it as a 'quality of the heart' in which the 'mind' plays no part. In Hinduism a useful distinction is made between the lower or rational mind (*manas*) and the higher intuitive mind or intellect (*buddhi*), which is equated with the heart and the praxis of attentiveness.

Are we dealing here with incommensurable religio-cultural traditions, or are we dealing with transcultural structures of the human psyche that reveal a universal form of knowledge which finds varied expression through different socio-linguistic frameworks? If the former, then our concern must be with pluralism. But if the latter, there may be justification for referring to a transcultural, universal way of knowing that is revealed only when the activity of the (lower) rational discursive mind is stilled or transcended. Since the genre of knowledge thus revealed is beyond discursivity and is no longer a function of an individual discursive subject, it is not without meaning, I think, to describe it as 'beyond words' because exceeds both discursivity and the duality of the subject/object relation. The term 'sapiential', from the Latin *sapere* meaning 'to taste', is sometimes used to describe this knowledge which 'cannot be attained except through being experienced and tasted' (Nasr, 1989:25).[10]

Some commentators refer to the instrument of this way of knowing as 'the heart' in order to distinguish it from the rational, discursive mind, while those from other traditions, seemingly for the same reason, refer to it as 'pure mind', 'lower mind' or 'intellect'. This may be of less import than the suggestion that these expressions and their associated doctrines, each within their own tradition, adequately point to practices essential for attaining this way of knowing. Whatever its name, the significance of this human faculty (be it 'heart', or 'pure mind', or 'soul') may be that it is not plural, and that it represents a domain of human consciousness which, since it is beyond both speech and rationality, has been referred to as post-representational (Alexander *et al*, 1990:293). Clearly, the question of a genre of nondual, post-discursive, post-rational, sapiential knowledge is intimately related to the possibility of a state of awareness or consciousness that apprehends that way of knowing. Because of this close relationship between epistemology and ontology, I earlier moved between defining a genre of spiritually-engaged knowledge and identifying that state of awareness, or subjectivity, through which such knowledge may be experienced. We will explore again this ontological aspect seeking, through a post-representational psychology, to identify the nondual state of being that is 'tasted' through sapiential knowledge.

Non-representational Psychology

Just as in the previous chapter I reviewed women writers in various fields in order to build up a picture of a distinctive stream of theory and practice, so here I review three religious traditions in order to explore the similarity between certain contemplative or meditative practices. The glimpses that I have given are deliberately short but are sufficient, I hope, to demonstrate the problem that has occupied commentators in the field of inter-religious studies. Are the similarities that can be pointed to between traditions merely examples of passages quoted out of context, taken from traditions that are distinct because they are the product of different religio-cultural streams? Or are there really some underlying epistemological, phenomenological and ontological features common to all religious traditions that might, like rationality and discursivity, constitute a domain within the human psyche that defines a universal potential?

Perennialism vs Constructivism

Forman (1990, 1993, 1996) offers a useful overview of the debate by looking at the two main schools of thought involved. The first is described by Forman as 'perennialism', and includes commentators such as Frithjof Schuon, Rudolf Otto, René Guénon, Seyyed Hossein Nasr, Huston Smith, Aldous Huxley, William James, Evelyn Underhill, William Johnston, W.T. Stace, and Mircea Eliade. The perennialists, according to Forman (1990:3), 'maintained that mystical experience represented immediate direct contact with a (variously defined) absolute principle'. After this common but ineffable experience of contact with the Absolute, mystics then *interpret* their encounters differently according to the language of their respective traditions. The mystical experience itself is therefore understood to be transcultural, concerned with sapiential knowledge of the Absolute, although its interpretation is subject to religio-cultural variations. On the basis of this sapiential knowledge the perennialists propose a transcultural 'perennial philosophy'.[11] Whilst Aldous Huxley (1945) popularised the term 'perennial philosophy',[12] it finds its most erudite and nuanced expression in the works of Perennialists, or Traditionalists, such as Guénon, Schuon and Nasr, all of whom are at pains to point out that both the perceived unity of faiths, and the sapiential knowledge that underpins it, are metaphysical, pertaining to a post-representational domain beyond the reach of philosophical, conceptual discourse.[13]

The second school of thought described by Forman is 'constructivism'. This school argues that 'mystical experience is significantly *shaped and formed* by the subject's beliefs, concepts, and expectations' (Forman, 1990:3). With the broader paradigm shift that occurred in the academy towards a postmodern understanding of experience and knowledge as socio-linguistically constructed, constructivism (or deconstructionism) tended to replace perennialism as the dominant paradigm in religious studies. Steven Katz (1983) emerged as one of the major proponents of constructivism, taking his lead from influential philosophers such as Wittgenstein, Derrida, and, in the field of religious studies, from thinkers such as Zaehner, and more recently Wayne Proudfoot, William Wainwright and Robert Gimello.

From the constructivist perspective, perennialism is epistemologically naive. The constructivists argue that there is no such thing as pure, unmediated experience. The articulation of a transcultural, 'perennial philosophy' is equated with the construction of a universalising metanarrative that necessarily rides rough-shod over the differences between religio-cultural traditions. From the perennialist perspective, the constructivists have succumbed to the desacralisation of knowledge characteristic of modernity. For the perennialists the Divine or Absolute is just that – absolute, unchanging, universal. Whilst they are happy to concede that each tradition is a unique product of its cultural, linguistic and historical context, they understand these traditions, not simply as cultural constructions, but as diverse determinations or expressions of the Absolute. *Every* determination of the Absolute is recognised by the perennialists as already in the realm of relativity, but the result is not a desacralised, nihilistic, spiritual relativism; it is a transcendent unity that respects the diversity of expressions while asserting that only the Absolute is absolute.

Incomplete Constructivism

The perennialist position, which might be described as incomplete constructivism, includes, but goes beyond, that of the constructivist;[14] the constructivist position, currently so popular in the academy, excludes that of the perennialist. The central issue seems to be *how much* of our experience is mediated. Whilst there is no doubt that a great deal of experience is socio-linguistically constructed it seems 'methodologically prudent' to 'leave open the possibility that trans-linguistic, unmediated experience is both possible and even reasonable, as well as the possibility that there is even an element of "trans-linguisticality" present even in those experiences in which culture and language play a prominent role' (Forman, 1996:78-9). It is possible to offer physiological examples, such as the universal need of the human body for food and water, to exemplify the way in which a model of incomplete or partial constructivism might work. There is little doubt that matters gastronomic are culturally mediated experiences, but this enculturation can be understood as an overlay on a universally, unmediated, physiological absolute – the need for food. There is, it can be argued, a level at which hunger and thirst are not culturally constructed. But rice and *saki*, are not beer and chips, and when we do hunger and thirst, it is for culturally mediated distinctive kinds of food.

Forman (1990) in his book *The Problem of Pure Consciousness* offers two additional arguments for incomplete constructivism. The first, which he refers to as the problem of 'novelty' (pp. 19-21), has also been described (in domains of knowledge other than religious studies) as the problem of 'creativity', or the problem of 'autonomy'. Constructivism, as Forman points out is a 'fundamentally conservative hypothesis' (p. 19). If all experiences are created and shaped by socially constructed knowledge and beliefs, then it is difficult to explain the occurrence of new or unexpected experiences or ideas that themselves shape new social beliefs and new knowledge. Forman's argument is primarily concerned with mystical or spiritual experience and he offers supporting examples of both inexperienced neophytes who, though not well-versed in a religious tradition, may have mystical experiences, and of experienced adepts who, though well-versed in a tradition, may still be surprised by the experiences that befall them.[15]

Forman's second argument for incomplete constructivism is more specific to the domain of religious experience but is particularly relevant to my own concern with attentiveness as an epistemology of radical empiricism. Forman

(1990:8) argues that a particular kind of mystical experience which he refers to as the 'Pure Consciousness Event' is common across religious traditions. This phenomenon is described as 'a wakeful though contentless (nonintentional) consciousness' (p. 8). Since the consciousness in question is contentless, Forman argues that it cannot be described as culturally constructed. Indeed, to arrive at this contentless experience 'the ordinary shaping processes of language must be dropped' (Forman, 1996:77). As Forman (1990, 1993, 1996), Rothberg (1990) and others suggest, it is possible to interpret the spiritual disciplines of religious traditions as systematically organised practices whose goal is to facilitate this bypassing of the usual socio-linguistic shaping processes. If pure consciousness events are accepted as unmediated experiences then the possibility of 'unlearning' our socio-linguistic conditioning must be acknowledged. If it is possible to reduce, or in the extreme case eliminate, the formative influence of socio-linguistic patterns, then it is not unreasonable to extend the claim, partially or otherwise, to include consciousness events with content, which returns us to the possibility of perceiving things-as-they-really-are[16] – the radical empiricism that I have already identified.

As Rothberg (1990:179) suggests, 'many mystical traditions can be read as offering paths of deconstruction or deconditioning of the fundamental forms by which experience and knowledge are mediated or constructed'. Rephrasing this in the terminology that has been developed in previous chapters, I would suggest that spirituality (mysticism in Forman's terminology) can be described as a disciplined path of deconstructing or de-automatising perception in order to approach an unmediated perception of reality. Spirituality might therefore be understood as facilitating a shift from our everyday, socially constructed epistemological modality to an epistemological modality of radical empiricism which fundamentally challenges the constructivist position that *all* experience is necessarily mediated. Whilst a post-constructivist spirituality does not deny that a great deal of our experience and knowledge is constructed, it affirms the possibility that the formative elements of a subject's socio-linguistic set can be progressively unlearned, or by-passed ('forgotten' as in Forman, 1993:36-37), in order to approach, and even ultimately attain, an unmediated experience of reality.

If we acknowledge this thesis of incomplete constructivism, then the pluralist thesis that has become so much a part of postmodern thought is also open to question. We are confronted with the possibility of 'human universals that function as the implicit meaning or rules behind language, human communication, and human development (cognitive, moral, or spiritual)' (Rothberg, 1990:178). There have, of course, been distinguished commentators in various fields who have advocated this position – Noam Chomsky's theory of language, Bernard Lonergan's method of knowing, Jurgen Habermas's communicative theory, and the developmental theories of Piaget, Kohlberg and Wilber, whom I mentioned earlier. In the domain of religious studies, the pendulum then swings back towards the more universal perspective of the perennialists.

Perennial States of Being

Forman (1996) argues for a *perennial psychology* (as opposed to a *perennial philosophy*) that proposes the existence of 'a perennial pattern of psychological change and new cognitive structure – i.e. a reasonably consistent trans-historical set of discrete psychological levels' (Forman, 1996:81).[17] These levels act as the 'deep' or universal structures that support the 'surface' or socio-linguistically constructed, variegated expressions of individual and social development. The thesis of a universal psychology does not, of course, originate with Forman. Freud, as we have already seen in the previous chapter, proposed a metapsychology, and Guénon (1984) described, from a traditional perspective, 'The Multiple States of Being'.[18] More recently developmental and transpersonal psychologists have sought to validate cross-culturally their claims that human development passes through an invariant sequence of stages on the way to maturity. For the most part the theories of developmental psychologists have focussed on the development of rationality and have not pursued the possibilities of post-representational modes of development. The clinical roots of modern Western psychology meant that, in contrast to spiritually based Eastern psychology, it concentrated more on the pathological aspects of adult development rather than on the highest potential of human development.

More recently, transpersonal psychology has focussed explicitly on these 'higher' or altered states of post-representational modes of development, but Forman (1996:81-2) seeks to distinguish his perennial psychology from transpersonal psychology (often associated with Ken Wilber, one of its main exponents[19]) by arguing that he offers 'a less complex typology of developmental patterns, i.e. [one that points] towards two or at most four discrete epistemological modalities or unusual states of consciousness ... [which] describe a path whose general features seem to centre on letting go of attachment and clingings' (pp. 81-2). Although I explore these alternatives below, what is significant here is that both the transpersonal and perennial psychologists recognise post-representational ways of knowing and being, and I will therefore refer to these as different articulations of a post-representational psychology that deal with non-rational, non-discursive, non-personal epistemologies and ontologies.

Post-representational psychology suggests that the capacity for radical empiricism, like the capacities for speech or rational thought, is a universal human capacity. The nondual state is not the exclusive experience of women or men, of environmentalists or postmodernists, of Hindus, Buddhists, Christians or any variety of spiritual practitioner, but is universal, unconstructed and potentially accessible to all. Post-representational psychology also suggests that the unmediated knowledge of the post-representational domain constitutes an important dimension of human knowledge and awareness. Forman and Wilber, however, offer different models of post-representational psychology, and in order to determine in what ways these models differ from each other, if indeed they do significantly differ, it is necessary to consider them in more depth.

To do this I explore the simplest version of Forman's thesis, which he himself has described as 'epistemological duomorphism'. This asserts that there are two distinct epistemological modalities (Forman, 1989). Forman (1996) argues that these two distinct modalities are ordinary experience and mystical experience. Ordinary experiences are intentional, changing, linguistic, structured by expectations, beliefs and concepts. They result from an epistemological modality in which 'the subject is aware of some object which is not the subject' (Forman, 1996:82). Forman contrasts this with (some) mystical experiences which appear to be non-intentional, unchanging, non-discursive, and not (completely) structured by expectations, beliefs and concepts.[20]

Forman (1996, 1993, 1990) gives various examples, all drawn from the domain of spirituality, to illustrate his claim. In his 1996 paper (p. 83), he offers the realisation of *Purusha* in Samkhya (a school of Hindu philosophy) in which all activities of the mind are stilled to reach a state of 'silent aloneness or silent awareness' (p. 83), and compares this to the dualistic knowledge of *Prakriti*, the opposite material pole of existence. Forman then points out the similarity between these two ways of knowing and the experience of the Flemish Christian mystic, Ruysbroeck, who also distinguished two kinds of knowing – ordinary knowledge, which is mediated by language and concepts, and a second form of knowing without intermediary in which 'the mystic attains a union with God which has no sensory or intellectual knowledge' (Forman 1996:83-84). Ruysbroeck, in turn, is compared with the experience of the ninth century Buddhist practitioner Yogacarin Paramartha who again described two modes of experience. The first is dualistic and involves the consciousness 'grasping' the object to be known. The second is 'the silent experience of cessation' in which no objects are grasped and the operations of the mind cease.

These examples, all of which seem to pertain to a non-discursive, non-rational state of nondual awareness, suggest a reading of Forman which is consistent with Wilber on many points. I would argue that this state of nonduality is what Wilber (1985:141-160, for example) refers to as 'the ultimate state of consciousness' or 'unity consciousness'. Now, whilst this sounds terrifyingly difficult to attain, Wilber's explanation is nonetheless illuminating. Describing this nondual consciousness he writes that it:

> is not a particular experience among other experiences, not a big experience opposed to a small experience, not one wave instead of another. Rather, it is every wave of present experience just as it is. And how can you contact present experience? There is nothing but present experience, and there is definitely no path to that which always is. There is no path to wetness if you're already standing shoulder-deep in water (Wilber, 1985:143)

Wilber makes it clear that whilst, from one perspective, this state of consciousness is the goal attained at the end of the developmental hierarchy which he proposes, from another perspective, this state of consciousness is never absent, contains within it every other stage or state of consciousness and can be accessed from any of those other stages. Wilber (1985:142) stresses that this state of Self-realisation, or nondual consciousness:

> is all-inclusive in the most radical way, much as a mirror equally includes all the objects it reflects. Unity consciousness is not a state different or apart from other states, but the condition and true nature of *all* the states. This is, from a rational viewpoint, difficult to grasp and leads to the paradoxical statements for which mystics are renown.

In the discourse of advaita Vedanta, where attainment of this state of nondual consciousness is often referred to as Self-realisation, Ramana Maharshi advises that: 'Realisation is nothing to be gained afresh; it is already there. All that is necessary is to get rid of the thought "I have not realised"' (Godman, 1985:19). Godman, in his explanation of Sri Ramana's teachings, writes that for Self-realisation: 'All that is required is an understanding that the Self is not a goal to be attained, it is merely the awareness that prevails when all the limiting ideas about the not-Self have been discarded' (ibid). It must be said, however, that this process of discarding involves deconstructing at a psychic and experiential level, the tide of conditioning that began with the first desire (and/or its repression), and which is constantly being reinforced by our contemporary society.

From the perspective of unity consciousness, it can therefore be said that *all* other states are relative. It is here that we come to both the strength and the weakness of Forman's argument. There is a sense in which Forman correctly posits an epistemological duomorphism, since beside this non-dual state, *all* other states are dualistic and relative, and can therefore be grouped together to constitute one epistemological modality. But this duomorphism cannot accurately be described as 'ordinary everyday knowing' versus 'mystical knowing'. It must be described as nondual versus dual epistemological modes, where the latter category includes, not only everyday consciousness, but also the states of dreaming, deep sleep and the many dualistic modes of altered consciousness that occur in mysticism. Even then epistemological duomorphism is a misleading term. By positing the dual and nondual epistemological modalities as simply alternatives, and refusing to make any qualitative judgement concerning their relative values, Forman seems to suggest that they are somehow 'equivalent' states of knowing. I argue that this is not so, since nondual consciousness includes within itself *all* forms of dualistic consciousness, including that of everyday life.

The explanatory framework offered by advaitic Vedanta again provides an illuminating contrast to Forman's duomorphic model. The advaitins postulate three epistemological modalities, or relative states of consciousness, which we all experience in an alternating, temporary manner – these are the states of waking, dream and deep sleep. These states are multiple and distinct, but not hierarchical as in Wilber's model.[21] They are, however, all temporary, coming and going within the field of awareness that might be said to support them and which, for that reason, is sometimes referred to by the advaitins as the *turiya avastha* or 'fourth state'. This fourth state, however, is also known as *turiyatita*, which means 'transcending the fourth', in order to convey the understanding that 'there are not really four states but only one real transcendental state' (Godman, 1985:10-11). Forman may be correct in assuming that for most of us the conditioning which constructs our everyday awareness is so strong that nondual 'mystical' consciousness is an epistemological mode we may glimpse only a few times in our lives, although this may be, in part, because we live in a society which not only fails to recognise this way of knowing, but which obfuscates any knowledge of it.

As I have already suggested, 'spirituality' or 'mysticism' are not the only discursive frameworks that can be used to convey this nondual experience. I have argued that some discursive streams of postmodernism, feminism and environmentalism offer alternative ways of framing the nondual experience. Roberts (1984:196) offers another alternative. She contrasts her 'mystical', nondual experience of no-self, to the experience of an elderly friend and acknowledges that two alternative views of what is apparently the same journey are possible. The first frames this journey to no-self within the discourse of mysticism as a 'supernatural event that constitutes, for the contemplative, the second major movement of his relentless journey into God'. The second view, frames it, within the context of ageing, as 'the final process of our natural life span, wherein self-consciousness is gradually relinquished as we come upon "that" which lies beyond the self'. This second view is a developmental perspective with much in common with both Kohlberg's and Wilber's work. However the association of spiritually-engaged knowledge with ageing frees this perspective from some of the hierarchical and goal-oriented errors that seem to easily attach themselves to other developmental models. Interestingly, Roberts goes on to suggest that children and intellectually handicapped people, who have not yet developed or locked themselves into the reflexive arc of self-consciousness, may also have access to this nondual mode of knowing. This makes sense if, as discussed above, this nondual mode is all inclusive. Anytime, when identification with the separate, constructed self is absent, we fall into it.

The significance of Wilber's 'pre/trans fallacy',[22] which attempts to distinguish pre-rational, pre-egoic, pre-discursive states from post-rational, post-egoic and post-discursive states, is confirmed on two counts. Firstly, the nondual state, as any parent knows, is not continuous for children, or for intellectually handicapped persons. The child-self is porous, and has moments of being absent because it is still being constructed. In the child, and perhaps the intellectually disabled person, the egoic self, which is still only in partially constructed or rudimentary form, can intrude at any time because it has not been 'seen through' or deconstructed. The self that comes and goes is an immature self that cannot yet take the position of another and which is identified, to varying degrees, with its individual physical and psychical desires. The pre-representational, nondual experiences of a child must therefore be distinguished from the post-representational, nondual experience of the adult, and particularly of the sage for whom the self has first developed and then has been deconstructed *so that it does not arise again*. Secondly, neither the child, nor the intellectually handicapped person, can tell us about the nondual experience. As Roberts (1984:197) writes:

> Without first having had the relative experience of self-consciousness, there is no way to describe or communicate this non-relative type of seeing and knowing. It seems that wherever this state occurs, it is wrapped in silence; and even when it is communicated – as only contemplatives can do – it is rarely understood. Truly it defies any form of intellectualizalion.

This clarifies, I think, a distinction that needs to be made. The nondual experience itself, which is non/trans-representational and non/trans-egoic, is accessible to both the child, the sage, and indeed everyone else. But the *knowledge* of that experience can only be *post-representational*, and as such is only available to a person who has already passed through the representational stages of rational and reflexive egoic consciousness. It is therefore correct to refer to a *post*-representational psychology since such knowledge can only be available to those who have passed through the representational stages.

We are now in a position to appreciate the strengths and weaknesses of Wilber's hierarchical transpersonal framework. Epistemological duomorphism is inclined to convey the impression that we can 'flip' from the dual to the nondual epistemological modality in an instant. Although this may be true for those brief glimpses of nonduality that befall us all from time to time, it seems to be incorrect for most of those adults who have managed to stabilise themselves in the post-representational nondual modality. The narratives of these people rarely describe an instantaneous transformation but, rather, often indicate an extended period of transition and adjustment through a variety of non-ordinary dualistic states of consciousness. It is these 'intermediate states' (such as the witnessing consciousness already mentioned) which Wilber maps in his hierarchical framework, although he would, I think, agree that they are all relative compared to the state of nondual consciousness within which they are ultimately contained.

As with Roberts's (1984:196) second reading of the nondual journey as 'the final process of our natural lifespan', Wilber frames the passage to nonduality within a developmental framework that represents it as a natural process of maturation across a human lifespan. It is a process that can be, and in contemporary conditions often is, blocked (through the individual or social neuroses and psychoses that Wilber explores).[23] Alternatively, it is a process that can be sped up, as Roberts and Wilber both suggest, through appropriate meditative or contemplative praxes. It is these contemplative praxes to which I now turn.

A Unified Theory of Meditation

As globalisation proceeds, dialogue between religious traditions has deepened and attempts have been made to formulate 'unified', or transcultural, theories about not only alternative 'spiritual' epistemological modalities, but about the dynamics and praxes of transformation from dual to nondual modalities within spiritual traditions. These theories explore the different epistemological modalities implied by meditative states, seeking to relate them to both altered states of consciousness and to transformative techniques of meditation and contemplation. Work in the 1970s by Goleman, Ornstein and Brown, as well as Washburn (1978), all contributed to attempts to articulate a unified theory of meditation. Recent work (some by these same commentators) that is more detailed and nuanced in its exploration of different religious traditions, continues to explore the possibilities of unified theories of transformational praxes within post-representational psychology.

All the major traditions document states of consciousness that lie beyond the boundaries of our contemporary, limited definitions of 'normal', and techniques for realising these states. Across a variety of cultures and traditions these techniques have invariably been connected to disciplined practices of attention and awareness. Although it has been variously described in different traditions, there is considerable evidence to support Schumacher's observation with respect to attention that 'no topic occupies a more central place in all traditional teaching; and no subject suffers more neglect, misunderstanding and distortion in the thinking of the modern world' (cited in Walsh and Vaughan, 1993b:3). It is my contention that the epistemological strategy of attentive love developed in the previous chapter is, as suggested by Mathews, Keller, and Donovan, a contemplative or meditative epistemology such as is found in religious traditions. I will therefore explore attentiveness as a meditative epistemology, demonstrate the relationship that exists between attentiveness and love in the domain of spirituality and show how this parallels the feminine praxis of attentive love.

Walsh and Vaughan (1993b) in their account of the 'common elements of transpersonal practices', list both *attention* and *awareness*. In the case of attention, they are concerned with the ability to sustain and focus attention, noting that 'attentional training and the cultivation of concentration are regarded as essential for overcoming the fickle wanderlust of the untrained mind' (Walsh and Vaughan, 1993b:3).[24] They point out the contrast between Western psychology, which asserts that attention cannot be sustained, and traditional spiritual teachings that advise that attention 'can and must be sustained if we are to mature beyond conventional developmental limits' (Walsh and Vaughan, 1993b:3). It is only through control of attention that we can exercise any control over our emotions or motives.

When considering awareness however, Walsh and Vaughan are concerned with 'refining awareness'. By this they mean that 'perception is to be rendered more sensitive, more accurate and more appreciative of the freshness and novelty of each moment of experience' (Walsh and Vaughan, 1993b:6). What is needed is to keep the mind focussed on the present moment, rather than roaming in the past and the future. As the mind becomes focussed and able to remain in the present, it becomes aware of more subtle levels of phenomena and can finally rest in awareness itself. This kind of present-focussed awareness is, according to Walsh and Vaughan (ibid), variously referred to in spiritual traditions as mindfulness (in Buddhism), *anuragga* (in Hinduism) or 'the sacrament of the present moment' (in Christianity). The capacity to sustain this focus in the 'now', relinquishing (the conceptual domains of) past memories or future dreams is generally known as meditation.

In a similar vein, Washburn (1978) and Brown (1986) propose that there are two basic types of meditation – concentrative and receptive – which can be identified across major religious traditions. Washburn (1978:46) maintains that the great majority of meditative practices can be understood in terms of these two categories. Although the practices and effects of the two meditative types differ, he argues that they 'may well have a common *telos*: illumined reflectivity, enlightenment . . . [which] many have held to be the highest realization of which man's consciousness is capable' (Washburn 1978:63). Whether or not Washburn's judgment that this is the *highest* realisation is accepted, it would certainly appear that these forms of meditation are concerned with altered states of consciousness, or altered epistemological modalities.

In his paper, Washburn (1978) tackles the question of how the two practices of attentiveness and awareness differ. In concentrative meditation the attention is focussed on a single object until the practitioner is completely absorbed in that object. The resulting state of absorption is known, according to Washburn, as *samadhi* in Hinduism, *jhana* in Buddhism, and contemplation in Christianity. Whilst some commentators (Walsh and Vaughan, 1993a,b; Naranjo and Ornstein, 1976) seem to understand concentrative meditation as simply an indirect way of enhancing receptivity (i.e. a first step, since one cannot be receptive to the present contents of consciousness if one cannot concentrate sufficiently to remain in present awareness), Washburn (1978:48) argues that the concentrative approaches aim 'not so much to open consciousness as to intensify it'. It is interesting to speculate how Washburn's suggestion that concentrative meditation intensifies consciousness or attention might usefully be related to Brennan's hypothesis, discussed in the previous chapter, of directed or concentrated attention as a form of energetic exchange.

The second type of meditation – receptive meditation – is also, according to Washburn, described as 'attentiveness', 'awareness' or 'insight meditation'.²⁵ Washburn (1978:46) offers the following explanation of receptive meditation which seems to align it very closely with the practice of attentive love that I described in some detail in the previous chapters.

> Receptive meditation . . . consists of the practice of open, nonreactive attention. Experience is witnessed nonselectively and without interference or interpretation. Continuous alertness also is required; for not only must experience be left untouched, but so too must the meditator keep himself untouched by the experience. That is, he must maintain attention in order to avoid becoming fascinated by, caught up in, or carried away by whatever may arise in his awareness. Major versions of this type of practice are the mindfulness (*satipatthana*) and insight (*vipassana*) meditations of the Buddhists, 'just sitting' (*shikan-taza*) of Zen, Krishnamurti's choiceless awareness, and Gurdjieff's self-remembering.

Prête (1990) in his study of the Catholic contemplative Thomas Merton explicitly links Merton's contemplative practice and understanding of attention to the theory and practice of Simone Weil's attentive love. If attentive love was 'impersonal' for Weil, Washburn describes receptive meditation as 'detached'. Other commentators also make clear the link between meditative/contemplative techniques and attentiveness.

In receptive meditation the identification of the subject is detached from the objects of awareness that arise in the field of cognition. These objects include not only perceptions of the 'outer' world but also 'inner' perceptions of emotions and thoughts, including the various constructions of self with which the subjectivity might previously have been identified. In order to be attentive the practitioner, initially at least, locates a witnessing subjectivity that views the discursively created self-construct, and the body and bodily sensations, as objective phenomena that can be observed along with all the other phenomena that come and go within the field of cognition (Holland, 1995).²⁶

This witness consciousness, however, is an 'intermediate stage' since the goal of meditation is not a form of subjectivism, or a separate (and therefore dualistic) 'witness' consciousness. As Holland (1995:305) suggests, with reference to advaita Vedanta, this dualistic witness stage is followed by another stage that 'involves a "sweeping outward", as it were, in which the Self is no longer a pole or focal point, but is realized as identical with the contents of its consciousness'. Thus Holland identifies three basic stages in the transition to nondual consciousness, which tallies with Ramana's succinct three-step summation of Sankara's advaitic position.²⁷

(1) *Brahman* is real,
(2) the universe is unreal, and
(3) the universe is *Brahman* (in Godman, 1985:187).

It is interesting to note that a misunderstanding has arisen, as Sri Ramana himself points out (in Godman, 1985:187), with regard to Sankara's teaching, as well as at the more popular level with regard to both meditation and Eastern spirituality. This misunderstanding is due to commentators taking the second statement (otherwise known as the doctrine of *maya*) out of its context within the advaitic tradition and considering it in isolation.

The Buddhist notion of 'emptiness' has often met with a similar fate, perhaps for similar reasons. In the different discourse of this religio-cultural tradition, Lodro Dorje of the Vajrayana tradition of Tibetan Buddhism describes three steps which resemble those described by Sri Ramana:

> In the Vajrayana tradition, there are three steps, crudely speaking. First is the dissolution of personal pride and the letting go of the reference point of personal ego. Then there is the notion of letting go of any conditioned experience whatsoever [emptiness]. Finally there is the level where you reappropriate the relative experience; in other words, the relative world is re-entered or brought back. This last stage corresponds to the notion of living in sacredness, or of transforming relative experience. So there is a process of going in – to union or dissolution – and then there is a coming out. Beyond that there is also the idea that relative and absolute reality are together already, from the beginning (cited in Walker, 1987:163).

Holland (1995) also suggests that meditation in Buddhist traditions passes through distinct stages to reach the ultimate realisation of nonduality. The objectless consciousness of *nirvana* and the continual flux of *samsara*, are realised, respectively, as the subjective and objective poles, or 'antipodal states within the field of Pure Consciousness' (Holland, 1995:309). Unlike Wilber's universal, hierarchical model of development, Holland is advocating that whilst the ultimate experience of nonduality is the same cross-culturally, the stages through which different practitioners pass to reach this nonduality differ across different religio-cultural systems. Holland's approach has some merit but it throws doubt on whether Wilber's formulation of transpersonal psychology, with its ten different stages of development that are traversed enroute to nonduality, can be applied cross-culturally.[28]

Forman's simpler hypothesis of two different epistemological modalities is certainly less complex and more easily supported by cross-cultural evidence, but it requires a clear acknowledgment that the modality of nondual consciousness stands in a special, inclusive relationship to all other dual modalities of consciousness. This returns us to the epistemological duomorphism of the more erudite expressions of perennialism which, whilst acknowledging the existence of multiple states of consciousness, posit only two basic epistemological modalities and two contrasting modes of consciousness, the absolute and the relative (Loy, 1988:69). These two different ways of knowing find expression in the different streams of spiritual discourse found within each tradition. The cataphatic stream expresses relative knowledge that takes as its starting point the reality of the ego, whilst the apophatic stream points to absolute knowledge that understands from the outset that the ego, and the duality which arises from it, are illusion.

Postmodern Spirituality

Re-defining the Spiritual

It is at this point that we can return to the working definition of spirituality with which I began. That definition had two components, one ontological and the other epistemological. In the former, I suggested, following Kovel (1991:1), that spirituality is what happens when the bounds of the ego give way. I began, in other words, with the assumption that the ego, the contained self, has some reality, some boundaries that firstly define it and, secondly, can give way in order to go beyond the ego. In the previous chapter, through the work of Teresa Brennan, I suggested that the ego, the contained self, is an illusion. This is the position of Buddhism, of Taoism, of some schools of Hinduism and of Christianity.[29]

It is also, significantly, the position of postmodernism which has (intellectually) deconstructed the subject. As I noted in chapter three, Derrida (1991:102) argues that: 'There has never been The Subject for anyone The subject is a fable.' But, he continues, 'to concentrate on the elements of speech and *conventional* fiction that such a fable presupposes is not to stop taking it seriously (it is the serious itself)' (ibid). Thus, Derrida justifies his own fall back into the play of signification as he re-grasps the subject, (mis)taking it for 'the serious itself'. It seems pertinent to ask whether, once we have seen that the subject is a fable, the ego an illusion, it makes sense to continue to take this ego or individual subject so seriously. Might we not pursue deconstruction's most radical implications and, having deconstructed the subject, escape our obsessive relationship with it by refusing to pick it up again? Then we might see that this discursive play of subjectivities is not the only alternative. The other possibility, as I have suggested, is a nondual subjectivity, defined through neither language nor objectification.

Many spiritual traditions can be read as pointing to the possibility of a non-discursive, or nondual, subjectivity that can be apprehended in the absence of the phenomenological self. Such an understanding is distinct from Derrida's since it understands this nondual realm, not as an epiphenomenon of discursivity, but as that which escapes and transcends discursivity.[30] From this perspective it would seem that the ontological component of the definition of spirituality which I offered as a working guideline at the outset, needs to be re-visited. That definition was based on an assumption of the ego's reality, but if we acknowledge that the ego is illusion then there can be no question of breaking through its boundaries, only of seeing through that illusion and breaking through the ignorance that has bound us into apparently separate selves. Something can hardly be *post-* egoic or *trans-* egoic if there never was an ego in the first place. It depends, of course, on the starting point.

The second epistemological aspect of my working definition of spirituality is, however, confirmed. What we see emerging with spiritually-engaged knowledge is exactly as Philippa Berry (1992:5) suggests:

> a new understanding of spirit, not as the opposite term of a binary couple, but rather as facilitating a wholly new mode of awareness, which not only invites the thinker to abandon their residual attachment to dualistic thinking, but also offers a potent challenge to their desire for subjective mastery and knowledge.

Spirituality emerges as the inclusive horizon capable of holding the tension of the binary dualisms of rational thought within a unified domain that preserves diversity and difference. It does this by reframing the project of knowledge and, as we next explore, shifting the emphasis from domination and mastery to submission and mystery.

The Way of Not-Knowing

As proposed above, many spiritual traditions contain within themselves two seemingly contradictory streams of doctrine which have different starting points. The first, referred to as cataphatic, is concerned with stating the doctrinal position in positive terms. In theistic traditions, for example, the cataphatic stream offers a particular representation of God, often by means of a list of preferred attributes, while in non-theistic traditions the representations may be concerned with particular states of consciousness. The second stream, referred to as apophatic (the *via negativa* of Christianity), is concerned with deconstructing the doctrine in order to overcome all conceptual formulations which, since they belong to the discursive domain, prevent access to the transcendent domain beyond discursivity. Again, to pursue the theistic example, the apophatic discourses deconstruct all of the positive attributes of God in order to point silently towards the domain of the godhead that exists beyond the domain of God(s). With the non-theistic example, the apophatic discourses deconstruct conceptual or dualistic notions of consciousness. The Madhyamika, Dzog Chen, or Zen traditions exemplify this in the Mahayana Buddhist tradition, while advaita Vedanta provides an example in Hinduism.

At least from the Western viewpoint, the cataphatic discourse has been presented as the primary doctrine. Postmodernism certainly facilitates a reading of the apophatic stream as a deconstruction of the primary cataphatic discourse. Hart (1989), for example, adopts this approach within the Christian tradition, framing the *via negativa* as a deconstructive reading of the primary cataphatic doctrine. Other more radical commentators, however, despite Derrida's apparent disclaimers (1989), read deconstruction as a negative theology[31] that passes beyond the ontotheological assumptions that have characterised Western philosophy and theology. Such a reading opens up the possibility of reversing the usual order and understanding the apophatic discourse as the primary stream of knowing which offers the absolute, nondual viewpoint.

Loy (1988:248-260) pursues just such an approach in his critique of deconstruction, suggesting that 'the problem with Derrida's radical critique of Western philosophy is that it is not radical enough' (1988:249). According to Loy, Derrida offers us a single deconstruction, but fails to apply the deconstructive strategy to deconstruction itself. By instituting itself as the un-deconstructed metanarrative that deconstructs all other metanarratives, Derridean deconstruction, it would seem, fails to grasp its own implication – the refutation of *all* prepositional truths, *including* its own, and the consequent establishment of the primacy of apophatic discourse.

If we pursue this more radical implication, which leads us beyond the deconstruction of all dualisms into the domain of nonduality, then we can see that Derrida's linguistic play of signs is not the only possible alternative:

> Although Derrida's difference constitutes a major philosophical insight, his employment of it does not develop its most radical implications. There is no transcendental signified that language can point to, because every signified is only a function of other signifiers; all we can ever have in language is a general circulation of signs. The importance of this can hardly be overemphasized, but from this sudden checkmate of all philosophy there are two directions to go. One is to make reasonable but solipsistic assumptions that, because language cannot point outside itself, we must remain forever inscribed in its sign-circulation. This may 'liberate' the proliferations of dissemination, but such 'free play' must be called nihilistic if it is motivated by having nothing else to do.
>
> The other possibility is that perhaps what metaphysics has sought in language can be found in some other way. Needless to say, contemporary Western philosophy is not sympathetic to such a possibility; but isn't that too a consequence of the frustration of its own attempt to point outside itself? *In language, such a possibility cannot be proven or disproven*, but the nondualist Asian traditions . . . are predicated on that possibility. Of course, examples are not lacking in the West either (Loy 1988:259).

When we try to comprehend this possibility through the application of the dualistic grammatical structure of language, we run into problems, or perhaps more accurately, paradoxes. As Loy (1988:62) states 'the "essence" of . . . revelation is indeterminable since our very oneness with it means we are unable to understand it'.

Although it cannot be conveyed discursively, this does not mean that nondual, spiritually-engaged knowledge cannot be suggested to someone else, cannot be pointed to, even though it may not be grasped and held. In Sino-Japanese culture, for example, as Johnston (1995:51) suggests:

> the tea ceremony, the flower arrangement, calligraphy and the martial arts ... [are all 'ways' in which] one identifies with the object and with the surroundings. In this way one enters into the state of consciousness whereby one identifies with the surroundings so closely that the separated self is lost. And all this leads to a supra-conceptual knowledge which is holistic and deeply human.

It is a knowledge based on connaturality, which might be called love. It is based, as Deborah Rose (1992:323) suggests, not so much on the dissolution of the self (which never was anyway), nor on its (imagined) incorporation into the Other, but on *total engagement with others*. It is this engagement with others that provides the ethical orientation of post-deconstructive spirituality that I formulated as an ethic of meeting. I would define it as a *kenotic* engagement, without remainder, in which the understanding of the self as empty leads to a nondual state that Thich Nhat Hanh (1996:37) refers to as *inter-being*. Inter-being is neither a *relational* engagement with others, nor absorption into the (terrifying) Other, since both of these require the acknowledgment (and therefore maintenance) of the self/other dualism. Interbeing is knowing things-as-they-really-are, as Adamson (1998) clarifies from the advaitic point of view:

> When the observer is completely absent, then there is unity. Not that you are united with all beings. Rather there is a feeling of complete non-being in which the division between you and the other ceases. This state without the word, without the thought, is the expanse of the mind which has no boundaries or frontiers, within which the I and not-I can exist.

There is nothing 'new' here, only a reformulation of the best of traditional wisdom. As I have already mentioned, in the well-known zen 'ox-herding' series of pictures which depicts the spiritual journey, the final picture is not absorption into a transcendent Other, but 'return to the market place',[32] having realised that not only are the waters, waters, and the mountains, mountains, but that the market is the market, the place of exchange, of the daily transmutation of secular into sacred.[33] Post-deconstructive spiritually-engaged discourse is not the revelation of a disembodied spirit, nor is its ethical demand one of imitation in the sense of following some universal set of ethical commandments, or imitating a particular life-pattern. Rather, it is based on a radical empiricism that is possible only through attentive love. This residue of love which emerges when the self is deconstructed gives rise to an excess of desire for the Other. Its ethical demand is kenotic, directing desire away from (the constant activity of maintaining) the self, towards the Other (who is already not-different from the Self). It seeks, as Wyschogrod (1990:xxiv) posits, the cessation of others' suffering and the birth of others' joy. But it also seeks to enlighten others, to release them from the pain of separation caused by the illusion of the individual self.

Although Wyschogrod writes in the language of alterity, privileging the other, she explains that the depth of this response to the Other is intimately related to the capacity to deflect desire away from oneself towards the Other. Such a task involves overcoming egoity, totally seeing through the illusion of the individual self: 'Self-renunciation to the point of effacement is', Wyschogrod (1990:96) tells us, 'the mark of saintly labour.' Humility, in other words, emerges as a necessary virtue. As we have already seen, if either the self or the other is completely deconstructed or effaced, then the opposing term of the self/other dualism, and dualism itself, collapse into nonduality.

This 'saintly labour' is not an ethereal praxis, but involves, as Falk (1992:15, 21) suggests, listening to the 'voice of conscience', which we might now understand as the imperative demand of the Other that issues, unformulated, from the non-discursive encounter.[34] Such a command will not necessarily conform to social convention. Indeed, if we consider the trends towards the establishment of a global corporate culture, then we can see how this understanding of spiritually-engaged knowledge runs directly counter to 'the culture of desire' (Korten 1995:151) propagated by corporate consumerism. Global corporate spending on advertising, which constantly titillates the self-directed desire for consumption, has increased seven-fold since 1950 (Korten 1995:153), representing a massive investment in directing desire away from the Other, as the fantasy of instant gratification and control is acted out on a global scale.

The post-deconstructive, spiritually-engaged knowledge that I have described stands in opposition to this culture of consumption advocated by global corporatism. It is for this reason that commentators such as Richard Falk point to the possibilities of a politically-engaged spirituality as a means of countering 'top-down', global corporate dominance. It is also for this reason that much environmental discourse sounds like a materially-engaged spirituality which, by deconstructing the human/nature boundary, undoes the resource-based rationality that would have us pollute or consume the earth upon which we stand. In the next chapter, I look at the relevance of spiritually-engaged knowledge in the socio-political domain. I return, in other words, to the woman on the bridge. But in concluding this chapter, we will remain with the yogi in the turban and the implications of the nondual, non-egoic way of being that he embodies.

Although, as I have argued, this way of being is post-discursive, belonging to the transcendent domain that exceeds the confines of a particular tradition. The yogi nonetheless, reached that domain through a tradition. My first meeting with him was not the one described in the prologue. I initially met him in the courtyard of a Shiva temple where he had been living as a renunciate for some years. Although he may embody a nondual state of being, the yogi is not a secular being, as he simultaneously embodies and transmits the sapiential knowledge of the Hindu tradition. It is this relationship between tradition and knowledge, a relationship fraught with tension for those who have been secularised by modernity, that I explore next.

Knowledge and Tradition

We have now traced the genre of spiritually-engaged knowledge through various domains, identifying it as a form of knowledge that is distinct from rational knowledge, which implies that spiritually-engaged knowledge represents a way of knowing, indeed *the* way of knowing for our global era. My approach has been phenomenological, persistently pointing to the praxis of attentiveness, or attentive love, in order to identify it as a transcultural, universal, human practice that offers a veridical form of knowledge. If the primacy of apophatic discourse is accepted, then there is no contradiction in arguing that spiritually-engaged knowledge, or attentive love, is simultaneously post-discursive and multi-discursive – it is universal and beyond words and yet it seeks expression in a multiplicity of discursive domains.

But 'love' is the wild card in the different accounts presented of attentiveness as a post-representational practice. Some commentators place it first in the sequence of perception, identifying 'bare' attention as 'loving' attention, while other commentators see it as the goal, or consummation, of attentive praxis. What seems to occur is a shift in the meaning of 'love'. When referred to as part of the early stages of practice, 'love' is generally employed as a transitive verb – one loves something, be it one's child, a flower or God. In the later stages of practice, however, when the practitioner has let go of the illusion of a contained self, love is employed intransitively – one loves – or more accurately, since these later stages are post-egoic and nondualistic – love is. Lonergan tried to convey this distinction by his final injunction, which was not Be Loving!, but Be in love! We cannot command ourselves to Be in love!, but when attentiveness reveals the egoic self as non-existent, that which remains is love.

Nisargadatta Maharaj (1981:109,112) says that 'When the sense of distinction and separation is absent you may call it love . . . You are love itself – when you are not afraid'. In the same tradition Gangaji (1996) speaks of love as that which lies beyond union, while in Tibetan Buddhism, Situ Rinpoche speaks of 'the inseparability of emptiness and compassion' (cited in Walker, 1987:149). Also in Mahayana Buddhism, but from the Zen tradition, Thich Nhat Hanh (1996) equates 'cultivating the mind of love' with 'the practice of looking deeply'. In Christianity, William Johnston (1995), implying that love is some kind of end-point, refers to mystical theology as 'the science of love'. In the same tradition, Bernadette Roberts (1984:179), in her experiential account of what remains when the self and the self/other dualism has dissolved, describes a 'dynamic, intense state of caring'.

It would be possible to effect a closure by concluding that the praxis of attentive love offers a postmodern, global form of spirituality which facilitates the deconstruction of the separate self and leads to a nondual way of knowing that we refer to as love. There is, I think, a degree of profound truth in such a statement, but if it is to avoid facile universalism it must be carefully explained. I am not advocating a 'lowest common denominator' kind of ecumenicism, which claims that the 'spiritual core' of all traditions and all secular paths is love, and therefore, since all ways are the same, we can practice a universal, non-doctrinal, spirituality of attentive love. Such an approach is anti-intellectual in that it ignores the very obvious differences, not only between secular and spiritual paths, but also between the different traditions with respect to the particularities of both doctrine and form with which they cultivate attentiveness. Such an approach is also naive because it ignores the degree to which the practice of attentiveness is constructed and supported by both the doctrines and methods, the discourses and praxes, of the various traditions and domains of knowledge.

To take the practice of attentive love out of its context within the spiritual traditions is, in many ways, to adopt a modern, technological approach to spirituality, to search for the 'quick fix', the one technique that will provide a short-cut to the goal. Attentiveness as an ongoing, disciplined praxis offers no instant gratification but an emptying of the very self which seeks that gratification. Within most of the major traditions, meditative praxes of attentiveness represent an advanced stage that is preceded by at least two preliminary stages of practice (Brown, 1986:223). The first, which is concerned with ethical training and the control of the body and mind, ensures that the attentiveness of the final stage is positively, not negatively, deployed. The second, which is concerned with the practice of concentration, increases the intensity of the attentiveness of the final stage, so that it can irreversibly break through the patterns of conditioning. The practice of attentiveness, as understood within the context of the traditions, represents one of the final stages of a disciplined science of transformation.

Although I have argued that attentive love constitutes a universal, human way of knowing that gives access to a nondual, post-discursive knowledge, it is neither a simple nor straightforward exercise to divorce attentive love from the traditions that have given it form. A comparison with language is helpful in clarifying why this is so. Language is undoubtedly a universal capacity of human beings, but if we wish to speak and be understood we must not only choose *one* language in which to express ourselves at any given time but, in order to speak with any degree of excellence, we must familiarise ourselves with the grammar and syntax of that language. Similarly, attentive love, I argue, is a universal capacity of human beings, but if we wish to practice attentiveness fully, to the point at which it dissolves into love, then we may need to familiarise ourselves with a tradition that will give context and form to our practice.

Commentators from the perennialist school of thought are unrelenting in their insistence that sapiential knowledge can only be realised by following the path set down in one of the spiritual traditions. To advocate the meditative practice of attentiveness or love outside the framework of a tradition is, from their perspective, to advance the desacralisation of both knowledge and form and to risk losing one's way in the labyrinths of the mind and ego. Until the modern and postmodern eras, of course, such an attempt was hardly possible, since, with very few exceptions, people were embedded in their traditions. The present proliferation of spiritual paths, both 'new age' and traditional, is possible only in the wake of modernity's secularism and globalisation's disembeddedness. From this contemporary sociohistorical locus we can recognise attentiveness as a universal way of knowing/being that might accurately be described either as 'postmodern spirituality' or as 'full human maturity', representing the final developmental stage of life. One of the great experiments of our time is, I think, to see whether people can reach this maturity outside the traditional spiritual pathways. My explorations in feminism, environmentalism, aesthetics and transpersonal psychology suggest that they can certainly make the attempt, and that the praxis of attentive love may be particularly significant for the many contemporary people who, though disembedded from their traditions, seek a deeper way of knowing and being.

At this point a distinction must be made between the spiritually-engaged knowledge that I have traced through various contemporary discourses, and the sapiential knowledge that represents the highest possibility of the world's spiritual traditions. I coined the phrase 'spiritually-engaged' to describe a genre of knowledge that was distinct from the rational, conceptual knowledge characteristic of the modern, secular era. This genre of knowledge, however, which I have identified within the contemporary Western episteme, points back to the contemplative and meditative praxes of spiritual traditions, and demands that we recognise them as noetic strategies, as authentic ways of knowing, that lead ultimately to a nondual knowledge which can be referred to as sapiential. Spiritually-engaged knowledge might best be described as the precursor of spiritual, or sapiential, knowledge which represents the full flowering of the wisdom of the spiritual domain. Spiritually-engaged knowledge can be thought of as the point of entry into the 'mazeway'[35] that leads to sapiential knowledge. Since spiritually-engaged knowledge, as I have shown, can be identified within a multiplicity of discursive universes, some sacred and some secular, I conclude that the sapiential mazeway can be entered through a diversity of doors. I suspect, however, that somewhere along the inter-connected paths of the maze a meeting with traditional spirituality, either in the form of a teacher or in the form of a teaching (doctrine), is likely to occur. Indeed, part of the significance of spiritually-engaged knowledge may lie in the way it facilitates a re-engagement with the spiritual traditions in the postmodern, global era.

I have argued that the epistemological strategy of spiritually-engaged knowledge is attentiveness, or attentive love, and this strategy is accessible to all – to the de-churched, the un-templed, the post-synagogued, secular peoples of the contemporary West. As Nisargadatta Maharaj (1973:126,324) says:

> Do not undervalue attention. It means interest and also love. All the blessings flow from it. The deepening and broadening of self-awareness is the royal way. Call it mindfulness, or witnessing, or just attention – it is for all. None is unripe for it and none can fail.

Maharaj's optimistic inclusiveness contrasts with the perennialist's insistence on a traditional path.[36] It could be, I suspect, that if the practice of attentiveness is pursued in a persistent and disciplined manner, then the other essential stages of development will occur. And while it may seem foolish to risk unchartered waters when maps and assistance are available from a tradition or a teacher, the traditions are not always perceived as accessible by contemporary, secular people. Nonetheless, I argue that the practice of attentiveness eventually draws its secular practitioners into conversation with the spiritual traditions, and it is this conversation that is giving rise to meaningful postmodern forms of spirituality.

The perennialists argue that as practitioners move from exoteric to esoteric practices, they simultaneously move into a nondual, post-discursive way of knowing that reveals a transcendent unity of faiths, not as something divorced from the traditions, but as their culmination. Traditional spiritual praxes, however, must be distinguished from secular discourses on attentiveness in that they offer ways and means of deconstructing, at the existential level, the individual self. Discipline and ethical training are given little consideration in the contemporary discourses of feminism, environmentalism and post-deconstructive ethics, so it might be that in by-passing these 'prerequisites', the praxis of attentive love becomes distorted or fails to reach its full potential. For sapiential knowledge is an incarnational way of knowing that, at its fullest, involves every aspect of the being – the will, the psyche, the emotions and the intellect.

If the perennialists' *transcendent* unity of traditions is accepted, it is possible to accurately conclude, I think, that the praxis of attentive love offers a mature, postmodern, global form of spirituality. This praxis finds different expression in different traditions, but in each one it facilitates the deconstruction of the separate self, and leads to a universal, nondual, form of awareness that is inextricably associated with love and nonduality. Such a spirituality, if it is to be a positive influence in the global domain, requires a spiritual resurgence that operates within the parameters of a *transcendent* ecumenicism based on a sapiential knowledge of the traditions, and not merely on a sentimentality which suggests that 'all we need is love'. But we also seem to be experiencing a spiritual resurgence outside the parameters of the traditions. It remains to be seen whether these 'secular pathways' can both guide the full development of human maturity and provide ways of nurturing that maturity in others.

However that may be, the practice of attentiveness provides common ground for a conversation between, on the one hand, the secular discourses of feminism, environmentalism, psychology and postmodern ethics and, on the other, existing spiritual traditions. These secular discourses challenge the traditions to make themselves more accessible by finding appropriate forms of both doctrine and practice for the contemporary global era; they interrogate sapiential knowledge, forcing it to distinguish more carefully between that which is truly revelation and that which simply perpetuates socio-historical prejudices; and they call upon spiritual practitioners to overcome the sacred/secular dualism that characterises modernity, as well as to incarnate that nondual, sapiential knowledge that is the acme of spirituality.

Such knowledge is inextricably associated with virtue which, Nasr (1989:312) argues, constitutes 'the *conditio sine qua non*' for the realisation of sapiential, or spiritual, knowledge, and which sets it apart from contemporary discursive knowledge. As Nasr (1989:313) explains:

> The association of realized [sapiential] knowledge with the spiritual virtues indicates how far removed this knowledge is from the purely mental grasp of concepts and judgements made upon them. This difference is to be seen also in the organic and inalienable nexus which exists between knowledge as here understood and love in contrast to purely mental knowledge that can and in fact does exist without relation to love or to qualities of the person who holds such a knowledge as far as love is concerned.

When nondualistic, post-rational, post-egoic knowledge is considered within the context of the major spiritual traditions, it is possible to understand how far both modern and postmodern Western knowledge has moved from a sapiential or radically empiricist way of knowing. As already argued, the modern and postmodern understandings of knowledge tend to equate knowledge with power. Knowledge is thus understood as instrumental, to be used for our human purposes. Many of the contemporary attempts to formulate postmodern, politically engaged spiritualities, or eco-spiritualities operate from this instrumental understanding of knowledge. Spirituality, and the spiritual knowledge associated with it, are seen as resources in the fight for social justice or protection of the environment.

As detailed in the next chapter, although that sapiential knowledge does impact positively on both social and environmental crises, Marion's (1991) warning about the risk of idolatry needs to be taken seriously by those who aspire to a politically or environmentally engaged spirituality. Sapiential knowledge is concerned with the truly universal and does not fix its gaze on any conceptual or sectarian determination. When the gaze is fixed on a conceptual determination rather than upon the Absolute, then, as Marion (1991:164) warns, we have:

> the imposture of an idolatry that imagines itself to honour 'God' when it heaps praises on his pathetic 'canned' substitute In this sense, profanation would increase with the bustle of a too obviously 'political' worship: political in the profound sense that the community would seek to place 'God' at its disposition like a thing, its thing, to reassure its identity and strengthen its determination in that thing.

Sapiential knowledge, as revelation, is concerned with receiving. It relinquishes the pretension to absolute knowledge that belongs to the domain of the idol (Marion, 1991:23) and understands through apprehension, rather than comprehension, through experience, or 'taste', rather than through conceptualisation. Only when we cease to idolise knowledge by directing our gaze beyond the conceptual to the spiritual horizon that bears witness to the limits of discursive knowledge and to the noetic power of love will we be able to apprehend alterity, or be able to meet the real/world/other without the distorting intervention of the 'fat relentless ego' (Murdoch, 1970:52). Weil suggested that the primary stance of the human being is as a recipient, dependent on the gift of the other – ultimately the wholly Other. To know the other, as Other, is only possible through the knowledge that comes when we wait attentively to receive the other's gift of self-revelation. Where knowledge of the other is wrested from him or her by violence, then we know nothing of the other's alterity, but only the results of our own power.

Spiritually-engaged knowledge implies a fundamentally different subjective stance. The attitude associated with both spiritually-engaged and sapiential knowledge is one of submission to mystery, rather than desire for mastery. This attitude is reflected in the traditional spiritual perspective where one is expected to submit to the authority of the tradition (either in the form of the revealed teachings, or of the teacher). It is an attitude that is alien to both the modern and postmodern understanding of how knowledge is acquired, and one that is fraught with difficulty when so many people, through the processes of globalisation and modernisation, have been disembedded from their traditions. Under such conditions, discernment and discrimination assume particular significance.

Sapiential knowledge is essential, I believe, to ensure that globalisation occurs in such a way that diversity is preserved within the embrace of a larger unity. As we come more and more into an awareness of our global unity which encompasses the planet's diversity, so we must grapple at the intellectual and spiritual level with a unifying way of knowing that can encompass, without absorbing, multiplicity. Sapiential knowledge is a unifying way of knowing, a *coincidentia oppositorum* that recognises the unity in diversity and which must therefore emerge as the world moves through the process of globalisation. This nondual, sapiential knowledge is not divorced from the world, but is intimately connected with it through the bond of love.

Love, however, is incompatible with the construction of the modern self as an individual, separate entity. With the insight of a great artist, D.H. Lawrence (1981:108) summed this up succinctly:

> We see, what our age has proved to its astonishment and dismay, that the individual *cannot* love. The individual cannot love: let that be an axiom.

To love, we must be able to break through the boundaries of the egoic, individual self and concede, as does Lawrence (1981:110), that the separate self is 'really an illusion'. Modernity depended on the construction of the self as a separate, isolated, individual but postmodernity offers new possibilities. Beyond the horizon of discursive truth, beyond the horizon of being, lies the horizon of love where the bounded, egoic modern self is discarded as the outgrown skin of an expanding subjectivity – a chrysalis cast off as the butterfly spreads her wings.³⁷

The next and final chapters draw together the threads of my argument and briefly explore the relationship of spiritually-engaged knowledge to the socio-political domain, the domain of the woman on the bridge.

Notes

1. Plotinus, cited in Walsh and Vaughan (1993:1) from *The Essential Plotinus*, tr. by E. O'Brien, Hackett, Indianapolis, 1964.
2. The approach that I adopt is in line with the school of thought known as 'traditionalism' or 'perennialism', which is discussed later in this chapter. Perennialism posits the existence of a *scientia sacra*, a science or praxis of transformation that is, from a transcendent point of view, common to all traditions, but from a relative point of view differs with respect to the doctrine and form of particular traditions (see Nasr 1989:130-159). Nasr also gives an excellent account, firstly, of the transcendent unity that unites the multiplicity of sacred forms and traditions (chapter 9), and secondly, of the significance of what he refers to as 'sapiential' or 'principial' knowledge as the means of moving beyond the present global crisis.
3. See Keating, in Walker (1987:108-9); also Nasr (1989), particularly chapter 1, for a more detailed account of the loss of sapiential knowledge in the Western tradition.
4. See Nasr (1989:24-26) for a summary of the influence of Nicholas of Cusa.
5. This phenomenological similarity, it can be argued, is not coincidental since, from an esoteric or sapiential perspective, Hinduism and Buddhism ultimately meet in a transcendent, metaphysical unity (Coomaraswamy, 1943; Schuon, 1975).
6. It appears first as 'the 10th Discourse of the "Middle Collection of Discourses"' (*Majjihima Nikaya*) and again as 'the 22nd Discourse of the "Long Collection"' (*Digha Nikaya*) where it has the title *Maha-Satipatthana Sutta*, i.e. 'the Great Discourse' (Nyanaponika, 1983:9).
7. The complete text of the *Supplication to the Gurus of the Kagyu Lineage*, from the *Kagyu Evam Institute*, Melbourne, is as follows:

    Great Vajradhara, Telo, Naro and Marpa, Mila, the lord of the dharma Gampopa; the knower of the three times, the omniscient Karmapa; the holders of the lineage of the four great and the eight lesser schools; Dri, Tak, Tsel, these three, Sri Drugpa and so on; and those who have completely achieved the profound path of mahamudra; to those incomparable protectors of all beings the Dagpo Kagyu – I supplicate you, the Kagyu gurus, I follow your tradition and example; please grant your blessing.
    Renunciation is the foot of meditation, as is said; not being possessed by food and wealth. To the meditator who cuts off the ties to such a life, grant your blessings, so that he ceases to be attached to honour and ownership.

> Devotion is the head of meditation, as is said. It is the guru who opens the gate to the mine of the profound oral teachings. To the meditator who always supplicates the guru, grant your blessing, so that true devotion is born in him.
>
> Awareness is the body of meditation, as is said. Whatever thought arises, its nature is nowness. To the meditator who rests there without effort, grant your blessing, so that the subject of meditation is free from conceptions.
>
> The nature of thoughts is dharmakaya, as is said. Nothing whatever, but everything arises from it. To the meditator who sees the unobstructed play of the mind, grant your blessing, so that he realises the identity of nirvana and samsara.
>
> Through all of my births, may I not be separated from the perfect guru and so enjoy the glorious dharma. Accomplishing the good qualities of the paths and the stages, may I speedily attain the state of Vajradhara.

8. In other contexts, Nyanaponika also adopts the terminology of 'bare attention'. When distinguishing between 'mindfulness' and 'clear comprehension' he explains that the 'mindfulness' referred to is: 'Mindfulness in its specific aspect of Bare Attention' (Nyanaponika 1983:30).

9. Both Sri Ramana Maharshi and Sri Nisargadatta Maharaj occasionally refer to 'God' but it is always in response to a questioner who frames his or her inquiry in that terminology.

10. The term 'sapiential' is commonly used by commentators within the traditionalist or perennialist school of thought. Within the domain of spirituality the term is more appropriate than the clumsier phrase 'spiritually-engaged' which I have employed. I have, however, persevered with 'spiritually-engaged' because in the discourses of feminism, environmentalism, psychology and postmodernism, I consider that the term 'sapiential' is not always appropriate since the spiritually-engaged knowledge to which I refer in these domains, while being post-rational and post-discursive, falls short of the 'fullest' realisation of sapiential knowledge.

11. The term *sophia perennis* (perennial wisdom) has sometimes been used in preference to *philosophia perennis* (perennial philosophy) in order to distinguish the perennialists' use of the term 'philosophy' from the discursive constructions of much Western philosophy. Guenon (1945:109), for example, makes it clear that the perennialists' concerns are metaphysical where metaphysics is understood as referring to a domain that is unlimited and beyond discourse. Schuon (1979:133) also supports this understanding:

> '*Philosophia perennis*' is generally understood as referring to that metaphysical truth which has no beginning and which remains the same in all expressions of wisdom. Perhaps it would here be better or more prudent to speak of a '*Sophia perennis*', since it is not a question of artificial mental constructions, as is all too often the case in philosophy.

12. Huxley (1945) claimed that he borrowed the term from Leibniz, but it appears to have been first used by Agostino Steuco (1497-1548), a Renaissance philosopher and (Augustinian) theologian. See Nasr (1989:69).

13. See Schuon (1975) for a thorough exposition of this viewpoint.

14. According to my reading of Guénon, Schuon, Nasr and others in the traditionalist school of perennialism they have always occupied the middle ground associated with the position of incomplete constructivism which we might now refer to as post-constructivism. The use of the term 'perennial philosophy' has, however, had an unfortunate impact on the interpretation of their work particularly in the postmodern era.

15. Bernadette Roberts' (1984) book, *The Experience of No-Self*, constitutes an interesting example of the contemplative's own experiences surprising her and exceeding the conceptual framework of her tradition.
16. In the tradition of advaita Vedanta, for example, *nirvikalpa samadhi* is equivalent to Forman's pure consciousness event; it is the state of cessation of all mental impressions and content. *Savikalpa samadhi*, however, is the ('higher') state in which the mind is stilled, but not without content since awareness of the world is present. A parallel can be drawn with the series of ox-herding pictures frequently used to depict the path in Zen Buddhism. Whilst some series of the ox-herding pictures end with the eighth frame of cessation ('both boy and ox forgotten!'), most series go on to the tenth frame of 'return to the market place', which can be interpreted as unmediated perception of the world (Johnson, 1982).
17. It can be argued, though I do not intend to do so here, that the perennial psychology being proposed by Forman is simply the *sophia perennis* in a different guise. Traditional wisdom has always been concerned with states of consciousness and, more particularly, with the attainment of an ultimate state of nondual consciousness. If this is now more easily expressed in Western idiom through the discourse of psychology rather than philosophy, this may well indicate the shifting disciplinary boundaries of Western thought more than the shifting premises of the *sophia perennis* where ontology and epistemology have always been recognised as inter-dependent. For my purpose here, I simply regard Forman's 'perennial psychology' as another way of stating that part of the perennial philosophy which deals with states of being or consciousness.
18. Guénon's (1984) book was entitled *The Multiple States of Being*.
19. Wilber's work (for example 1980, 1981, 1983, 1985, 1986a,b,c 1990, 1991, 1995, 1997a,b) which consists of a number of magnificently constructed meta-narratives, is regarded with suspicion, at least in part, because it runs counter to the current trend of socio-historical particularity and deals, according to some commentators, unreflexively with cross-cultural universals. See Zimmerman (1994) for a balanced account of Wilber's contribution.
20. Forman uses a very limited definition of mystical experience, restricting it, at least in his 1990 book, to what he refers to as 'pure consciousness events'.
21. Wilber has enlarged upon his model in many of his books. See for example, Wilber *et al* (1986), particularly chapter 3 – *The Spectrum of Development* – where he outlines his model and relates it to a developmental perspective.
22. See note 16 in chapter three.
23. See Wilber *et al* (1986), particularly chapter 4 – *The Spectrum of Psychopathology* and chapter 5 – *Treatment Modalities*.
24. This can be compared to Weil's (1973) description of attentiveness in her 'School Studies' essay. In that essay it seems likely that Weil is referring, in the first instance, to concentration as it is applied to school studies. But in the second instance, where she is considering the way that we meet with others, she seems to be referring to the 'refined awareness' of Walsh and Vaughan. Weil's vocabulary and the terminology of those who follow her in feminist studies, do not adequately distinguish between the two different meanings of the terms, hence some of the confusion that was noted in the previous chapter.
25. Again the problem of terminology – Washburn's terms are not consistent with those of Walsh and Vaughan.
26. Thus there is a 'return of the body' as the practitioner observes with great attention the coming and going of bodily sensations and embodied experiences. But this 'return to the body' is distinct from the postmodern call for a 'return to the body'.

Although it involves the release of repression and careful attention to bodily desires, functions and sensations, it does not involve identification with the body (and therefore a continuing identification with a separate contained individual), but is the precursor of an outward sweep of consciousness towards a position of nonduality beyond subject and object.

27. In the advaitic tradition Ramana Maharshi is widely recognised as one of the greatest practitioners of nonduality and Sankara as one of its greatest theoretical exponents (see Sharma, 1993a,b).
28. Brown (1986), on the other hand, suggests another alternative from his study of 'Hindu Yoga', Theravada, and Mahayana Buddhism. He argues that the progression of stages through these different traditions is the same, but the 'end-point' of enlightenment is not. Brown's conclusion is the reverse of the traditionalists' 'many paths to one goal' position; he argues for one path to many goals.
29. The situation in Christianity is complex, but particularly in the Eastern Orthodox churches an understanding of the ego as illusory has been retained. See for example Fr. Timko's assertion that 'Ego is an imaginary projection' (in Walker, 1987:163).
30. See Coward (1990), who tries to locate Derrida's work within the spectrum of Indian philosophical thought.
31. See, for example, Williams (1992:72).
32. See Johnson (1982).
33. This refers to the Zen saying, generally attributed to Ch'ing-yuan (d.740), that before a person studies Zen, mountains are mountains and waters are waters; after a first insight into the truth of Zen, mountains are no longer mountains and waters are not waters; but after enlightenment, mountains are once again mountains and waters are waters.
34. See Bauman (1995:74). Bauman cites both Kierkegaard's 'continual commandment' ('I hear it, as it were, even when I do not hear it, in such a way that, although it is not audible itself, it muffles or embitters the voice bidding me to do other things') and Levinas's work ('the command which is binding before it has been spoken' so that one must attempt the ambivalent if not impossible task of 'obeying the order before it has been formulated') as examples of this post-discursive ethical demand.
35. The term is Hargrove's (1988).
36. It must be acknowledged that Nisargadatta Maharaj himself was situated within the Hindu tradition. He was the direct disciple of Siddharameshwar Maharaj within the Inchegeri Sampradaya of the Navanath lineage that claims direct descent from the Rishi Dattatreya.
37. Reanney (1995:266) also uses this metaphor.

PART IV: CONCLUSION

Chapter 6

A Handful of Leaven

> Do you think you can take over the universe and improve it?
> I do not believe it can be done.
> The universe is sacred.
> We cannot improve it.
> If you try to change it, you will ruin it.
> If you try to hold it, you will lose it
>
> *Tao Te Ching*[1]

Drawing on biblical imagery that compares the kingdom of heaven to a handful of leaven, feminist commentator Andrea Nye (1994) likens the contemporary philosopher's vocation to bread-making and, by implication, the philosopher to the biblical woman who, taking a handful of leaven, 'hid [it] in three measures of meal until the whole was leavened' (Matthew, 13:33). Nye's metaphor seems particularly apt for the work undertaken here. Although we began with the image of a woman on a bridge committing infanticide, an image intended to capture the marginalisation, social injustice and environmental degradation that constitute the present global crisis, the path taken in seeking to address these issues arose from the handful of leaven that the yogi threw into my world. Exploring questions concerning the nature of knowledge and the adequacy and validity of our modern Western, rational way of knowing involves a retreat from the socio-political domain of the woman on the bridge. Yet, as I suggested in chapter two, when a problem is tackled on a fundamental level, the approach may not seem immediately relevant 'to the causal eye', but the impact may in the long run turn out to be 'more widespread and efficacious' (Crowe, 1987:8).

It is increasingly apparent that within the postmodern global context, the impact of the globalising capitalist system, and of the modern Western system of knowledge that underpins it, is destructive both for the majority of the global population and for the biosphere. Under such circumstances the attempt to re-orient, or re-frame, that knowledge may itself be regarded as a long term political action. I have presented here an analysis of a new form of knowledge, which is emerging in response to our postmodern, global context. This spiritually-engaged knowledge goes beyond rationality to include the ethical, affective and spiritual aspects of knowing. This way of knowing, defined through the course of this exploration reframes the project of knowledge within a transcendent or spiritual horizon.

If spiritually-engaged knowledge is likened to leaven, then just a handful of such knowledge introduced within the meal of the modern Western episteme would produce a very different loaf – a postmodern genre of knowledge more appropriate to our global context. Introducing the leaven of spiritually-engaged knowledge necessitates reframing Western discourse within ethical and spiritual horizons, and this task involves reclaiming both recessive and pre-modern aspects of the Western heritage. If I am correct that there is currently a re-emergence of spiritually-engaged knowledge, then these tasks of reclaiming and reframing may define important aspects of the intellectual work of the post-modern global era.

I refer to some of the implications of this intellectual work in the final part of this chapter, but before doing so we will retrace my steps to provide a summary of the arguments in support of my thesis concerning the re-emergence and definition of spiritually-engaged knowledge. We then consider how such knowledge might come through into the socio-political realm. A postmodern genre of spiritually-engaged knowledge may prove more effective than modernism in sustaining, not only the woman on the bridge and her global companions in poverty, but also the global environment, during this new millennium.

The Rise of Spiritually-engaged Knowledge

Before moving to my conclusion, we will first return to the preceding chapters, weaving together the ideas that bring us towards a new way of knowing. My inquiry into spiritually-engaged knowledge was divided into two parts. The first was concerned with the logic of inquiry – why this genre of knowledge might be emerging in the contemporary context. The second part was concerned with genre analysis – with describing the emerging genre of spiritually-engaged knowledge. In summarising my argument here, I consider these two parts again, beginning with the logic of inquiry. I argued in chapter two that, from a Western point of view, globalisation and postmodernity define our contemporary context and, while these two theoretical frameworks exist in tension with each other, both lead to a crisis of knowledge within the Western episteme that can be addressed by the emergence of spiritually-engaged knowledge.

Considering the global context first, I argued, in line with globalisation theory, that it is now possible to consider, and take as the object of our analysis, the global domain as a whole. Within this domain, we can identify an ongoing process of 'globalisation' that involves, through the increasing inter-dependence and inter-penetration of nations, political economies and cultures, both a 'compression' of the world into a global unit and an intensification of our awareness of the world as such a unit. Globalisation theory establishes a global horizon within which all human knowledge systems operate. The effect of this more inclusive global horizon, however, is to relativise all of those systems of knowledge, revealing them as particular, historically situated, cultural constructs.

Whilst although globalisation pushes us towards relativism, I proposed that it simultaneously puts limits on that relativism. By defining a global horizon our individual, national or cultural identities are set within the broader context of a shared human identity. By confronting us with the biophysical limits of the Earth, globalisation provides us with some external referents (such as environmental destruction, population control, poverty, war or famine) against which we might assess the adequacy and validity of our ways of knowing. By confronting us with systems of knowledge different from our own, our way of knowing can be brought into 'conversation' with other ways of knowing. Thus globalisation can lead us beyond relativism to a reflexivity that involves a deeper questioning and critique of our own cultural episteme through conversation with other cultural epistemes that exist side-by-side within the global ecumene. The larger global context, however, pushes us still further beyond this reflexivity to search for 'human universals' that might be common across different cultural systems of knowledge.

I have argued for the emergence of a universal, transformative way of knowing that is spiritually-engaged and thus related to a re-emergence of the sacred. The global context stimulates us to ask deeper questions concerning humanity and our role on the planet, questions concerning the meaning of human existence that have, in all but our modern culture, previously fallen within the domain of religion or spirituality. Within the global horizon, however, we are confronted with the multiplicity of religious traditions, and while for some this confrontation precipitates a loss of belief in their particular tradition and a fall into nihilistic relativism, for others this diversity of religious expression appears as confirmation of a more universal truth that adopts different cultural forms in different cultural settings.

In chapter one I defined the distinction between religion and spirituality as the difference between the translational and transformational functions of traditions. I identified 'religion' with the translational function and 'spirituality' with the transformational function in which the boundaries of the ego are dissolved to reveal more expanded forms of subjectivity. These two different functions might be identified respectively as the exoteric and esoteric aspects of traditions.[2] I contend in chapter two that globalisation also calls forth more expanded forms of subjectivity as it reveals the culturally idiosyncratic nature of our modern, individual, independent, nationalistic selves, and places these constructed selves within a more inclusive global horizon. A constructive response to this relativisation of our culturally constructed selves leads towards a relinquishing of the boundaries of the separate, egoic, individual self, and thus to a transformation that results in more expanded forms of subjectivity – a movement, in other words, in the direction of spirituality.

Postmodernity is also a significant feature of our contemporary context, particularly for those peoples whose dominant way of knowing has been defined by the Western episteme. In chapter two I argued that, like globalisation, postmodernism leads us into relativism and, if responded to constructively, creates the conditions for moving beyond relativism into non-dominative, post-discursive ways of knowing. In the second, third and fifth chapters, I explored the relationship of postmodernism to this post-discursive way of knowing. Postmodernism deconstructs the metanarratives of modernity, rupturing, at least in the intellectual domain, the hegemony of modern knowledge. Postmodern deconstruction confronts us with the limits of the rational, discursive, logocentric way of knowing that has dominated the Western episteme in the modern era. Modern knowledge is revealed as a discursive construction, a play of inter-dependent signifiers that keeps us entangled within a discursive web. Having understood this however, we have two alternatives: the first is simply to remain within that discursive web, playing with the signifiers and signs at our disposal; the second, with which I have been concerned here, is to move into the non-discursive domain which, from the modern Western point of view, is relegated to the domain of spirituality and mysticism. Postmodernism, I therefore posited, can be read as leading us back to a spiritually-engaged knowledge that is post-discursive and post-rational.

I concluded that both postmodernism and globalisation can direct us away from the form of knowledge that governed the modern era, towards a spiritually-engaged, nondual way of knowing that: transcends rationality, but is not irrational; that deconstructs moral metanarratives, but is profoundly ethical; that functions within the spiritual domain, but is not other-worldly; and that is capable of multiple forms of expression, while not being logocentric. Both globalisation and postmodernity help to create the conditions necessary for the emergence of such knowledge, but while globalisation theory does not, and indeed cannot, articulate this spiritually-engaged knowledge, some strands of postmodernism go further, marking out the ethical and spiritual horizons of this emerging way of knowing.

The second part of my argument was concerned with identifying and defining the genre of spiritually-engaged knowledge. The process was one of garnering rather than of critical argument. My intention was to bring together examples of the emerging genre and, by identifying similarities, move towards a definition of spiritually-engaged knowledge. In chapter three, I explored the ethical horizon of spiritually-engaged knowledge within the context of post-deconstructive ethics and that spiritually-engaged knowledge was constituted, in part, by an 'ethic of meeting' that had its origin in the encounter with the other. This ethic of meeting does not involve a moral metanarrative but a decision, before the face of the other, to 'be for' the other, to intend good rather than evil for the other. Such a moral stance, I noted, always involves ambivalence because there is no certain way of deciding what is a 'good' response to the other. It also involves, however, an inescapable moral responsibility, and the recognition of the moral demand that is addressed to us through every encounter with another.

The 'ethic of meeting' which I proposed was personal because it arose from the domain of inter-personal encounter, and operated only in terms of the first and second person pronouns. I argued that it could be extended from the inter-human to the environmental domain, since it is possible to address other species or aspects of the environment, as well as other persons, as 'thou'. To do so however requires a particular epistemological strategy that has been variously identified as 'care', 'attentiveness', 'love' or, combining the last two, as 'attentive love'. Such an epistemological strategy allows us to meet the other as Other, as one who is not defined by discourse, but whose potentialities extend beyond the confines of discourse into a transcendent, non-discursive domain.

In chapter three, I referred to such a way of knowing the other as a 'craft of Othering' and a variety of sources were cited to provide evidence for this ethical way of encountering the other. Since the construction of self and other are so closely inter-related, this craft of Othering, I argued, implies a form of subjectivity which extends beyond the boundaries of the individual, rational, egoic self. Thus both self and other are set within a transcendent horizon which, exceeding discursivity, is ultimately nondual. I argued that this way of knowing can be characterised as post-discursive and post-egoic, and provided evidence to suggest that it is connected with a mature stage of human subjectivity which can be described as post-rational. This expanded form of subjectivity is defined, not through domination, but through surrender and a recognition of inter-being. As such it has particular relevance to radical environmental discourse which seeks to relate to both Earth-others and the Earth in a non-dominative way.

Having clarified that spiritually-engaged knowledge provides an ethical way of encountering the Other, I then sought to define more closely this genre of knowledge, which, I argued, constitutes a form of radical empiricism. In chapter four, I considered, through the discourse of feminism, the epistemological strategy of attentive love associated with spiritually-engaged knowledge. Within the heterogeneous domain of feminism there is a stream of thought, having its origins in the work of Simone Weil, which valorises this epistemology of attentiveness or attentive love as Weil called it. It was this particular stream of feminist thought upon which I drew. My goal was not to claim attentiveness as either an exclusively feminist, or feminine, praxis but to build up both a theoretical and phenomenological understanding of attentiveness as a way of knowing, through the work of contemporary women commentators. I demonstrated, as might be expected of a way of knowing associated with a mature form of subjectivity, that attentive love can be found across the diverse spectrum of knowledge with which women are now involved. Women theorists in science, literature, environmentalism, politics and philosophy have all described this more immediate, unmediated, way of knowing. Particularly significant is their understanding of attentiveness as a quotidian way of knowing intimately associated with, rather than divorced from, the daily activities of their lives. Attentive love, according to the women whose work I explored, is a way of knowing as pertinent to good science as to good mothering.

Since attentive love constitutes a non-dominative way of knowing, I argued that it is less likely to be expressed by the dominative way of being that in the modern era was associated with masculinity. Again through the work of women theorists, I explored, in chapter four, the construction of the modern masculine and feminine forms of subjectivity in order to demonstrate the deficiencies of each. Although attentive love can not be associated with a dominative masculinity, neither can it be associated with a subordinated femininity. I employed the strategy of considering attentiveness as an interactive form of energy in order to grasp the ways in which it points beyond both of these limiting modern forms of subjectivity towards an expanded, non-dominative form of subjectivity. Attentive love implies a reframing of both masculinity and femininity such that they can be viewed as iconic ways of being in the world.

This led me to the domain of spirituality, which in chapter four, I began exploring through the work of women theorists. Attentiveness as an epistemological strategy has long been practised in spiritual traditions, and I turned in chapter five to a consideration of spiritually-engaged knowledge in the spiritual domain. The feminist perspective of chapter four, however, had significant implications not only for framing spiritually-engaged knowledge within a transcendent horizon, but also for reframing spirituality within a nondual horizon that does not differentiate between an 'other-worldly' spiritual realm, and a 'this-worldly' quotidian, material realm. Women's understanding of attentive love as a quotidian way of knowing, one which is at once spiritual and a part of daily life, is essential to guard against slipping back into a dualistic understanding of spirituality as somehow opposed to the materiality and physicality of our immediate experience.

Despite a preponderance of male commentators, it is in the spiritual domain, I argued in chapter five, that attentiveness as a way of knowing finds its most complete exposition. Practised as part of a disciplined path of transformation, attentiveness gives rise to a nondual, sapiential knowledge which the spiritual traditions regard as the most desirable form of knowledge. Within the spiritual domain, what I had call spiritually-engaged knowledge leads into sapiential knowledge, an integrated, incarnational way of knowing that involves the whole being. Such knowledge has been referred to as wisdom, or gnosis, within the Western tradition. It is distinct from the dominant modern or postmodern forms of knowledge because it is ethically based, is associated with virtues, is non-instrumental, and it requires the stance of recipient rather than master. It is a way of knowing that offers new possibilities for progressive action in the world.

I argued that the reframing of knowledge within a spiritual horizon has profound implications for our understanding of spirituality, no less than for our understanding of philosophy. Spirituality itself is reframed, not as standing in opposition to 'material' reality, as modern dualistic thought would have us believe, but as a form of nondual awareness which holds in tension these supposed opposites and unites them within a transcendent horizon. Whilst much of the discourse concerning spirituality as a mode of nondual awareness occurs within the meditative or contemplative streams of the major religions, I suggested that it is now possible, from a psychological perspective, to offer an understanding of spirituality freed from some of its religio-cultural trappings. I explored the possibilities of a post-representational psychology as one model for understanding some aspects of spiritually-engaged knowledge within the framework of a contemporary discourse. Within such a framework attentiveness can be understood as a meditative, post-discursive epistemology which finds expression through a multiplicity of discourses, both secular and religious, yet which ultimately transcends discursive representation to give access to a nondual, spiritually-engaged knowledge.

This does not mean however that attentive love constitutes a universal form of spirituality which can simply be divorced from any cultural or traditional context. Within religious traditions, attentiveness is represented as an advanced meditative practice which leads to the flowering of sapiential knowledge. It may be that without the preliminary ethical and concentrative practices found in the religious traditions, attentive love does not reach its full potential. Although I have argued that such a way of knowing cannot be claimed by any particular gender, race, religion or group of people as exclusively their own because it arises from the universal cognitive, affective and ethical capacities of human beings, it would seem that certain of those cognitive, ethical and affective capacities do need to have matured before the attentiveness of spiritually-engaged knowledge can give rise to sapiential knowledge. As such, spiritually-engaged knowledge offers the possibility of new alliances which cut across the divisions of gender, race, or religion to recognise both a universal way of knowing, and an innate human ethic.

Since it is readily identifiable in the world's religious traditions, spiritually-engaged knowledge cannot accurately be referred to as a 'new' genre of knowledge, except in the sense that the human capacity for attentive love is always seeking alternative forms of expression, more appropriate to changing socio-historical contexts. In the preceding chapters, I have attempted to capture the play of spiritually-engaged knowledge through a diversity of descriptive systems. On the one hand, I have used this method to build up a more complete picture of this way of knowing – taking a post-deconstructive ethic, adding some attentive love from feminism, a little nonduality from spirituality, a transpersonal self from psychology and the sapiential wisdom of spiritual traditions. On the other hand, I have been trying to point towards a way of knowing which slips out between all of these universes of discourse, uncaptured by any of them, because it is a way of not-knowing, a way of escaping the fixity of views, while retaining an ethical orientation towards the world.

Such knowing can be described as non-discursive or post-representational. It transcends thought, going beyond the subject/object dualism inherent in all discursive expression into a realm of nonduality that can, nonetheless, be experienced. In all of the world's major spiritual traditions reference can be found to this thought-free, sapiential knowledge. Some two and a half millennia ago the sage Astavakra said:

> There are those who think that the world exists and that the world is real. There are others who think that the world does not exist and that the world is not real. Rare indeed is that blessed one who does not think, but who is ever calm, abiding in the absolute (*Astavakra Gita*).

I conclude, therefore, that it is possible to identify a genre of spiritually-engaged knowledge which is re-emerging in response to the twin impulses of postmodernism and globalisation. This knowledge is ethically based and arises from an epistemological strategy of attentiveness. It is a way of knowing which I have shown can be found across a broad spectrum of human knowledge. It seems to be dependent, not on the object of that knowledge, but on the maturity of the human subject. The knowing subject of spiritually-engaged knowledge is not the individual, bounded subject of modernity, but the extended, interdividual subjectivity which is re-emerging in the postmodern era. Spiritually-engaged knowledge thus reframes both knowing and being within a transcendent horizon which exceeds the limits of discursivity.

This genre of spiritually-engaged knowledge constitutes a kind of radical empiricism which cognises what is. Although it is non-conceptual, it does not reject concepts or language but utilises them as a means of liberation from the fixity of the *said*. Recognising both the ambiguity of any descriptive system and the multiplicity of the globe's various descriptive systems, spiritually-engaged knowledge finds expression in a plurality of discursive universes, attached to none as the correct formulation, exceeding all as beyond the duality of subject and object. Unlike the perennialist perspective discussed in the last chapter, which confined access to spiritually-engaged knowledge to the religious traditions, I suggest that the multiple forms of expression of spiritually-engaged knowledge offer multiple 'entry points' into this way of knowing. For some the point of entry may be postmodern ethics, for others feminism, Buddhism, mothering, an encounter with death, a moment of oneness with nature or another person, a meeting with a woman on a bridge – anything which truly captures our attention or that draws us outside of our bounded concept of self. If we hold to the practice of attentiveness, then we will move past the entry point into other pathways, other expressions of attentive love, which interweave with different discursive universes. Hargrove (1988) captures this multiplicity of entry points and interwoven paths with her description of the 'new mazeways' by which we might journey to a 'larger vision of global responsibility and economic rethinking'.

One of the tests of any ethically based knowledge is, of course, how it impacts upon the realm of politics and the moral problems of our times. It is therefore necessary, albeit briefly, to conclude this philosophical consideration of the genre of spiritually-engaged knowledge and relate it back to the sociopolitical domain – the global domain of social injustice and environmental degradation inhabited by the woman on the bridge. Although my approach has been philosophical, ultimately spiritually-engaged knowledge is an incarnational knowledge that finds true expression in lives that are lived 'for the Other'.

From the perspective I have taken, to will 'Good' for the Other has nothing to do with imposing a universal metanarrative or forcing some impersonal order upon the cosmos. The Good can only be defined in the particular, in the specificity, concreteness and historicity of lived time. The particular Good arises out of a certain kind of relationship between self and other – between person and person, between person and cosmos, between person and the sacred. This relationship is not necessarily concerned with spectacular acts, but with the minutiae of everyday living. It gives rise to a politics which, as Giddens (1994) suggests, is 'beyond left and right', or to a 'life-style politics' (Giddens, 1994) which is concerned with a 'right', or harmonious, relationship with the cosmos, However, I refer to this relationship as spiritually-engaged politics because that 'right' relationship is not framed within the limited political or secular horizons of modernity, nor within the terminology of left and right, but within the ethical and transcendent horizons of a different way of knowing and being in the world.

Spiritually-engaged Global Politics

It is possible now to explore how spiritually-engaged knowledge refers us back to the political task of creating an ethical, global politics of difference which institutes a just relationship with strangers, while also preserving their otherness.[3] Although spiritually-engaged knowledge places politics in a secondary domain, the domain of the third person (or entity) and therefore of plurality, it by no means abdicates political responsibility. Instead it reframes politics within the *universal* ethical demand of responsibility before the face of the Other, and it requires a radical reorganisation of political space in order to strive for a just society, or for a world which confirms the 'multiplicity of non-additive, unique beings' (Levinas, 1993:118).

An ethical politics requires a just global polity which draws us into an ethical relationship of interpersonal responsibility and obligation to the strangers who, in a globalised world, are our neighbours. An inclusive global community, in turn, requires the transformation of the ways in which we, as human beings, conceive of ourselves. Far from being inimical to questions of justice and ethics, as some commentators have suggested, the contemporary postmodern interval can be seen as leading us into a universal re-articulation of human responsibility within the contemporary global situation which daily confronts us with alterity. As Bauman (1995:43) suggests:

> The denizens of the postmodern era are, so to speak, forced to stand face-to-face with their moral autonomy, and so also with their moral responsibility. This is the cause of moral agony. This is also the chance the moral selves never confronted before.

I do not think that the new religious and social movements which give expression to spiritually-engaged knowledge in the political domain have yet coalesced into a sufficiently formidable force to counter the present form of barely restrained transnational capitalism. I do think, however, that the potential is there for an effective alliance that could restructure the global political domain and institute a spiritually-engaged global politics. I therefore consider three essential aspects of such a politics: a politics of conscience; an inclusive Earth community; and a postmodern global identity.

A Politics of Conscience

In order to discuss an ethical politics of conscience it is first necessary to rehabilitate the notion of conscience. Due to influences as disparate as constructivism and Freudian psychology, conscience has been relegated to the position of a socially contrived super-ego which merely echoes the voices of parental and social authority in order to discipline the subject within the limits of socially constructed norms. However, in the post-discursive realm that I have proposed, conscience assumes a far more prominent role as the amplifier of the unspoken, but imperative, demand of the Other. This demand does not necessarily conform to social convention or follow the imprints of the super-ego. It is the 'continual commandment' that issues unformulated from the non-discursive encounter; it is the Levinasean 'command which is binding before it has been spoken' so that one must attempt the ambivalent if not impossible task of 'obeying the order before it has been formulated' (cited in Bauman, 1995:74).

Kohlberg and Ryncarz (1990) suggest that the authority of conscience can be grounded, within the Western philosophical tradition, in the doctrine of natural law which, they argue, is closely connected to the mature, post-egoic, post-rational, nondual stage of human moral development I outlined in chapter three. This mature and final stage of human development is rooted in a nondual, cosmic perspective in which human nature is understood to reflect the natural or cosmic order. From this cosmic, or transcendent, perspective the ethic of meeting, and the virtues, or the human values, associated with spiritually-engaged or sapiential knowledge, are not socially constructed. Rather, they are reflections of the order and harmony of (the natural law of) both the fully integrated, mature human being, and of the cosmos.[4] As Kohlberg and Ryncarz (1990:195) put it:

> Natural law theory generally holds that human responsibilities, duties, and rights are not arbitrary or dependent upon social convention but are objectively grounded as laws of nature.

However, Kohlberg and Ryncarz then assert, erroneously I believe, that natural law theory 'further holds that individuals can apprehend the laws of nature through the exercise of reason'. Kohlberg and Ryncarz thus perpetuate the error of the Western episteme in giving priority to reason and the inherently dualistic function of the rational mind. I argue that, at this mature stage of development, another way of knowing comes into play which is post-rational and post-discursive. I have called this way of knowing spiritually-engaged and have argued for its recognition as a veridical form of knowledge which, although post-rational, can be indicated by means of a rational argument.

The instrument of this kind of knowledge is not the rational mind, but a faculty of which we have almost lost sight and which is therefore difficult to name within the contemporary Western vocabulary. This instrument can be referred to as the intellect,[5] or the heart, and it is the organ of apperception both for spiritually-engaged knowledge and for the revelations of conscience. I have already quoted Hillman's (1983:6) diagnosis of Western society that 'we are bereft in our culture of an adequate psychology and philosophy of the heart'. There is, however, a way to find the heart and this, according to Needleman (1982a:157), is through attentiveness. We contact conscience in the same way and this contact is made, not through the rationality of the mind, but through the attentiveness of the heart.

Having heard the voice of conscience we must then acknowledge its primacy. This primacy is grounded in the recognition that conscience emerges from the most mature state of moral development of which humans are capable. The dictates of this conscience guide the ethical global politics I am advocating. Only conscience is able to challenge the supremacy of the secular state, questioning the legitimacy of its modernist goals and opposing where necessary its unjust laws or systems (Falk, 1992:21). As I mentioned in chapter three, this primacy of conscience has already been given some recognition in international law through the Nuremburg principles.

Mahatma Gandhi, Aung San Suu Kyi, Sulak Sivaraksa, Archbishop Desmond Tutu, His Holiness the Dalai Lama, Thich Nhat Hanh, Nelson Mandela, A.T. Ariyaratne and Martin Luther King[6] are amongst well-known contemporary figures who have fought (or continue to fight) unjust laws and civil systems through campaigns of civil disobedience which are informed by respect for a higher, natural law grounded in the spiritually-engaged knowledge of the heart, or conscience. King, in his 'Letter from Birmingham Jail' states the case: 'One has not only a legal but a moral responsibility to obey just laws. Conversely, one has a moral responsibility to disobey unjust laws ... [though] one ... must do so openly, lovingly, and with a willingness to accept the penalty' (cited in Kohlberg and Ryncarz, 1990:196). As is apparent from the above-mentioned practitioners of a politics of conscience, these assumptions are not particular to any philosophy, religion, race or gender, but are common to those who are willing to engage in a politics of conscience which counterposes 'natural', 'moral' or 'spiritual' authority against the secular authority of nation states.

Mahatma Gandhi gave classic expression to a politics of conscience with the non-violent, civil disobedience campaign he waged to win India's independence. In his comment on that campaign, Cohen (1985:13) captures the qualitatively different dynamic involved in spiritually-engaged politics, which does not operate from a technology of power but from what I have described as a craft of attentive love:

> When in the late 1930s the British colonial administrators asked Gandhi what he expected from his annoying non-violent agitation, the Mahatma replied that he expected the British would quit India. They would quit India on their own because they would come to see that they were *wrong*. Moral force is a scandal for ontological thinking, whether that thinking is gently attuned to being or imposing its subjective will Ethics is forceful not because it opposes power with more power, on the same plane, with a bigger army, more guns, a finer microscope or a grander space program, but rather because it opposes power with what appears to be weakness and vulnerability but is responsibility and sincerity.

As can be seen from the above example, a politics of conscience arises from the conscience of the activist and addresses the conscience of the opponent. It is not just heart politics, as Fran Peavey (1986) suggests, but heart-to-heart politics that challenges modernist assumptions concerning the loci of authority and power. There is a shift away from the State as the locus of power and authority in two different directions – firstly, towards the person who understands that obedience to the state no longer exhausts the meaning of good citizenship; and secondly, towards the global domain where international laws, treaties and organisations attempt to represent the universal responsibilities, rights and obligations necessary for the harmonious survival of the planet. Ideally, the global expressions of ethics and law should mirror the natural law of the mature human conscience and provide a safeguard for action based upon it. In the world of *realpolitik* such mirroring will be only partial because not all human consciences are mature and because international law-making can be co-opted by dominant locals. Nonetheless, I argue that we are seeing the emergence of a politics of conscience, and with it a new ethic which I have referred to as an ethic of meeting. Inchausti (1991:123) captures the spirit of this ethic in the global domain as follows:

> A new ethic has walked unexpectedly onto the stage of world history looking very much like an ordinary person. Clothed in prison fatigues from Buchenwald and the Soviet gulag, in a Polish workshirt and homespun cloth from Calcutta, this ethic has already toppled governments and reconciled what was once thought irreconcilable. It expresses itself through the concrete deeds of simple people who insist on finding their own bearings in history without sacrificing their integrity or personal sense of the sacred.

This alternative ethic and politics finds expression in the new social and religious movements which operate within the global domain.[7] I have already mentioned these movements in chapter two, and here distinguish again between those social and religious movements which seek to reconstruct or strengthen a clearly demarcated identity boundary and those 'new', or 'transformative', movements, as I call them, which facilitate a more complex, 'porous' identity construct.

As Hannigan (1991) notes, the new religious movements have much in common with the new social movements, 'both structurally and ideologically'. He suggests that 'three processes – contestation, globalization, and empowerment – are identified as characteristic of [these new] contemporary movements'. In seeking to define spiritually-engaged politics, I consider these in turn here, and add a fourth characteristic of my own – the epistemological strategy of attentive love. First, I propose that the critical and defining area of contestation for spiritually-engaged politics is the self/other boundary, and at stake is not simply the positioning of that boundary but its deconstruction. Hannigan expresses this as the contestation of the boundary between the private and public domains, whereas I go further by pointing to a growing realisation that there is no duality – no 'private' domain as opposed to a 'public' domain, because there is no private self that can stand in opposition to the universal (public, in a sense) domain of inter-being. Whilst this may sound theoretically complex, I believe it was encapsulated in the early feminist realisation (and slogan) that 'The personal is political'. Although this realisation gives rise to a politics of conscience, there is also another political form it might assume, a point to which I return shortly.

The second of the three processes characteristic of spiritually-engaged politics is globalisation, which I have already discussed in some detail in chapter two. The new politics exceeds the boundaries of nation states, as it is transnational in both scope and concern. I will elaborate on the significance of this shortly and here simply point out that, because of its global reach, spiritually-engaged political movements define 'colloidal' or dispersed communities of persons around the globe.

The third process that Hannigan identifies is empowerment. I argue that the process of empowerment, if it is to result in long-term change, must be intimately related to the process of maturation which I have considered in some detail. I have argued that both postmodernism and globalisation push us towards a spiritually-engaged way of knowing which implies an expanded way of being. The contemporary global condition, in other words, challenges us to attain a new level of moral and psychological development. The way of knowing characteristic of that level is a post-rational, post-egoic, spiritually-engaged knowledge that situates the source of power and authority within the expanded self which we eventually come to recognise as our own. This is the ultimate form of empowerment and responsibility to the Other is crucial to it, for, as I have argued, the process involved is not one of individuation but of interdividuation, or of coming into the full understanding and expression of inter-being.

Attentive love is an essential element of this maturation and constitutes, I suggest, the fourth process that needs to be added as characteristic of the spiritually-engaged politics of the new social and religious movements. At their best these movements operate on the basis of a radical empiricism which not only allows them to see what is, but which also shows them what needs to be changed in order to bring that 'what is' into line with the natural harmony and laws of the cosmos. Whilst this may sound grandiose, a task for highly evolved intellects/consciousness, at the pragmatic level, or at the level of the heart, there is in fact widespread understanding of what the laws of the cosmos are *not*. Falk (1992:14) captures this with the phrase 'reaction to the intolerable'. In the inter-human realm, torture, starvation, murder, enslavement, humiliation, rape, genocide, destitution, female infanticide, are all recognised by most people as intolerable – or against the natural law. In the broader biospheric domain, human sensitivities are less developed and we are only just beginning to recognise that the accelerated extinction of species, the pollution of soil and waterways, the destruction of forests and other natural ecosystems, dried up wells and river beds and so forth are also intolerable – or against the natural law that protects and defines the harmony of the cosmos.

Whilst I am arguing here for a recognition of the similarity which exists between the new social and religious movements, I do not want to lose sight of their differences. The similarity is important because it identifies a potential alliance which has yet to come to fruition as a political reality. But the difference between the new social and religious movements is also important because it helps us to understand the major shift that is occurring with regard to the re-organisation of political space. So far I have considered a politics of conscience which is somewhat more characteristic of the new social movements than of the new religious movements, though the line is very blurred.[8] The new social movements, I argue, tend to manifest most often in a reactive way as movements opposing certain features of what is, and their associated politics of conscience can be thought of as a reaction against the intolerable. Generally this politics of conscience involves contestation in what has traditionally been regarded in the West as political space.

The new religious movements, on the other hand, are more likely to be involved in defining and constructing what should be. This might be described as a politics of consciousness rather than conscience, and it operates less in the traditional domain of politics than in the domain of life-style where the adherents try to live out their lives in harmony with the natural law. This approach at first sight appears to be apolitical, but it may in the long-term prove to play a significant role in reframing our understanding of political space. In a global world, the personal and the political are intermeshed as never before. As Singer (1999) writes in reference to climate change:

> What once seemingly innocent activities does this [global warming] make wrong? Perhaps a Sunday afternoon drive in the country? What about motor racing? Driving cars round and round in circles to see which one goes faster might be fun, but how can it rank alongside rising sea levels that threaten to inundate low-lying Pacific island nations?

In an ecologically beleaguered world life-style *is* a political issue. From an environmental perspective it is crucial that the affluent people of the globe adopt a much simpler subsistence, or survival, life-style (Mies and Shiva, 1993:297-334). The new religious movements may have crucial roles to play in giving form to sustainable alternatives which could replace the high-energy, resource-intensive life-styles of the global (but predominantly Western) affluent classes. By addressing the deeper, spiritual needs of their adherents, and empowering them by offering access to expanded modes of subjectivity, such alternatives offer incentives which compensate for the necessary reduction in material wealth and resource use.

As can be seen from the exemplars of spiritually-engaged activists mentioned above, in the mature practitioner the politics of conscience and the politics of consciousness are synergistic, working together to create a life narrative that is structured around the response to the Other. The significance of the new social and religious movements is not limited to a handful of charismatic leaders, but is embodied in grass roots communities of resistance living out their sense of both integrity and the sacred in the everyday events of their lives. The members of these communities refuse to be distracted from the truth as they understand it, and they refuse the inconsistency of employing dominative means to achieve nondominative ends.[9] The politics of conscience and of consciousness can therefore be understood as synergistic, and although such a spiritually-engaged politics requires both tenacity and sacrifice, it ultimately contributes to building an inclusive, sustainable Earth community, which is the subject of the next section.

An Inclusive Earth Community

I have already suggested that the new social and religious movements, due to their transnational constituencies and concerns, constitute colloidal global communities. The question then arises whether an alliance of these transformative movements might facilitate the formation of a global civil community with a shared understanding of the common good and of an appropriate common future. I think that this model has some merit, but before looking at it more closely I want to consider two different ways in which community can be understood.

Borrowing again from Sharma's (1993a:59-60) discussion of religions, two kinds of communities can be distinguished. First, there is the model, presented above, in which a community comes together around a common core of shared goals or understanding. The contemporary religious communities of Christianity, Buddhism and Islam provide examples of such communities. The second model of community operates differently, as it describes the situation in which a common core emerges from a pre-existing togetherness. Sharma offers the primal religions of Hinduism and Judaism as examples of this second model. As he notes, these two different kinds of community differ in the way they deal with the universal. Those which come together around a common core tend towards universalism as they seek to expand their constituency. Sharma likens this process to 'circumferences radiating from a centre'. Those which seek out a core to articulate their pre-existing togetherness tend towards universality, and Sharma likens this to a circumference seeking to identify its centre.

As discussed in chapter one, universalism, because it is the absolutisation of a particular, tends to reduce diversity, while universality, because it identifies a meta-level praxis which finds diverse forms of particular expression, nurtures diversity. Clearly the distinction is important in a globalising world. If we wish to avoid a hegemonic form of globalisation where one particular so extends its reach as to encompass the global domain, then we must eschew the kind of global community which tends towards universalism and, indeed, seek to establish a global community which will protect diversity and particularity through universality. In Sharma's terminology, we need to identify a circumference, a pre-existing togetherness, and then articulate its core. When considering global issues a circumference for a community readily presents itself – that of the planet or biosphere – and we are then able to begin, not from philosophical notions, or metanarratives of the common good, nor from narrow anthropocentric notions of a human community, but from an inclusive, embodied community extending beyond humanity. As Thomas Berry (1992:43) suggests:

> We cannot aim our efforts precisely, and certainly not exclusively, to the human community, because the human is an abstraction if this designation is taken in isolation from its larger context. There is no such thing as

> 'human community' without the earth and the soil and the air and the water and all the living forms. Without these, humans do not exist. There is, therefore, no separate human community. Humans are woven into this larger community. The large community is the sacred community. The earth is a very special sacred community.

There is no duality in this earth community, only inter-being, and it is from this point that our thinking about a global civil community must begin or we will too easily fall back into the anthropocentric model of community as something dependent on the shared aspirations and understandings of human minds. The pre-existing unity, the nonduality, of the earth community must be our starting place, and though we may identify a need to define a human, global civil (sub-) community, the inescapable context of that human sub-community is the larger earth community which issues its own demands for responsibility.

The paradigmatic shift needed is brought into focus by Lingis's (1994)[10] phrase: 'the community of those with nothing in common'. From the perspective of the modern, rational, autonomous individual, an inclusive earth community requires the amalgamation of diverse forms of being – fish, mountains, ants, eagles, streams, dung beetles, humans, trees – which have nothing in common. But when we look from a nondual perspective, from the perspective of spiritually-engaged knowledge, then this community of those who have nothing in common is reframed and the challenge becomes, not finding a common ideological construct, but deconstructing those ideologies and ways of knowing which have divided the community of those who, sharing the same Earth, have everything in common. This inclusive model of a global community, according to Lingis (1994:10-12):

> demands that the one who has his own communal identity, who produces his own nature, exposes himself to the one with whom he has nothing in common, the stranger. [This] other community forms when one recognises, in the face of the other, an imperative. [It] forms when one exposes oneself to the naked one, the destitute one, the outcast, the dying one. One enters into community not by affirming oneself and one's forces but by exposing oneself to expenditure at a loss, to sacrifice. Community forms in a movement by which one exposes oneself to the other.

The themes of self-emptying and responding to the other, which repeatedly emerged in my exploration of spiritually-engaged knowledge, emerge again here, for it is only through the practice of attentiveness that we can really open to difference and unknowability. It is only through attentive love that strangers can be transformed into neighbours, neighbours into members of a common community or community into the warp and weft of our own Self.

There is no need to construct an inclusive earth community as it is already there, but not all of its members, most notably at the moment humankind, incarnate the responsibilities and restraints which such a community implies. It is for this reason that a human, global civil community is needed to articulate and implement those responsibilities and restraints. The challenge is to move into the broken middle, the domain of discourse, and attempt to articulate at the global level an ethics and a law which reflect, as accurately as possible, the natural law of the earth community. This is a challenge fraught with risk for when universality is distorted into universalism, global unity becomes, as Sachs (1992:107) says, 'a menacing fate'. There is much that is distorted about the contemporary form of globalisation. The word has become almost synonymous with extreme free-market capitalism and the inequities which that implies for a distorted global community.[11] However, as Wiseman (1999) suggests:

> Globalisation is neither a panacea nor a catastrophe. It is a word that describes the many ways in which space and time have been compressed by the acceleration of financial, resource, and information flows. These developments create a far wider range of strategic options than economic rationalism on the one hand and racist nationalism on the other.

Contemporary global developments and the words which describe them create, for the first time in history, the possibility of an inclusive earth community being consciously recognised, articulated, and embodied. Yet as Wiseman warns, such words must be more than a panacea. To transform globalisation from a menacing fate to a worthwhile process, the present political and economic systems must be transformed. Wiseman (1999) reports that at a recent World Economic Forum meeting in Davos, world leaders agreed that 'extreme free-market globalisation' is an idea whose time is gone, but there seemed to be a 'leadership vacuum'[12] concerning new ways to tackle the issues of globalisation.

Perhaps Wiseman was looking in the wrong place for such leaders, as a politics of power is unlikely to facilitate the emergence of an inclusive global community. That can only eventuate from a politics of conscience, a politics that can recognise the existing inclusive earth community, and be attentive to its natural laws. Such a politics must relinquish the absurd myth of unending economic growth, challenge the obscene disparity between the rich and the destitute and halt the environmental holocaust. This politics of conscience must also be a politics of consciousness which embraces simplicity of lifestyle and seeks to both attain and maintain, through the practice of attentiveness, a sufficient level of spiritually-engaged knowledge to be able to discriminate between universalism and universality, between the egoic, separate self and the inclusive Self, between a technology of power and a craft of love and to act in accordance with that discernment. An inclusive earth community must be supported by the wisdom of its members, and I shall consider next by whom the membership of this emerging community is constituted.

Citizen Sadhaks

I suggested in chapter two that globalisation has called forth new ways of being, and I argued for a spiritually-engaged politics of conscience/consciousness. I also argued for the establishment of a global civil community which might allow humankind to participate consciously and constructively in the pre-existing earth community. I now bring these components together to tackle the question of identity, and I explore what form of identity might both support a spiritually-engaged politics and constitute a global civil community. As noted in chapter two, the concept of global citizenship has emerged as an identity construct that could potentially bring together the diverse porous identities now emerging around particular axes of analysis such as gender, ecology, peace and/or ethnicity.

Various re-conceptualisations of citizenship have been undertaken to 'recover the radical character that it possessed during the struggle against absolutism' (Mouffe, 1992:3). Nerfin (1987) adopts the capitalised term 'Citizen' to signify a common political identity between the new social movements that struggle against various forms of domination. His understanding of global Citizenship is related to praxis, or mobilisation, with respect to certain libratory themes – feminism, environmentalism, peace, alternative development, alternative lifestyles and human rights. Nerfin's Citizens are thus constituted by a porous identity constructed around various axes of difference. While I support the notion that a fluid, or porous, identity is politically strategic for the global Citizen, I argue that it can only be constructively employed when the emptiness of all identity is understood. Citizens, in other words, need to find their 'true' identity in the unchanging awareness that supports the changing play of identifications, otherwise their politics will always be partisan and partial.

Richard Falk (1992, 1993a,b) attempts to capture this way of being with the term 'citizen pilgrim'. While Falk's evocative concept of the citizen pilgrim suggests an alliance between the transformative social and religious movements, it is still the citizen who seems to dominate that alliance by providing a vision of the future towards which the pilgrim partner is journeying. Although this vision of the future seeks to avoid universalism by offering an 'aspirational community in time', rather than a substantive community in space,[13] the citizen in Falk's construct pulls his pilgrim partner into his domain of exteriority, the domain of the secular, the shared geo-political field which constitutes the realm of the Western-based concept of citizenship.

Falk calls on his global citizens to leave the certainties of the present and to become pilgrims journeying towards an aspirational community in time – an imaginary future of an inclusive global community. But these pilgrims, journeying towards their imaginary future of an inclusive global community, are still trapped within the secular horizon of modernity. Bauman (1995:88) concurs with this interpretation of the pilgrim as a modern figure, insisting that 'the world is not hospitable to pilgrims any more'. He sees pilgrims as carrying too much modern baggage, their sense of purpose and identity only being possible as projects of self-creation within linear time (Bauman 1995:86).

I suspect that Falk's use of the term 'pilgrim' is inappropriate,[14] and I believe that we cannot afford to empty the postmodern global identity of its spiritual connotations so as merely to tie it to a secular utopia, albeit an aspirational one. It is the spiritual horizon which keeps open the boundaries of our gaze, referring us beyond the political to the ethical, and beyond the ethical to a transcendent which continually deconstructs our reified utopias and identities. The spiritual horizon ensures that we are concerned, not only with politically transformative praxis, but also with the interior journey of epistemologically and ontologically transformative praxes which constitute the only long-term safeguards against domination and hegemony.

If epistemological and ontological transformation does not underpin political change, then history will merely repeat itself and a new hegemony, or a new regime of domination, will be instituted. It is the domain of interiority, so ignored in the modern era, that transmutes our concern with the other. It calls a halt to obsessive modern plans to develop, educate, reform or otherwise 'improve' the other, and it reframes the Other as an icon, a doorway to the sacred which has immense import for our own Self. The domain of interiority uncovers the fragility of the boundary between self and other, opening us to the realm of inter-being where the needs of the self and the needs of the other are perceived as coinciding rather than competing.

Just as we have no suitable term in English to describe 'the place of the heart', so there is a dearth of words to refer to one who travels within, exploring the domain of interiority which is the realm of attentive love. 'Pilgrim' seems too easily associated with journeys in space and time to capture this meaning, and so I offer the Hindu term '*sadhaka*' to convey this meaning of one who journeys inwards. I put this term forward for two reasons: firstly, because of the accuracy with which it conveys my meaning – a sadhaka is a spiritual practitioner; and, secondly, because it is a term from a non-Western tradition of knowledge. If a non-hegemonic global episteme is to develop it must include knowledges of non-Western origin. Chambers (1994:22) identifies the contemporary Western prejudice when he writes that:

> It still obviously strikes us as a paradox to consider an idea of 'knowledge' that is not in the end of occidental origin.

The identity 'citizen sadhak' denotes the bringing together of the secular and the spiritual, but it connotes the meeting of the Western and Eastern traditions of knowledge within an over-arching global episteme. From the West comes the political tradition of democracy and citizenship which rests on a sound metaphysical basis of equality and mutual responsibility. From the East comes the spiritual tradition of nonduality and attentiveness which offers the epistemological and ontological means for realising the sapiential knowledge which underpins all metaphysical realisation.

In this construct of citizen-sadhak, my use of the term 'citizen' is, I think, in broad agreement with Falk's usage, as well as with the work of Nerfin (1987) and Inchausti (1991). The aspect of citizenship that is being particularly invoked for the global identity construct of citizen-sadhak is responsibility. The citizen responds to the demands of the community's others, and the term 'global citizen' can be understood as implying an identity which is for the embodied Other within the global domain. Citizens are attentive to the backgrounded Other and understand themselves as standing in a relation of responsibility to that Other. Such an understanding is postmodern because it reframes the modern notion of the citizen, whose primary responsibility is to the State. The postmodern citizen, by contrast, stands naked before the others of the global domain, and the locus of responsibility shifts from the political relationship with the State to the ethical relationship with the Other.

Nerfin (1987) argues that this postmodern global citizenship is not a political given, but an ethical process with which one engages in order to express solidarity with others. Although, like Falk's Citizen Pilgrim, Nerfin's Citizens are journeying towards a vision of the future, Nerfin acknowledges their Citizenship only when they have entered actively into this process and mobilised themselves to actively work for the realisation of their vision. Nerfin's work casts the concept of citizen in terms of desire for the (socio-political wellbeing of the) Other. Such desire requires a degree of self-transcendence which starts to dissolve the distinction between the needs of the self and the needs of others.

My use of the term 'sadhak' is intended to throw into question what kind of 'work' is really required to meet our responsibilities as citizens in the global domain. The Western heritage, particularly during the modern era, has been outwardly directed and action-oriented. Yet as Tolstoy[15] wrote:

> It appears that people are busy with trade, negotiations, wars, the sciences, the arts, and so on. But there is only one thing which really matters – their understanding of the moral law by which they live.

The spiritually-engaged identity of citizen-sadhak suggests a new mode of being in the world. It is a way that grounds action in attentiveness, by turning towards the Other. Attentiveness to the Other affirms the worth, the uniqueness, the alterity, and the ultimate mystery of our Earth others. It affirms that our desire to respond to them is not socially constructed, but is an expression of the love which constitutes the substratum of consciousness when the boundaries of the self give way. Such love marks out the natural law of an inclusive global community based on the ontological truth of inter-being. No doubt there is risk involved in trying to articulate that natural law, bringing it from the post-discursive realm to the broken middle, the discursive realm where it needs to be given imperfect expression in systems of ethics and laws. The discernment of sapiential knowledge is needed for the task and yet, as Gandhi implied, this knowledge of the heart is not so difficult to discern:

> I will give you a touchstone for truth. Whenever you are in doubt, or when the self becomes too much with you, apply the following test. Recall the face of the poorest and the weakest man whom you may have seen, and ask yourself, if the step you contemplate is going to be of any use to him? Will he gain anything by it? Will it restore him to a control over his own life and destiny? In other words, will it lead to *swaraj*[16] for the hungry and spiritually starving millions? Then you will find your doubts and your self melting away (Gandhi).[17]

Gandhi's words, like any other, reflect his times and alert us to the changing particularities of the broken middle. Now the poorest and the weakest persons whom we might recollect in the global domain are likely to be women, and the most exploited are likely to be the non-human Earth others who also demand our attention. Nonetheless, Gandhi's life revealed clearly how the sadhaka component of the citizen-sadhak is oriented primarily towards the transcendent domain which exceeds discursivity and rationality. It is a non-discursive domain before which words recoil,[18] being essential for preserving both the alterity of the Other and a realm beyond the rule of law from which that law can be continually questioned and deconstructed.

The citizen and the sadhaka can be seen as representing the complementary faces of postmodern spirituality: without the citizen, the sadhaka's spirituality remains trapped in the dualism of 'other' worldliness; without the sadhaka, the citizen's vision is confined to the secular and reduced to a materialism which easily succumbs to technologies of domination. The postmodern citizen-sadhak thus reframes spirituality as a nondual awareness which unites the transcendent and material realms by directing the love and compassion of spiritual practice back into the material world. The sadhaka, however, retains the upper hand by continually deconstructing the identity of the citizen, and by reframing the relative goals of any political agenda within the eternal now of the Absolute.

Not By Bread Alone

Falk (1992:2) writes that globalisation 'will ensue, but its nature and human consequences remain in the crucible of choice and struggle out of which the future will emerge'. I have argued here that although, to date, globalisation has assumed an economic focus which has been less than positive, this need not be so. When consideration is given to the social, cultural and spiritual aspects of globalisation then resources and trends can be identified which could lead to a very different form of globalisation – on which would preserve the diversity of the earth community within the universality of a transcendent horizon.

In the contemporary conditions of the postmodern, global world, we are seeing the emergence of a new way of knowing which could support this inclusive form of globalisation. I have identified this genre of knowledge as spiritually-engaged, explored spiritually-engaged politics, and very briefly indicated some of the ways in which our current understanding of politics might be reframed within a spiritual horizon. A spiritually-engaged politics does not, however, exhaust the task of reframing which spiritually-engaged knowledge implies. By challenging the foundational, dualistic distinction between subject and object, spiritually-engaged knowledge demands the reframing of the entire Western episteme within a nondual transcendent horizon.

It is for this reason that I do not adopt the terminology of Falk and others who refer to 'politically engaged spirituality'. Spiritually-engaged knowledge is not an instrumental form of knowledge which can be applied in the realm of politics to achieve our pre-conceived ends. Rather, spiritually-engaged knowledge indicates the horizon within which not only politics, but education, economics, science and the arts must be reframed in order to escape from the confines of modernity. What is called for is an epistemological revolution which Tarnas (1991:433-40) argues is already underway. He notes, however, that for this new way of knowing 'a developed inner life is indispensable for cognition' (p. 434) and I argue that the indispensable practice for any inner life is attentiveness.

Having described the emerging genre of spiritually-engaged knowledge, the ramifications of this new way of knowing are manifold, and beyond the scope of this book. It would be possible, for example, to pursue the emergence of spiritually-engaged knowledge in education through the increasingly popular methods of Rudolf Steiner, or to follow the possibilities of spiritually-engaged knowledge into the domains of science, economics or history. As I suggested at the start of this chapter, the task of reframing the Western episteme within a transcendent horizon may prove to be the intellectual task of the postmodern era. But there is a more immediate task, a task of inner exploration that confronts each one of us. For the emergence of spiritually-engaged knowledge is dependent on our own realisation. Although in the contemporary world the forces of the global marketplace and electronically mediated information undermine spiritually-engaged knowledge, it nonetheless demands our attention, or more accurately, our attentiveness. Spiritually-engaged knowledge is always before us, awaiting only our recognition. The truth of nonduality lies hidden in the heart and is never further away than the face of the Other, before whom all things perish.[19]

Notes

1. Lao Tsu, *Tao Te Ching,* XXIX, tr. by G. Feng and J. English. Vintage Books, Random House, New York, 1972:v29.
2. This is the terminology used by the traditionalists. Since it keeps both the exoteric and the esoteric functions firmly under the umbrella of tradition, it militates against the post-modern split between religion and spirituality which perhaps too easily slides into a 'new age' spirituality that, in its concern with 'feeling good', becomes divorced from traditional or sapiential knowledge.
3. See Critchley (1992:219-235) for an account of a 'Levinasian Politics of Ethical Difference'. I have drawn upon Critchley's account in formulating this section.
4. Such an argument is based on two assumptions: firstly, that mature, correctly discerned, human conceptions of moral law are the 'outcomes of universal human nature developing under universal aspects of the human condition, and in that sense they are *natural*'; secondly, that 'our consciousness of justice or moral law is parallel to, or in harmony with, our consciousness of the ultimate power or laws governing the larger cosmic order' (Kohlberg and Ryncarz, 1990:196).
5. I use the term here in the way that the perennialists employ it, to represent the functioning of the 'higher', intuitive mind, or *buddhi* in Hindu terminology.
6. Several of these people are included in Ingram's (1990) book, *In the Footsteps of Gandhi*, in which she offers a brief history of, and interviews with, a number of 'spiritual activists'.
7. The terminology of new social movements (NSM) and new religious movements (NRM) is already established in the literature. In line with the distinction which I have already drawn between religion and spirituality, I would have preferred the phrase 'new spiritual movements' to 'new religious movements' (despite the fact that it generates the same acronym, NSM, as the new social movements), but I have followed the current usage in the literature to avoid confusion.
8. Movements such as liberation theology (Boff, 1986, 1995; Guttierrez, 1973; Berryman, 1987) or socially engaged Buddhism (Sivaraksa, 1986, 1988, 1992: Queen and King, 1996), for example, fall right on the (imagined) boundary between the new social and new religious movements.
9. Contemporary examples of this kind of politics are not lacking. The resistance of the Tibetan people to the occupation of their land offers such an instance. Although His Holiness the Dalai Lama leads the Tibetan community in exile and consistently upholds a non-violent attitude towards the Chinese, many of the 'ordinary' Tibetans who continue to live within the territory claimed by the Chinese constitute a community of resistance that refuses to be distracted from their just claims for independence. See also Welch (1985) – *Communities of Resistance and Solidarity: A Feminist Theology of Liberation* – for examples based on Christian liberation theology and the communities of resistance in South and Central Americas.
10. The phrase is the title of Lingis's (1994) book, although the text makes it clear that, like Levinas, Lingis's thought seems constrained by the limits of a human community.
11. See Melbourne newspaper, *The Age*, 6 February 1999. In the article 'Global Backlash', p. 19, Claude Smadja, the managing director of the World Economic Forum held at Davos, Switzerland, is quoted as saying:

    The concept of globalisation – thought of until now as an unstoppable trend – is under attack and reconsideration, leading to a perception of global capitalism in retreat.

12. Melbourne newspaper, *The Age*, 6 February 1999:22.
13. Falk (1995) from lecture 'Global Citizenship and Postmodernity' presented at La Trobe University, July, 1995.
14. Falk refers to Paul's letter to the Hebrews 11:13-16 for his use of the term pilgrim. Interestingly, in my 'revised standard version' of the Bible, the term pilgrim is not used in this passage. My text refers to 'strangers and exiles on earth' who were 'seeking a homeland'. The difficulty with Falk's interpretation of the term 'pilgrim' can be explained by this textual difference. I agree that strangers and exiles are seeking homelands, aspirational communities perhaps, where they belong, but this is not the case for the pilgrim. Pilgrims leave their homes in order to experience the transcendent, but they then return with that experience, in order to imbue their daily lives with immanence.
15. The quotation is taken from *Leo Tolstoy: A Calendar of Wisdom – Wise Thoughts for Every Day*, tr. by P. Sekirin, Hodder and Stoughton, London, 1997:140.
16. *Swaraj* means freedom, self-rule, or independence, and while Gandhi used the term in its political sense of independence from colonial rule when referring to India, when referring to the people, and particularly when elaborating his ideas on the form of development appropriate for an independent India, *swaraj* often assumed the meaning of self-sufficient, free from dependency or self-sustaining.
17. I first saw this quotation written on the wall in Jaipur airport many years ago and I copied it down. I later found it quoted in *Manushi* (1992, 73: title page).
18. The Taittirya Upanishad (1986, II. IX:i) describes this domain as one where words, along with the mind, turn back.
19. 'All things perish save His Face' is a Quranic verse (Nasr, 1989:326).

Epilogue

Meeting I

Dawn is breaking as a woman walks over the bridge.[1] Already the village is alive with voices and movement. Women and girls form a queue at the well, waiting to fill their water pots. They call to the woman as she passes. A few of the girls will meet her at the Women's club later, but first she must visit some families. The woman stops outside Parvati's house. It is a thatched hut, made out of mud. From inside a child wails, weakly but persistently. A man, going out, pushes roughly past the woman. Parvati comes to the door in response to the woman's call. She is carrying the crying child awkwardly for she is eight months pregnant. The little girl has diarrhoea, and the woman gives Parvati the ingredients for a rehydration solution.

Water pot on her head, Parvati's mother returns from the well. She greets the woman warmly, and, putting her own pot down, takes the brass vessel off the head of a seven year old girl who accompanies her. The child smiles shyly, and offers the woman a drink of water. With two daughters already, Paravti's new born, if a girl, is considered a 'high risk baby' – one likely to be killed at birth. Parvati's husband, an agricultural labourer who works only seasonally, insists that a third daughter must be killed. It is impossible to pay three dowries, he says, and he is right. But Parvati's mother was one of the first members of the Women's club. For three years she has chanted at each meeting:

> As a member of the Women's club, in my home, in my village, in my society, the killing of female children, directly or indirectly, will not be allowed to happen.[2]

She protected the last baby, allowing Parvati to stay with her until this woman had talked with the husband and his family, and convinced them to take wife and daughters back. But three *daughters! Mentally the woman weighs the strength of the mother and grandmother against the despair of the husband and the will of the mother-in-law. She talks of a loan from the Women's Club that could buy a cow, that could give milk, that died of a fever, they say.[3] The doctors say that Janaki's husband will die too. The woman talks of a gift of clothing for a baby girl child. She praises Janaki that her two older girls have done so well at school. She talks of training – Janaki might learn tailoring – but all the time she sees the tears filling Janaki's eyes and feels the weight of her despair.*

'Why should the newborn suffer like me?'[4] Janaki cries.

The woman walks back over the bridge and has some tiffin before the meeting. She is glad that it is the teenage girls this morning, and not the Women's Club. She loves these girls. Over two years she has taught them about the dowry laws, about their rights, about motherhood, about the way they see themselves. Teaching them, she teaches herself – reminds herself, through them, that she is proud to be a woman; that she is strong; that she can speak out; that working with other women they have brought change to the village. Instilling self-confidence in these girls is her way of answering Janaki's question, her way of responding to the face of her own daughter who would have been just this age.

Before leaving the meeting room the woman fills out a form marked 'Statistics'. 'Wednesday: three visits to high risk families; one education session – 17 adolescent girls; fifteen minutes for tiffin; fifty-five minutes travelling time – on foot; total four and a half hours work.' Each month she adds up these daily statistics and prepares a report for her supervisor in Madras. Dr. Arunachalam tells her that these reports are sent all around the world – to Australia, to Sweden, to Germany – all the places that provide money for the Girl Child Project. The woman smiles as she packs up her things and locks the door. 'Imagine', she muses as she crosses the bridge, 'someone, on the other side of the world interested in how long I take to eat my tiffin, interested in Janaki's cry, interested in the face of my own daughter!'

Meeting II

Though he sits on a red velvet chair in a large hall, the yogi is dressed in rags, a scruffy turban around his head.[5] A woman stands behind him, holding an outrageously large palm leaf fan with which, despite the whirring electric fan overhead, she fans him. The hall is part of an ashram constructed by a wealthy benefactor. On the other side of the compound there is a mandir where bhajans *are sung and a canteen where devotees sit on the floor to eat rice and curry off banana leaves. There are small concrete rooms where visitors are accommodated.*

Although his devotees refer to him as Bhagavan, *or Lord, the yogi reserves the term for a famous sage who used to live in the same town, and continues to refer to himself as 'this beggar'. He laughs uproariously at the stories the devotees tell about him. 'Father's grace!' he says, dismissing tales of healings, blissful experiences, and wishes come true. 'Why have you come to see this beggar?' he demands of those in the* darshan *line that shuffles past him twice a day after the* bhajan sessions. Many of the people do not respond but some, Indians and foreigners, stop to talk, to put a question, or seek advice.

'Do you meditate?' asks a tall angular Frenchman. 'Yes', responds the yogi, 'this beggar is meditating now.'

'Why do you meditate?' a German woman asks. 'To maintain this beggar's love,' replies the yogi.

'The Vedas say that the liberated sage has no need of meditation', a grey-haired Indian man comments. 'This beggar is not meditating,' says the yogi.

'But you just said', the Frenchman interrupts, 'that you were meditating.'

'This beggar did', says the yogi with a bellow of laughter, 'but he is not meditating.' The Frenchman, to the yogi's amusement, looks exasperated. He struggles to frame a question but the yogi continues, 'Meditation is occurring continuously, without a break, so intensely that there is no room for the thought I am meditating. There is a state of constant integrated awareness.'

'What is the nature of this awareness?' asks the German woman. 'Awareness is attention, and pure awareness is that which remains when all that distracts attention, all self-identifications, are given up as false. Pure awareness is Saccidananda,' says the yogi.

'Existence-consciousness-bliss,' translates the Indian man.

'How can you sit there in bliss, speaking of love, but doing nothing to change the poverty and suffering around you?' demands a young American woman. 'What is it you want to change?' the yogi asks her. 'The environment is being destroyed', replies the young woman, 'and millions starve, whilst others die from the effects of over-indulgence.' 'So what would you change?' the yogi asks again. 'The destructive ways that people are living.' 'And why are they living that way?' questions the yogi. 'Because of their own desires and fears.' 'Yes', says the yogi, 'and to help those people you must be free of desire and fear. When you have seen through every desire, and dismantled every fear, that which remains is desireless and fearless. It has no desire to help and yet it offers true help, for it points to reality. Relatively speaking, what causes suffering is wrong, and the alleviation of suffering is right. But from the perspective of the Absolute, what brings you back to reality is right, and what dims reality is wrong.' The woman ponders the answer for a few minutes, and then asks another question. 'How can I know that what you call reality is not just a construct of your own mind, your own culture?' The yogi roars with laughter, 'You cannot,' he says. 'This idea of "knowing" must be surrendered. The Truth is. All is Truth.'

You will not experience the arbitrary nature of your beliefs by reading more scientific, analytical books, or just by thinking about them. Something or someone outside of yourself must jolt you into opening your eyes, perhaps just for a moment, to an aspect of reality that does not fit comfortably into your present belief structure. If this happens, hang onto it. Expand on it, explore it. Do not suppress it and deny it. Rather ask whether some of your previously held beliefs need to be opened up to make room for a richer reality.[6]

Notes

1. The material in this first part of the epilogue is based on printed material from Plan International, the Indian Council for Child Welfare (Tamil Nadu), the Tamil Nadu Government, and my own experience when visiting villages where female infanticide was practised. Names have been changed.
2. Quoted from material prepared by Plan International Australia in 1997 to publicise their work. Plan International Australia works in conjunction with partner agencies in India – the Indian Council for Child Welfare and the Community Services Guild – to implement projects aimed at reducing female infanticide and raising the perceived value of girls and women. The projects adopt a holistic approach and include a number of components such as vocational training, health care, credit/saving funds, women's groups, literacy classes, home study units, income generation, counselling and attitudinal change for both men and women.
3. The practice of leaving the village seems to be relatively recent and is related to the increase in prosecutions for infanticide. Infanticide is illegal, and agencies working on this issue are often faced with conflicting demands. On the one hand, they need to gain the trust of villagers in order to work with them; on the other hand, they do not wish to be party to illegal acts and may consider prosecutions as a deterrent against future infanticides.
4. This response is quoted from Venkatachalam and Srinivasan (1993:50), who found that many female respondents in their research perceived their own lives as so harsh, they wished to protect their daughters from a similar fate. The women's logic is analogous to the logic employed in contemporary Western constructions of infanticide for grossly handicapped infants.
5. The material in this second part of the epilogue is written largely from memory. Since, as far as I am aware, there are no books, to date, presenting the teachings of the yogi whom I have described, I have checked the statements attributed to him from memory against the works of other advaitic teachers such as Sri Ramana Maharshi, Sri Nisargadatta Maharaj and Yogaswamigal, and have utilised their teachings to ensure accuracy of expression.
6. Taylor (1980).

Appendix
Female Infanticide in India

Having included in both the prologue and epilogue brief glimpses of the problem of female infanticide in India, I offer in this appendix a deeper analysis of the issue. Female infanticide persists in India today, although it has been illegal in all states for over one hundred years. It is by no means a common practice, but it represents the extreme end of a spectrum of discrimination against girl children that is pervasive.[1] Female infanticide occurred in India before colonial rule, but the ensuing political waves of colonisation, independence, modernisation and globalisation have all had an impact on its construction in contemporary India.

The British became concerned about female infanticide in India during the late eighteenth century, when as an expanding colonial power, they sought to re-order first the economy and then the civil administration of the sub-continent to their own economic and political advantage. As mentioned in chapter one, practices such as female infanticide, *sati* (widow burning) and child marriage provided legitimisation for colonial intervention. One of the important signifiers of the 'good' society adopted by the British as a point of entry for their reconstruction of Indian society was 'the protection of women' (Spivak, 1988:298). Another was religion, and these discourses, whether through orientalist tendencies, as Said (1979) might suggest, or not, became inextricably intertwined. There can be no pretence that the Hindu scriptures condone female infanticide, although the existence of direct scriptural sanction for *sati* was (and still is) the subject of much dispute. However, a high degree of gender differentiation in which men were given authority over women, and sons were favoured over daughters, did appear to be sanctioned by certain passages from Hindu sacred texts.[2] This was perceived as laying the foundation for the secondary social status of women, and indirectly for the grossly discriminatory practices which became the focus of British concern.

Although the practices of female infanticide and *sati* were not universal, but confined to incidents within certain areas of India,[3] by conflating incidents (*ghatana*) with custom or tradition (*pratha*),[4] the British constructed an entry point for colonial interference, legislation and control in the private sphere. Whilst certainly not advocating these discriminatory practices against women and girl children, it is important to understand how, within colonial India, discourse concerned with the rights and status of women was inscribed with the colonial agenda of the British (Spivak, 1988). Such discourse must be 'read against the grain',[5] so that its 'humanitarianism', or supposed 'feminism', can be interpreted within the broader context of that colonial-era social restructuring, from land ownership to administration, which disrupted certain traditional patriarchal practices *in order to replace them with others*. Within this colonial horizon, a number of well known (male) Indian reformers, later anti-colonialists or nationalists, responded by making the status of women central to their own projects of opposing the British and modernising India on their terms.[6] Thus, from the colonial era the discourses concerning the rights and status of women, religion, nationalism and modernity became intertwined and entangled.

The response of the British was to eventually make female infanticide, along with *sati* and child marriage, illegal. Almost one hundred years after the 'discovery' of female infanticide by a colonial official, Jonathan Duncan, in Uttar Pradesh in 1789, the British government passed the Infanticide Act of 1870 officially outlawing the practice (Miller, 1981:50-51).[7] The difficulties of actually eradicating infanticide, however, were related not just to political concerns but to the construction of gender and ethnicity within the horizon of colonial India. Miller suggests that 'the general attitude of the British toward the Rajputs and other 'manly' groups of northern India was inhibiting, and it was such people as these who were mainly guilty of practicing [female] infanticide' (ibid p. 51). It seems that female infanticide was a phenomenon primarily of 'the higher social groups of the North' (ibid, p. 55).[8]

The practice seemed, according to the historians, to have arisen from overly stringent requirements for prospective husbands, and from the economic pressures of the dowry system. Rather than be economically ruined by the excessive demands of dowry, socially embarrassed by marrying a daughter to a man of lower social status or suffering the ongoing humiliation of unmarried daughters at home, these social groups solved their dilemma by killing their daughters shortly after birth. The motivation was generally summed up as 'pride and purse' (Miller, 1981:56; Gaur, 1989:83-102).[9]

This type of widely accepted analysis of the problem obscures its gendered construction. Clearly the motivations proposed are offered from a male standpoint, and the women's perspective is not recorded. It was men who paid dowries, it was generally women who disposed of the infants, by poisoning, suffocation or exposure soon after birth. The British (male) colonial officers collected their information from the males of the groups concerned. A gendered analysis of the situation suggests that the motivation may have been more accurately summed up as 'patriarchy, pride and purse', or perhaps 'power, pride, and purse'.

The 'pride and purse' interpretation, however, allowed the British to cast themselves in a positive role as 'white men, protecting brown women from brown men' (Spivak, 1988). Through such legitimating ruses the patriarchal British colonial service was able to construct itself as the bearer of 'civilisation', assuming the 'white man's burden'. This deception was aided by the different status accorded to white women in the colonies compared to their status in Britain (George, 1993), and by the different construction of infanticide in Britain. For it must be noted here that, during the colonial era, infanticide was not an uncommon practice in Britain. In 1845, Benjamin Disraeli, with delightful irony, wrote in his novel *Sybil:* 'Infanticide is practised as extensively and legally in England as it is on the banks of the Ganges; a circumstance which apparently has not yet engaged the attention of the Society for the Propagation of the Gospel in Foreign Parts' (cited in Rose, 1986:36).

In Britain infanticide was practiced primarily by the lower social classes in response to poverty and illegitimacy, or 'vice' as it was commonly referred to. Rose, describing the situation in Britain says that 'in the early nineteenth century infant life was held cheap, especially bastards' (ibid, p. 35). The dominant or 'official' discourse on infanticide in Britain was constructed from the subjective position of the ruling upper class male in opposition to the lower class female. It was used to legitimise existing constructions of both class and gender, including the controlling notions of 'good' and 'bad' women, meaning in this context, decent married paupers and unmarried 'fornicators' or 'adulterers' (ibid, p. 31). Although the subject position of the women involved in infanticide was heavily circumscribed, the court and welfare systems did provide limited opportunities for them to represent themselves. Both male and female infants seem to have been equally at risk if construed as 'bastards'.

The different position of the discursive subject in the discourse on infanticide in India led to a focus on race rather than gender and class. It seems to have been constructed from the subjective position of British, Christian colonial male in opposition to the Indian Hindu male, and was, as mentioned above, used to legitimise colonial (administrative and missionary) restructuring of 'native' discourse. The absence of a subjective position for Indian women, and the fact that infanticide was mainly perpetrated upon female infants, allowed for the interpretation of Indian women as victims, requiring British protection from Indian men. Since this provided useful ideological legitimation for the colonial enterprise, comparatively little effort was made by the British to eradicate female infanticide. According to Panigrahi (1976:145), the British perception of the Rajputs as a 'martial race', and their reliance on Rajput participation in the Indian army, made the British reluctant to 'offend their sensibilities', so for some time the British invoked 'the inviolability of the home' (Miller, 1981:52) as the rationale for not acting more vigorously on female infanticide.

Within the context of colonial India, it can be seen that the construction of gender, race, modernity and nationality intersected, providing the British with a means of casting Indians as 'barbarous others' in need of British rule. For the Indian (male) reformers who emerged from the privileged literati, the low status of women became a signifier of the backwardness of both India and Hinduism. The reconstruction of women by these (male) Indian modernisers therefore became one of the signifiers of modernity and of India as a modern nation. Koylaschander Bose, for example, writing of Indian women of his time (1846) suggested that: 'She must be refined, reorganised, recast regenerated . . .' (quoted in Sangari and Vaid, 1993:1). For other Indian males such as the Rajputs, the status of women became entangled with discourses of ethnicity (as distinct from nationalism) and cultural independence which continue to the present day.[10] What does seem clear is that the discourses concerning the status and rights of women, whether wielded by male British colonialists or by male Indian reformers, were largely concerned with the reconstruction of gender for the purpose of reconstituting patriarchies across all levels of society (Sangari and Vaid, 1993:6). If the British took action to outlaw some of the more extreme patriarchal practices of traditional Indian society, they did so as part of the process of reconstituting that society within the patriarchal framework of colonialism and capitalism.

The British deliberately, though at times inadvertently, cut across traditional caste, religious and ethnic boundaries in order to codify a single, homogenised, 'unifying' system of administration and law, as well as to create classes of Indians who could both rule (for the British) and be ruled. The reconstruction of gender was only one among several reconstructive projects occurring at the time which interacted with each other in complex ways, these often tending to exacerbate existing inequalities of both gender and caste.[11] In matters of law 'the colonial regime codified the customs of the dominant land owning and other rural groups. This froze particular customs into universal laws and gave a juridical sanction to certain patriarchal practices regarding marriage, succession and adoption' (ibid, p. 7). In addition it was often high caste Hindu norms which were codified rather than the customary practices of other groups, and this further disadvantaged 'all Hindu women whether rural or urban' (ibid).

Within this fluid context, Indians themselves were not passive recipients of British-constructed identities. There was a multiplicity of subject positions from which some joined the modernising trend and jockeyed for power in the reconstitution of traditional hierarchies, while others opposed the colonial impact by attempting to re-assert traditional identities. For the purpose of focussing on gender, I have so far homogenised other identities, using the term 'Indian' and at times 'Hindu'. But within the historical context, the construction of these 'Indian' and 'Hindu' identities was only just beginning.

A major factor in the colonial reconstruction undertaken on the sub-continent, was the melding together of multiple ethnic and religious identities to create the imagined community of 'India' under one colonial administrative system.[12] Simultaneously, the reconstruction of religious discourse was undertaken to create a unitary religion of 'Hinduism' (in the mould of the Christian/British understanding of religion) from the existing plurality of non-Islamic rituals, practices and texts. This task, which was also taken up by Indian reformers (such as Rammohun Roy[13] who initiated the *Brahmo Samaj*), exacerbated tensions between the existing Islamic communities and these imagined communities which resulted from the articulation of the new nationalist, and Hindu discursive positions and identity constructs. Since the Indian nation was formed within the horizon of the modernising project, the rise of Indian nationalism and particularly the post-independence path after Gandhi's assassination, tended to encode as normative the patriarchal values of the modern capitalist rather than traditional society. Both the construction of a national Indian identity and the construction of the modern nation state of India have affected on women and men differently.

The construction of female infanticide in the contemporary world operates in a different context. In Western, or 'developed', countries pregnancy and birth have been reconstructed as 'medical events' and brought under the supervision of that profession. Changing sexual mores and gender roles, access to reliable contraception, foetal screening, abortion and falling rates of infant and maternal mortality have all contributed to the greatly reduced occurrence of infanticide. The remainder has been constructed largely as the concern of bioethics, dealing as it does with the continued provision of life-support systems for infants with gross abnormalities. Such incidents of infanticide are no longer read in terms of 'vice', but rather in terms of a 'concern' which weighs the prospective quality of life of the infant against possible suffering. This contrasts strongly with the residue of socially disapproved incidents of infanticide in Western nations, resulting from severe physical abuse. This form of infanticide is still constructed in terms of 'vice', albeit a different kind of vice from the eighteenth century British category. Different, though no less far-reaching, changes on the Indian sub-continent have also reconstructed infanticide in that context.

In 1986 female infanticide was 'rediscovered' by the national weekly, *India Today*[14] in Madurai district, later research also uncovering its practice in other states. The construction of the discourse is revealing. The media reports identified dowry as the main cause (Krishnan, 1991:34), the implication being that this outdated traditional practice, already outlawed (by legislation that is difficult to enforce, even if the attempt is made), needs to be abolished in practice. However, the negative influence of two other factors which defy this modernist interpretation was also acknowledged: (a) the greatly increased availability of consumer goods, which appears to have exacerbated the impact of the dowry system – motor scooters, televisions, videos, refrigerators and other consumer items are now common amongst the increasing dowry demands (Krishnan, 1991:38); and (b) the spread of the dowry custom to social groups, particularly the scheduled castes (SC) and tribes (ST), who previously did not pay dowry. Venkatachalam and Srinivasan (1993:42) describe the complete reversal of custom amongst tribal groups:

> It is an irony to see that even the ST community has started to consider the female as a liability because of dowry. Even a decade before, in most of the tribal communities, the bridegroom had to pay a bride price to get the hand of the girl and the expenditure for the girl's parents was only the feast on the wedding day. It is disheartening to see that the present day mores have an impact even on tribal culture due to this unhealthy custom which is getting imbibed gradually into their culture too.

Significantly, however, most analyses of female infanticide by women researchers conclude that dowry is not a primary causal factor but an indicator, along with the rising number of 'dowry deaths',[15] of the increasing commodification of women in the modern Indian state. Both Vasant (1991a:74) and Krishnan (1991:41-42) mention the impact of the media on the construction of gender. The cinema, and increasingly video and television, through both programmatic and advertising material, have played an important part in establishing the consumer culture and in reconstructing gender roles. Women are offered two conflicting images, one of the 'bad modern girl' in Western dress who is sexually exploitable, and the other of the 'good traditional' wife and mother who is a devoted but simple creature (Krishnan, 1991:41-42). The combination of these images of women, combined with the promotion of positive images of heterosexually active males, seems to have increased the perceived need to discipline girls, while leading to a relaxation of some of the traditional controls on male sexual behaviour. In Venkatachalam and Srinivasan (1993:39) the vulnerability of girls to sexual attack was given by women as a reason both for not sending their daughters to school and for the necessity of an early marriage as soon as they reach puberty.

The reorganisation of labour and agriculture has also played a role in reducing the 'value' of females. Miller (1981:28) suggests a more benign attitude to daughters in the south of India due to the prevalence of swidden and wet-rice cultivation which creates a high demand for female labour. Venkatachalam and Srinivasan (1993:38) suggest that this may still hold for 'low income groups, where girls . . . start working at a very early age and bring home their earnings' but, additionally, forces such as the disruption of agricultural practices through changing cropping patterns,[16] the centralisation of land ownership, the mechanisation of agricultural work, natural and man-made environmental changes[17] and so forth, have combined to erode the 'asset value' of girls. Privatisation of the traditional village commons and forests has closed economic options such as breeding and grazing animals (Krishnan, 1991:38) or the collection of forest products, previously available to girls in some social groups as an independent source of income. The difficulty in finding any paid work, the absence of property rights for women and the fragmentation through inheritance of already small land holdings, all exacerbate the economic plight of women and increase the perception of marriage as the only path to survival.

Within marriage, traditional ideologies such as *pativratya* (Dhruvarajan, 1989) – the subordination of the woman to her husband – exist in tension with the changing roles and employment opportunities arising from modernisation, these differentially affecting men and women and reshaping existing definitions of gender (Dass, 1994:57). Even where employment opportunities favour women over men, the resulting replacement of the male as the family provider within an institutional marriage which subordinates the woman, may lead to an intensified gender conflict that translates into violence against women (ibid, pp. 58, 60).

Traditional cultural practices and beliefs[18] perpetuate the widespread perception that daughters are a liability while sons are an asset. A Telegu proverb *Bringing up a girl is watering a neighbour's plant*, sums up this perception.

It appears that the preference for sons is widespread and not confined to any particular class or caste. As Dass notes: 'In countries such as India, all institutions may be described as having a double articulation in both tradition and modernity' (ibid, p. 53), and this leads to ambiguities and contradictions. One such ambiguity, which has impacted negatively on the survival of female foetuses/infants, arises from the articulation of the Government's campaigns for reduction in family size, with the traditional preference for sons. Government publicity campaigns suggest that the 'ideal family' is one male and one female child, but Venkatachalam and Srinivasan (1993:41) found most of the families in their study had one female and two male children, a number of female infants (in this study, foetuses in the broader context) being likely to have been killed to reach this position. Since the poorer and less-educated social groups have inferior access to contraception and abortion, or to amniocentesis, scanning and other tests which can determine the sex of a foetus,[19] their expression of this widespread cultural devaluation of females is more likely to find expression through female infanticide.

In India as elsewhere, the lower caste and poor communities are confronted with 'the failure of the promises of tradition *and* modernity' (Dass, 1994:56). Their lives trace out the ambiguities arising from the rupture of traditional frameworks by modernity. Women, as the perceived bearers of cultural or communal identities, are particularly subject to the tension between these two frameworks.

> [T]he new settings of the school and the work place, as well as . . . the new forms of culture that are being produced provide opportunities for women to imagine other stories for their lives. Simultaneously the configuration of material conditions such as the working of the economy and the reproduction of inequalities in the family make it difficult for most women to realise any other stories except the ones transmitted to them through their traditions (Dass, 1994:61).

This traditional/modern dichotomy can be misleading as well as illuminating. If teased apart, it reveals the construction of identities as 'an interaction between economic, political, socio-cultural and religious structures' (Bhasin, Menon and Khan, 1994:v) and discourses, some of which may operate on individual lives only indirectly. In the global domain, the integration of India into the world economy by means of IMF or World Bank structural adjustment programs causes the shadow of global economic discourse to fall across the lives of women in India. As the national economy becomes more export-oriented and internal spending cuts slash health, welfare, education or nutrition programs, the negative impact is felt more by women than men, and the feminisation of poverty emerges hand in hand with accelerated investment, modernisation, and globalisation.[20]

If the commodification of women is related to female infanticide, then might we not trace it, as Nandy (1987c) does in the case of *sati*, to 'the emergence of market morality as the only moral principle in social relations, . . . [due to] the emergence of modern political economy as the only organising principle of material life'? There seems little doubt that as high economic growth rates and capital inflows promote rapid modernisation, the associated modern constructions of identity and lifestyle compete with, and often displace, traditional patterns of living and identity based on kinship and interdependence.

Whilst modernist interpretations of infanticide read it as the pathological expression of outdated tradition, another possible interpretation would be to see it as the pathological expression of modernity or, more accurately still, the pathological articulation of modernity and tradition in contemporary India. For many women trapped in the dual marginalisation of modernity and tradition, the situation is one of conflicting loyalties. The Women's Movement in India has long campaigned against issues such as dowry deaths, female infanticide and domestic violence in order to establish a porous identity construct of (Indian) 'women' which traverses ethnic and religious divisions. However, the rising Hindu nationalist parties have also developed campaigns around the same issues in order to win the allegiance of women for the construction of fundamentalist, non-porous Hindu identities which deal with the relativisation of identity in the global context. The nationalist parties do this by constructing a rigid 'religiously' defined discourse which prescribes a home-bound role for good Hindu women and excludes others from the imagined, exclusive, Hindu community and nation. In the absence of other alternatives, the situation for women can be (mis)represented as choosing between one's 'womanness' and one's religion or culture. Although not all regions of India are similarly afflicted by the extremes of fundamentalism and communalism, the articulation of discourses, one to another, requires a re-presentation, not only of women, but of spirituality, of development and of politics, in order to weld together a libratory context in which any one of these discourses may give rise to a libratory praxis.

Just as in the colonial context female infanticide was used to create an unbridgeable difference between the British and the Indians in order to justify the imposition of Britain's 'civilising influence', so failure to recognise the varied constructions of (m)other love under certain circumstances may lead to the justifications for the further imposition of 'development', or modernisation, in contemporary India. But do the structural adjustment programs which mark the globalisation of the Indian economy stand in causative or curative relationship to issues such as female infanticide? Do they, as instruments of foreign capital penetration and modernisation, simply 'take away the meaning of life of millions . . . reduc[ing] them to being cogs in the wheels of an enormous, homogenising machine, as we further push to the wall all those who are already living at the margins of cultural survival' (Nandy, 1987c)[21] or do they still open the way to the liberal humanist dream of global equality, progress and inclusion for all?

The voices of women committing infanticide are more disturbing than these sociological ponderings might convey. The cost of raising children and the expense of the dowry for girls are frequently cited as motivations for infanticide, but other factors emerge. Venkatachalam and Srinivasan (1993:42) cite their respondents' discussion of sexual practices within the extended family, domestic violence and the onerous work load of women whose responsibilities include collecting firewood, fodder and water (Krishnan, 1991:40), tasks made infinitely more difficult and time-consuming in the face of deforestation, recurrent drought and increasing environmental destruction.[22] Several of the respondents claim that they were pressured by husband or family members to commit infanticide (Venkatachalam and Srinivasan, 1993:50), but some seem to have been under no direct coercion other than the prevailing ideologies which devalue women[23] and construct lifeworlds of extraordinary physical harshness. Many, disturbingly, express neither grief nor remorse.

Is infanticide of a newborn different in kind or merely in degree from aborting a female foetus after amniocentesis? Are the women moral agents or passive victims? Morgan (1988) refers to 'moral madness' as the condition induced in women living in a patriarchal society, suggesting that the moral double binds created for women by patriarchal ideology can be resolved, in some cases, only through insanity. Is female infanticide a symptom of this condition in which a woman is set up to believe that she can be a 'good' wife and mother (to her sons) by destroying her own image in the form of her daughters? The woman I saw on the bridge: was she, as the law would label her, a murderer? Was she involved in some heinous crime or in a courageous act of protest? If she had already preserved four daughters, was the destruction of the fifth a capitulation to the moral madness of patriarchal ideology, a common sense decision concerning her own reproductive rights or acquiescence to impossible economic and environmental pressures?

Notes

1. The following quotation from *India Today*, XI:11, 15 June 1986, provides a summary of the facts:

    India is the only country in the world where the ratio of women to men has been declining over the years. The sex ratio declined from 972 females per 1,000 males in 1901 to 935 in 1981. And India is one of a handful of countries where female infant mortality exceeds that of the male notwithstanding the fact that the female child is biologically stronger at birth.

Girl babies are breast-fed less frequently, and for a shorter duration than boy babies. When they grow up, they are provided [with] less nutrition than their brothers. A recent survey of infants, toddlers and pre-schoolers showed that within their combined age groups, 71 per cent of females suffered from severe malnutrition, as against 28 per cent of the males. A related statistic reveals that boys are taken to hospital for treatment of common diseases in twice the number as girls. Boys do not fall ill more frequently than girls, they are merely provided more health care by parents who value sons more than daughters.

In the widening gender gap in India the female literacy rate – 24.88 per cent – is barely half that of males – 46.74 per cent. And the gap continues to widen. In the 6-14 age group, nearly 84 per cent of boys are enrolled in schools, as against 54 per cent in the case of girls. The plight of India's girls aged 15 and under – about 140 million of them – cries out . . . for caring and sensitive attention.

2. A situation not dissimilar to Christianity, it should be noted.
3. According to Miller (1981:53-4) in colonial times:

   . . . female infanticide was confined mainly to the northern part of India from Gujarat in the west to the eastern border of present-day Uttar Pradesh the only example of infanticide from north eastern India is that of the tribal Nagas. Examples from the area south of the Central Provinces (Madhya Pradesh today) are few: the Todas of the Nilgiri Hills in the state of Madras; mention of its occurrence in Vizakhapatam District of the present state of Andhra Pradesh; and the tribal Khonds of what is now mostly Koraput district in the state of Orissa. These scattered examples of infanticide outside North India are provocative cases demanding their own explanation.

   It is interesting to note the changed distribution today. Infanticide seems more frequent in the southern state of Tamil Nadu, although it continues in Rajasthan and seems to be spreading in Bihar. The present distribution seems as related to economic factors – extreme poverty and destitution – as to traditional cultural factors.

4. See Nandy (1987c). Nandy was actually referring to the practice of *sati*, but the same would seem to hold true for female infanticide. Just as in Britain over the same historical period, infanticide was relatively common, but could not correctly be referred to as a 'custom' of the British, which was the logical consequence of Christian scriptural injunctions. So, with respect to India, there is a flaw in the logic that presents female infanticide as an Indian or Hindu custom.
5. Mohanty (1991) writes of this way of reading, although not with particular reference to infanticide.
6. I am thinking here of reformers such as Rammohun Roy, the founder of the Brahmo Samaj (Killingley, 1993).
7. Venkatachalam and Srinivasan (1993:19) cite Kali Kinkar Datta from his book *A Social History of Modern India* (1875) to suggest that the East India Company's officers took action much earlier. In the Bengal Regulation XXI of 1795 (later extended by Regulation III of 1804) and Regulation VI of 1802, female infanticides were declared murders. However, Datta notes that 'detection was not an easy task'. More optimistically, he continues: 'these practices gradually disappeared throughout the country with the growth of education and thanks to the energetic efforts of some "military political officers"'.
8. Some writers (for example Dickeman, 1976:2) suggest that this may have been due to the British lack of interest in collecting data amongst the lower castes, but Miller (1981) suggests that, in fact, the census data collected by the British was class/caste specific. Whilst the problem is probably one of degree in areas where infanticide was endemic, it seems likely that it was more frequent amongst the

higher social groups, even to the extreme cases of villages where no daughters at all were preserved (Miller, 1981:55).

9. Gaur (1984:83-102) gives much detail on the social difficulties of finding appropriate husbands for girls, particularly amongst the higher castes, and the complexities of the cost of the marriage which were not solely due to dowry but to other customs as well.

10. See, for example, analyses of Roop Kanwar's *sati* in 1987 and the power play between the Central and State (Rajasthan) Governments that pitted nationality against ethnicity. The *Manushi* (1987, 42/43) issue on *sati* provides many insights into the political, traditional and social dimensions of the practice.

11. For example, the introduction of individual property rights led to a concentration of property in the hands of males from the dominant land-owning groups, this 'further impoverished both tenants and agricultural labour' (Sangari and Vaid, 1993:6), and marginalised women belonging to these groups, as well as female members of the propertied elite.

12. At the time to which I am referring, this imagined community of India included both Pakistan and Bangladesh.

13. Killingley (1993) suggests that Roy was probably the first 'Hindu' to use the term in a self-referential way to describe his religious affiliation. Originally the term 'Hindu' was a geographic term, referring to the region and peoples around the Indus valley.

14. *India Today*, 1986, XI:11, 1-15th June.

15. See Kumar (1985); Stone and James (1995:125-134). Dowry deaths, or dowry murders, have been increasing in India. They occur most often in arranged marriages and involve women being murdered, usually burned to death, by their husbands or in-laws who are dissatisfied with the dowry payments made by the wives' families.

16. For example, the change to sugar cane, which is a less labour-intensive and more water-intensive crop, or the move to export-oriented crops.

17. These include persistent drought brought about, at least in part, by the damming of rivers, widespread deforestation and the drawing of (particularly irrigation) water from tube wells which lowers the water table, causes salination and eventually dries up the wells.

18. The patriarchal devaluation of females seems to have ancient roots in the Indian tradition. Although it is suggested that in pre-Vedic times women enjoyed 'equal rights with men from education to inheritance' (Venkatachalam and Srinivasan, 1993:30), this changed in the Vedic era. In the Atharva Veda there are descriptions of 'charms and rituals to ensure the birth of a son in preference to that of a daughter' (Krishnan, 1991:34) and the Manu Shastra mentions that 'a woman must be her father's shadow in childhood, her husband's in her youth, her son's in old age' (cited in Venkatachalam and Srinivasan, 1993:30).

19. Sex-determination of foetuses, and the selective (female) abortions that often follow, have been controversial issues in India, with many women's organisations campaigning, successfully in some states, for a ban on amniocentesis (Kishwar, 1995).

20. See Bakker (1994); Vickers (1991) particularly chapters 1,2, and 3; Danahar (1994) particularly chapters 23 and 24.

21. Nandy (1987c) is writing about the practice of *sati* but his argument can equally be applied to female infanticide.

22. See Agarwal's (1985:372) section on 'Environment and Women'. He argues that:

The maximum impact of the destruction of biomass sources is on women. Women in all rural cultures are affected, especially women from poor landless, marginal and small farm families. Seen from the point of view of these women, it can be argued that all development is ignorant of women's needs at best, and anti-women at worst, literally designed to increase their work burden.

23. One of the effects of the ideology of *pativrata*, which constructs a particular constellation of female personality traits, is that it militates against decisive moral action in the face of disapproval by the husband, family or community (Dhruvrajan, 1989).

Select Bibliography

This bibliography contains only a selection of the more important references used in the book. For the full bibliography please visit www.ashgate.com.

Abu-Lughod, J. (1991) 'Going Beyond Global Babble', in A. King (ed.) *Culture, Globalization and the World-System*, Macmillan, London, pp. 131-138.
Bauman, Z. (1993) *Postmodern Ethics*, Blackwell, Oxford.
Bauman, Z. (1995) *Life in Fragments*, Blackwell, Oxford.
Berry, P. (1992) Introduction in P. Berry and A. Wernick (eds) *Shadow of Spirit: Postmodernism and Religion*, Routledge, London, pp. 1-10.
Beyer, P. (1994) *Religion and Globalization*, Sage, London.
Blaney, D, and Inayatullah, N. (1994) 'Prelude to a Conversation of Cultures in International Society? Todorov and Nandy on the Possibility of Dialogue', *Alternatives*, 19, pp. 23-51.
Brennan, T. (1992) *The Interpretation of the Flesh: Freud and Femininity*, Routledge, London.
Brennan, T. (1993b) *History After Lacan*, Routledge, London.
Buber, M. (1994) *I and Thou*, tr. by Ronald Smith, T. and T. Clark, Edinburgh. First published 1923.
Cixous, H. (1990) *Reading With Clarice Lispector*, tr. by V. Conley, University of Minnesota Press, Minneapolis.
Coomaraswamy, A. (1943) *Hinduism and Buddhism*, Philosophical Library, New York.
Coomaraswamy, A. (1981) *Sources of Wisdom*, Ministry of Cultural Affairs, Sri Lanka.
Cowan, J. (1989) *Mysteries of the Dreaming*, Unity Press, Lindfield, New South Wales.
Crawford, J. (1993) *The Sustainable Self: An Inquiry into the Metaphysics of Sustainability and the Self*, Environmental Paper No. 10, Graduate School of Environmental Science, Monash University, Melbourne.
Crawford, J. (1995) 'Weaving Webs', *Cappuccino Papers*, 1, pp. 18-21.
Derrida, J. (1976) *Of Grammatology*, The Johns Hopkins University Press, Baltimore.
Derrida, J. (1978) 'Violence and Metaphysics: An Essay on the Thought of Emmanuel Levinas', in *Writing and Difference*, tr. by Alan Bass, Routledge and Kegan Paul, London, pp. 79-153.
Derrida, J. (1981) *Positions*, tr. by A. Bass, University of Chicago Press, Chicago.

Derrida, J. (1989) 'How to Avoid speaking: Denials', in S. Budick *et al* (eds) *Languages of the Unsayable: The Play of Negativity in Literature and Literary Theory*, Columbia University Press, New York.

Derrida, J. (1991) '"Eating Well", or the Calculation of the Subject: An Interview with Jacques Derrida', in E. Cadava, P. Connor and J. Nancy (eds) *Who Comes After the Subject?*, Routledge, New York.

Derrida, J. (1992) 'Force of Law: The "Mystical Foundation of Authority"', in D. Cornell, M. Rosenfeld and D. Carlson (eds), *Deconstruction and the Possibility of Justice*, Routledge, New York.

Donovan, J. (1996) 'Ecofeminist Literary Criticism: Reading the Orange', *Hypatia*, 11:2, pp. 161-184.

Dunkley, G. (1997) *The Free Trade Adventure: The Uruguay Round and Globalism – A Critique*, Melbourne University Press, Melbourne.

Falk, R. (1992) *Explorations at the Edge of Time*, Temple University Press, Philadelphia.

Falk, R. (1993a) 'Politically Engaged Spirituality in an Emerging Global Civil Society', *ReVision*, 15:3, pp. 137-144.

Falk, R. (1993b) 'Democratising, internationalising, and globalising: a collage of blurred images', *Third World Quarterly*, 13:4, pp. 627-640.

Forman, R. (1990) *The Problem of Pure Consciousness*, Oxford University Press, New York.

Foucault, M. (1988) 'Technologies of the Self', in *Technologies of the Self: Seminar with Michel Foucault*, L. Martin, H. Gutman and P. Hutton (eds) University of Massachusetts Press, Amherst.

Fox, W. (1990) *Towards a Transpersonal Psychology*, Shambhala, Boston.

Gilligan, C. (1982) *In A Different Voice*, Harvard University Press, Cambridge, Massachusetts.

Gilligan, C. (1986a) 'Remapping the moral domain: New images of the self in relationship', in T. Heller, *et al* (eds) *Reconstructing Individualism: Autonomy, Individuality, and the Self in Western Thought*, Stanford University Press, Stanford.

Gilligan, C. (1986b) 'Exit-voice dilemmas in adolescence development', in A. Forley, *et al* (eds) *Development, Democracy, and the Art of Trespassing: Essays in Honour of Albert O. Hirschman*, University of Notre Dame Press, Notre Dame.

Gilligan, C. (1987) 'Adolescent development reconsidered', in C. Irwin (ed.) *Adolescent Social Behaviour and Health*, Jossey-Bass, San Francisco.

Gilligan, C. *et al* (1990) 'Moral Development Beyond Adolescence', in C. Alexander and E. Langer (eds) *Higher Stages of Human Development*, Oxford University Press, New York.

Heidegger, M. (1958), *The Question of Being*, tr. by W. Kenback and J. Wilde, Tvayne Publications, New York.

hooks, b. (1990) 'Postmodern Blackness', in *Yearning, Race, Gender, and Cultural Politics*, South End Press, Boston.
Huntington, S. (1993) 'The Clash of Civilizations?', *Foreign Affairs*, Summer.
Inchausti, R. (1991) *The Ignorant Perfection of Ordinary People*, State University of New York Press, Albany.
Kohlberg, L. and Ryncarz, R. (1990) 'Beyond Justice Reasoning', in C. Alexander and E. Langer (eds) *Higher Stages of Human Development*, Oxford University Press, New York.
Levinas, E. (1979) *Totality and Infinity*, tr. by A. Lingis, Duquesne University Press, Pittsburgh.
Levinas, E. (1981) *Otherwise than Being or Beyond Essence*, tr. by A. Lingis, Martinus Nijhoff, The Hague.
Levinas, E. (1985) *Ethics and Infinity*, Duquesne University Press, Pittsburgh.
Levinas, E. (1993) *Outside the Subject*, tr. by M. Smith, The Athlone Press, London.
Levinas, E. (1995) 'Ethics of the Infinite', in R. Kearney (ed.) *States of Mind: Dialogues with Contemporary Thinkers on the European Mind*, Manchester University Press, Manchester, pp. 177-199.
Lonergan, B. (1972) *Method in Theology*, Herder and Herder, New York.
Loy, D. (1988) *Nonduality: A Study in Comparative Philosophy*, Yale University Press, New Haven.
Lugones, M. (1989) 'Playfulness, "World" – Travelling and Loving Perception', in A. Garry and M. Pearsall (eds) *Women, Knowledge and Reality*, Unwin Hyman, Boston.
Lugones, M. (1991) 'On the Logic of Pluralist Feminism', in C. Card (ed.) *Feminist Ethics*, University Press of Kansas, pp. 30-44.
Lyotard, J. (1988) *The Differend: Phrases in Dispute*, University of Minnesota Press, Minneapolis.
Lyotard, J. (1992) *The Postmodern Explained to Children*, Power Publications, Sydney.
McCann, D. and Strain, C. (1985) *Polity and Praxis*, Winston Press, Minneapolis.
Macy, J. (1991) *Mutual Causality in Buddhism and General Systems Theory*, State University of New York Press, Albany.
Macy, J. (1993) *World as Lover, World as Self*, Rider, London.
Main, J. (1989) *The Way of Unknowing*, Darton, Longman and Todd, London.
Mander, J. (1992) *In The Absence Of The Sacred*, Sierra Club Books, San Francisco.
Mathews, F. (1989) 'Attentive Love: An Epistemology of Interconnectedness', Paper presented at Ecopolitics IV Conference, Adelaide University, South Australia.
Mathews, F. (1993) 'To Know the World', in Kelly Farley (ed.) *On the Edge of Discovery: Women in Australian Science*, Text Publishing, Melbourne.

Mathews, F. (1994) 'Cultural Relativism and Environmental Ethics', *IUCN Ethics Working Group Circular Letter*, 5, pp. 5-7.
Mathews, F. (1995) 'Community and the Ecological Self', *Environmental Politics*, 4:4.
Midgley, M. (1989) *Wisdom, Information, and Wonder: What is Knowledge For?*, Routledge, London.
Mies, M. and Shiva, V. (1993) *Ecofeminism*, Spinifex, Melbourne.
Milbank, J. (1992) 'Problematizing the secular: the post-postmodern agenda', in P. Berry and A. Wernick (eds) *Shadow of Spirit: Postmodernism and Religion*, Routledge, London.
Mouffe, C. (1992) *Dimensions of Radical Democracy: Pluralism, Citizenship, Community*, Verso, London.
Murdoch, I. (1970) *The Sovereignty of Good*, Routledge and Kegan Paul, London.
Nandy, A. (1987a) *Traditions, Tyranny and Utopias: Essays in the Politics of Awareness*, Oxford University Press, New Delhi.
Nasr, S. (1989) *Knowledge And The Sacred*, State University of New York Press, Albany.
Noddings, N. (1984) *Caring: A Feminine Approach to Ethics and Moral Education*, University of California Press, Berkley.
Plumwood, V. (1990) 'Women, Humanity And Nature', in S. Sayers and P. Osborne (eds) *Socialism, Feminism and Philosophy*, Routledge, London.
Plumwood, V. (1992) 'Feminism and Ecofeminism', *The Ecologist*, 22:1.
Plumwood, V. (1993) *Feminism and the Mastery of Nature*, Routledge, London.
Robertson, R. (1992) *Globalization: Social Theory and Global Culture*, Sage Publications, London.
Rodda, A. (1991) *Women and the Environment*, Zed Books, London.
Rose, D. (1985) 'Consciousness and Responsibility in an Australian Aboriginal Religion', *Nelen Yubu*, pp. 3-15.
Rose, D. (1992) *Dingo Makes Us Human: Life and Land in an Australian Aboriginal Culture*, Cambridge University Press, Cambridge.
Rose, G. (1992) *The Broken Middle: Out of our Ancient Society*, Blackwell, Oxford.
Rose, G. (1993) *Judaism and Modernity: Philosophical Essays*, Blackwell, Oxford.
Ruddick, S. (1989) *Maternal Thinking*, Beacon Press, Boston.
Sahliyeh, E. (1990a) 'Religious Resurgence and Political Modernization', in E. Sahliyeh (ed.) *Religious Resurgence and Politics in the Contemporary World*, State University of New York Press, Albany, pp. 1-16.
Sahliyeh, E. (1990b) 'Concluding Remarks', in E. Sahliyeh (ed.) *Religious Resurgence and Politics in the Contemporary World*, State University of New York Press, Albany, pp. 297-306.

Salleh, A. (1984) 'Deeper than Deep Ecology: The Eco-Feminist Connection', *Environmental Ethics*, 6, pp. 339-44.

Salleh, A. (1992) 'The Ecofeminism/Deep Ecology Debate: A Reply to Patriarchal Reason', *Environmental Ethics*, 3:14, pp. 195-216.

Schumacher, F. (1973a) *Small is Beautiful: Economics as if People Really Mattered*, Abacus, London.

Schumacher, F. (1973b) 'The Age of Plenty: A Christian View', in H. Daly (ed.) *Economics, Ecology, Ethics*, Freeman, San Francisco, pp. 126-137.

Schumacher, F. (1978) *A Guide for the Perplexed*, Abacus, London.

Schuon, F. (1975) *The Transcendent Unity of Religions*, tr. by P. Townsend, Introduction by H. Smith, Harper and Row, New York, Revised edition,

Schuon, F. (1976) *Islam and the Perennial Philosophy*, World of Islam Festival Publishing, London.

Schuon, F. (1990) *To Have A Centre*, World Wisdom Books, Bloomington, Indiana.

Spivak, G. Chakravorty- (1988) 'Can the Subaltern Speak?', in C. Nelson and L. Grossberg (eds) *Marxism and the Interpretation of Culture*, University of Illinois Press, Urbana and Chicago.

Ungunmerr, M-R. (1988) 'Dadirri', *Compass Theology Review*, 1-2, pp. 9-11.

Washburn, M. (1978) 'Observations Relevant to a Unified Theory of Meditation', *The Journal of Transpersonal Psychology*, 10:1.

Weil, S. (1952) *The Need For Roots: Prelude to a Declaration of Duties Towards Mankind*, Routledge and Kegan Paul, London.

Weil, S. (1962) *Selected Essays*, Oxford University Press, London.

Weil, S. (1970) *First and Last Notebooks*, tr. by Richard Rees, Oxford University Press, London and New York.

Weil, S. (1973) *Waiting on God*, Collins, London.

Weil, S. (1977) *The Simone Weil Reader*, George A. Panichas (ed.), McKay, New York.

Weil, S. (1987) *Gravity and Grace*, Routledge and Kegan Paul, London.

Wilber, K. (1985) *No Boundary: Eastern and Western Approaches to Personal Growth*, New Science Library, Shambhala, Boston.

Wilber, K. (1990) *Eye to Eye: The Quest for a New Paradigm*, Expanded edition, Shambhala, Boston.

Wilber, K. (1995) *Sex, Ecology, Spirituality: The Spirit of Evolution*, Shambhala, Boston.

Wilber, K. (1997a) *The Eye of the Spirit*, Shambhala, Boston.

Wilber, K. (1997b) 'A Spirituality that Transforms', *What Is Enlightenment?*, 12, Fall/Winter.

Wyschogrod, E. (1990) *Saints and Postmodernism: Revisioning Moral Philosophy*, University of Chicago Press, Chicago.

Index

Aborigines, mysticism 135
Abu-Lughod, J. 26, 45
Adamson, B. 157, 174
adhyasa 42
Advaitic Vedanta 152, 164, 169, 172
Alexander, C. 75
alterity *see* othering
anamnesis, knowledge 4-5, 150
anuragga 168
Astavakra 196
Atman 90, 153
attention
   and awareness 167-8
   and the ego 128
   Nisargadatta on 152-3, 178-9
   positive/negative 126, 137
   Ramana on 153
   as vigilance 139
attentive love 13, 15, 51, 98, 107-40, 177, 202
   Donovan on 119, 120, 133
   as feminine craft 109-22, 121
   Keller on 133
   language, compared 177
   and maternal love 114
   Mathews on 117, 118-19
   Murdoch on 112-13, 116-17, 120-121, 132, 137, 148
   and otherness 122
   praxis 179
   as psycho-physical energy 126-8, 132-3
   Ruddick on 113-14
   self-directed 132-3
   and self-transcendence 123-4
   and spiritually-engaged knowledge 13, 107-40, 193
   Weil on 111-12, 137, 148, 169
   Weil's life 109-10
attentiveness
   Brennan on 126-8, 138
   and conscience 199
   Frye on 124-5

   and identity formation 129-30
   as interconnection 117-19
   and meditation 167
   as meditative awareness 119-22, 177
   as objectivity 115-17
   and racism 125
   and self-construction 125
   to the Other 209
awareness, and attention 167-8

Basho 80, 81
Basu, A. 35
Bateson, Gregory 137-8
Bauman, Z. 65-6, 75, 207-8
   on morality 67-8, 198
   on the unspoken ethical command 95
Bellah, Robert 37
Benhabib, S. 91
Berry, Philippa 12-13, 48, 172
Berry, Thomas 23, 204-5
Bertens, H. 47
Beyer, P. 21, 24-5, 31
bhakti xii, 141 n.15
biosphere 21, 29, 90, 91, 189, 204
Bird-Rose, Deborah 134
Blaney, D. 6, 7, 79
Bordo, J. 88
Bose, Koysaschander 221
Brahman 50
Brennan, T. 10, 78, 81-2, 83, 108-9, 115, 118, 125, 131, 132, 136, 139, 146, 171
   on attentiveness 126-8, 138
   on the ego 128-9
Brown, D. 168
Buber, M. 94
   I and Thou 79, 87
   on othering 79-80, 82
Buddhism
   Mahayana 172, 176
   Tibetan 154-5, 170, 176

Cantwell-Smith, B. 37, 42, 44
care, ethic of 71-3, 74, 87, 101 n.11
Carroll, W. 24
Cassian, John 150, 151
Castoriadis, C. 54-5
Chambers, I. 208
Chiroco, J. 32
Chodorow, N. 117
Chomsky, Noam 161
Christian Meditation Network 150, 151
'citizen pilgrim' 207, 209
'citizen sadhak' 208-9, 210
citizenship
  global 207
  as process 33
Cixous, H. 119-20
'clash of civilizations' 5, 36
Cohen, R. 52, 53, 200
Communion and Liberation 31
conscience
  and attentiveness 199
  politics of 198-203
consciousness, nondual
  Forman on 163, 164, 170
  Wilber on 163-4, 165-6
constructivism
  incomplete 160-162
  vs perennialism 159-60
conversation
  and the Other 7, 52
  spiritually-engaged knowledge as 6-7
'conversation of cultures' 5, 36
Cornell, D. 49
Cowan, J. 135
Crowe, F. 53
culture, meaning 25

dadirri 134, 135
Dass, V. 53, 225
deconstruction 47-9
  criticism of 173
  as nihilism 49
  as positive inquiry 49-50
Deikman, A. 83
Derrida, J. 45, 46, 47, 48, 49, 93, 173
  on empiricism 70
  on prayer 50-52, 67
  on the Subject 92, 171
  on violence 53
Dietz, M. 136
discourse, environmental 84-5

discourses, linking 8, 43
Disraeli, Benjamin, on infanticide 221
doctrine
  apophatic 172, 173, 176
  cataphatic 172
Donovan, J. 155
  on attentive love 119, 120, 133
dualism, subject/object 42, 45
Dunne, T. 98

Earth, as Other 87-90
earth community, inclusive 204-6
ecofeminism 10, 58 n.23, 85, 91, 105 n.45, 119
ecumenicism, and fundamentalism 29, 32
ego
  and attention 128
  Brennan on 128-9
  deconstruction of 126
  formation 128-9
  Lacan on 126, 127
Eliot, T.S. 109
empiricism
  Derrida on 70
  post-deconstructive 70
empowerment, and spiritually-engaged knowledge 202
emptiness
  and inter-being 174
  notion of 170
environment
  and globalisation 23
  and life-style 203
environmental discourse 84-5
environmentalism 10
epistemology
  authority 36
  framework, globalisation 37-46
erasure, 15 n.4
  and knowledge 4, 54
ethic
  of care 71-3, 74, 87, 101 n.11
  meaning 66
  of meeting 66-7, 69, 70, 75-6, 79, 84, 145, 192-3, 201
  post-deconstructive 67-71, 75, 92-3, 121

Falk, Richard 33, 46, 175, 202, 207, 210, 211

Featherstone, M. 37
female infanticide, India xvii-xviii, 5-6, 215-16, 219-27
   and colonialism 219-20
   dowry reasons 220, 223
   origins 220
femininity, construction of 117-18, 127
feminism 10
   postmodern 35
   transnational 33
Forman, R. 159, 162
   on nondual consciousness 163, 164, 170
   The Problem of Pure Consciousness 160
Foucault, Michel 47
   technology of power 77, 78
Fox, E. 123, 124, 137
Friedman, M. 80
Frye, M., on attentiveness 124-5
fundamentalism 25, 31
   and ecumenicism 29, 32

Gandhi, Mahatma 7, 90, 200, 210
Gangaji 138
   on love 176
Garrett, G. 23
Gellner, E. 38
genre analysis 13
Giddens, A. 26-7, 197
Gilligan, Carol 74, 75, 122
   In a Different Voice 73
Global Ethic 30, 99 n.2
globalisation
   approaches to 21-2
   and the environment 23
   homogenisation 25
   and identity
      alliance 31
      construction 32-3, 34-5, 35-6
   as imperialism 24-5
   knowledge framework 37-46
      reflexivity 41-2
      relativism 39-41
      superiority 38-9
      transformation 42-6
   local impacts 27
   meaning 3
   model, Robertson's 26-8
   opportunities 77, 210-11
   relativism 191
   resistance to 25
   theory 190-191, 192
   Wiseman on 206
globalisation theory 23-9
   and knowledge 36-7
   and postmodern theory 22-3
Godman, D. 164
Goldstein, J. 155
Graham, A., on mindfulness 148-9
Grail legend 111
Grewal, I. 24, 35, 43
Grosz, E. 139
Guénon, R 162

Habermas, Jurgen 161
Hannigan, J., on new religious movements 201-2
Hargrove, B. 196-7
Hart, K. 49, 172
Heidegger, Martin 4, 81-2
   on thinking 48-9
Hillman, J. 38, 199
Holland, R. 169, 170
Huntington, Samuel 5, 32
Huxley, Aldous 159

iconic understanding 88, 135
identity
   construction
      and globalisation 32-3, 34-5
      through othering 78
   ecological 34
   female, Salleh on 117-18
   formation 128-9
      and attentiveness 129-30
      female 131
      male 130-131
   and knowledge 35
   nondual 78
   spiritually-engaged 36
   types 33-4
imperialism, globalisation as 24-5
Inayatullah, N. 6, 7, 79
Inchausti, R. 112, 137, 201, 209
India
   female infanticide 5-6, 219-27
   sons, preference for 225
   traditional/modern dichotomy 225, 226
   Women's Movement 226
infanticide

Britain 221
Disraeli on 221
see also female infanticide
injunctions, transcendental 96-8
inter-being 202
and emptiness 174
interiority, and reflexivity 41
Irigaray, L. 137, 138
Iroquois, and othering 89

jhana 168
jnana 148, 152
Johnston, W. 97, 174, 176
justice
Rawls on 111
Weil on 110-11

Kaplan, C. 24, 35, 43
Katz, Steven 159
Keller, E. Fox
on attentive love 133
on knowledge 115-16, 117
King, Martin Luther 199-200
Klein, A. 82, 131, 134
on mindfulness 135-6, 148
knowing, praxis 43-4
see also consciousness; not-knowing
knowledge
anamnesis 4-5
and awareness 4
constructivist 8
and erasure 4, 54
as ethical process 65-6, 197
framework, globalisation 37-46
and globalisation theory 36-7
Hindu philosophy 42
and identity 35
Keller on 115-16
as love 115
objective/subjective 42
postmodern critique 55
as power 115
relativisation 29-31
sapiential
and mindfulness 156-8, 178
Nasr on 180
as revelation 181
and spiritually-engaged knowledge 17, 194
and tradition 176-82

translation 4-5
see also spiritually-engaged knowledge
Kohlberg, L. 76, 77, 113, 115, 198, 199
moral development, model 73-4, 74-5, 101 n.13
Kothari, R. 24
Kovel, J. 11, 12, 138, 171
Krishnan, R. 224
Kristeva, J. 137, 138
Kung, Hans 30

La Vallée Poussin, L. 6
Lacan, J., on the ego 126, 127
Laclau, E. 24
language
attentive love, compared 177
universal 8-9, 43
Lawrence, D.H.
on love 181-2
'Snake' poem, and othering 85-7
Levinas, E. 52, 67, 69, 70, 75, 79, 87, 93, 94, 110
'ethic of the face' 84, 100 n.10
life force 129
life-style, and the environment 203
Lingis, A. 205
Lloyd, G. 121-2
logic of inquiry approach 13, 14
Lonergan, B. 43-4, 138, 146, 156-7, 161
Method in Theology 97-8
love
Gangaji on 176
Lawrence on 181-2
Nisargadatta on 176
Thich Nhat Hanh on 176
see also attentive love
Loy, D. 48, 49, 173
Lugones, Maria 125
Luhmann, Niklas 21
Lyotard, J. 14, 55

McCann, D. 13-14
Mackie, F. 46
Macy, J. 82
Maharshi, Ramana 12
Main, John 157
on meditation 150-151
Mani, L. 6

INDEX 241

mantra technique, meditation 151
Marion, J.-L. 81, 180
masculinity, construction of 127
maternal love, and attentive love 114
Mathews, F. 131
    on attentive love 117, 118-19, 133
Mazrui, A. 32
meditation
    and attentiveness 167
    concentrative 168
    kinds of 168
    Main on 150-151
    mantra technique 151
    receptive 169
    unified theory of 167-71
meeting, ethic of 66-7, 69, 70, 75-6, 79, 84, 145, 192-3, 201
Merton, Thomas 169
metapsychology 146
Meyer, John 21
Midgley, M. 40
Miller, B. 220, 224
mindfulness
    Advaitic awareness 152-4
    Buddhist 154-6
    Christian 148-52
    Graham on 148-9
    Klein on 135-6, 148
    Nyanaponika Thera on 155
    religious traditions 147-58
    and sapiential knowledge 156-8, 178
missionary work, Third World 6
modernisation theory 23, 25, 26, 29, 56 n.8
modernity, spirituality as critique of 12
moral development
    gendered 73-4
    Kohlberg's model 73-4, 74-5, 101 n.13
    non-rational 75
morality, Bauman on 67-8, 198
Morgan, K. 227
motherhood, as social construct 114-15
Mouffe, C. 24, 33
Murdoch, Iris, on attentive love 112-13, 116-17, 120-121, 132, 137, 148
Myss, Caroline 129
mysticism 146-7

Aboriginal 135

Naess, A. 90
Nagarjuna 42, 45
Nandy, A. 7
Naranjo, C. 168
Nasr, S. 146, 150
    on sapiential knowledge 180
natural law theory 199
Needleman, J. 149, 150, 199
Nerfin, M. 33, 207, 209
Nicephorus the Solitary 149, 150
Nicholas of Cusa 152
    doctrine of ignorance 151-2
Nietzsche, Friedrich 48, 49
nihilism, deconstruction as 49
nirvana 146, 155, 170, 182 n.7
Nisargadatta, Maharaj
    on attention 152-3, 178-9
    on love 176
Noddings, Nell 77, 94
    Caring 71
    ethic of care 71-3, 74, 87
not-knowing 172-6
Nuremberg Principles 94-5, 199
Nyanaponika Thera 154, 156
    on mindfulness 155
nyani xii
Nye, Andrea 189

objectivity, attentiveness as 115-17
ontotheology 48, 49, 53, 112, 173
Ornstein, R. 168
Other, the
    attentiveness to 209
    and conversation 7, 52
    the Earth as 87-90
    Oriental, and spirituality 12
    and responsibility 68-9
    self
        boundary deconstruction 76-7, 201
        dualism 12, 65, 76
    spirituality as 12
othering
    Buber on 79-80, 82
    craft of 78-84, 193
        de-automatising perception 83-4
        direct seeing 80-81
        I-Thou relationship 79-80

nondualism 83
  surrendering to the Other 81-2
  and identity construction 78
  and the Iroquois 89
  in Lawrence poem, 'Snake' 85-7
  and spiritually-engaged knowledge 54
otherness, and attentive love 122

Panigrahi, L. 221
pativratya 224, 230 n.23
Peavey, Fran 200
perception
  in Buddhism 156
  de-automatising 83-4
  socio-linguistic basis 76
perennialism 179
  vs constructivism 159-60
Philokalia 149, 150
Plumwood, V. 78, 91
postmodern theory, and globalisation theory 22-3
postmodernism
  critical 47-8
  deconstructive 47
  ludic 38, 39-40, 41, 47
  political 47
  relativism 192
  and the Self 182
  and spirituality 14, 45, 171-82
  and spiritually-engaged knowledge 46-55, 192, 196
Prakriti 163
prayer, Derrida on 50-52, 67
Prête, T. del 169
Pseudo-Dionysius, *The Mystical Theology* 151
psychology 11
  non-representational 158-67
  perennial 162
  post-representational 162-3, 195
  see also metapsychology; transpersonal psychology
Purusha 163

racism, and attentiveness 125
Rajputs 221-2
Ramana, Maharshi 169
  on attention 153
  on the Self 154, 164
Rawls, J., on justice 111

reflexivity, and interiority 41
relativisation
  definition 31-2
  knowledge 29-31
  processes 32
religion
  communities 204
  models 204
  new movements 201-3
  spirituality, distinction 11-12, 191
  transformation 11, 29
  translation 11, 29, 30, 31, 191
  and transpersonal psychology 11
responsibility, and the Other 68-9
Roberts, Bernadette 165, 166, 176
Robertson, Roland 14, 21, 22, 29, 31, 34, 37, 38
  globalisation model 26-8
Rose, Deborah 134-5, 174
Rose, Gillian 72, 94, 110
  on the 'holy middle' 95
Rosset, C. 48
Rothberg, D. 161
Roy, Rammohun 222
Ruddick, S., on attentive love 113-14
Ruysbroeck, Jan van 163
Ryncarz, R. 74-5, 76, 198, 199

Sachs, W. 87, 206
sacred/secular boundary 12
sadhaka 208
Said, Edward 12, 219
saintliness 109
Salleh, A., on female identity 117-18
samadhi 168, 184 n.16
Sankara 42, 169
sati 6, 219, 220, 226, 228 n.4, 229 n.10, 21
Self
  Other, boundary deconstruction 76-7, 201
  dualism 12, 65, 76
  postmodern view 182
  Ramana on 154, 164
  and spirituality 11, 12
self-construction, and attentiveness 125
self-transcendence, and attentive love 123-4
Shankaracharya 45
Sharma, A. 8-9, 43, 204

Simeon, St 150
Singer, P. 203
spirit, definition 11
spirituality
    definition 11-12, 171-2
    ethical dimension 12
    modernity, critique of 12
    and new awareness 13
    and Oriental Other 12
    as the Other 12
    post-deconstructive 174, 175
    and postmodernism 14, 45, 171-82
    religion, distinction 11-12, 191
    and the self 11, 12
    Yarralin people 134-5
spiritually-engaged knowledge
    and attentive love 13, 107-40, 193
    as conversation 6-7
    emergence 54, 55, 211
    and empowerment 202
    genre analysis 13, 192
    and global politics 197-210
    meaning 4
    nature of 176
    and othering 54
    and postmodernism 46-55, 192, 196
    resistance to 139
    rise of 190-197
    and sapiential knowledge 17, 194
    and transformation 42-6
Spivak, G. xvii, xviii
Srinivasan, V. 223, 224, 225
Steiner, Rudolf 211
Stockton, E 134, 135
Strain, C. 13-14
Subject, the, Derrida on 92, 171
sunyata 50
Suzuki, D.T. 80
syncretism 8

Tacey, D. 83
Tarnas, R. 44, 211
technology
    meaning 102 n.21
    of power, Foucault 77, 78
Tennyson, Alfred 80, 81
Thich Nhat Hanh 174
    on love 176
thinking, Heidegger on 48-9
Third World, missionary work 6

Tiryakian, E. 28
Tolstoy, L. 209
tradition, and knowledge 176-82
transcendence, male/female 121-2
    see also self-transcendence
transformation
    religion 11, 29
    and spiritually-engaged knowledge 42-6
translation, religion 11, 29, 30, 31, 191
transpersonal psychology 162
    and religion 11
    roots 11
    scope 11
turiyatita 165

UN Development Programme 36
Ungunmerr, Miriam-Rose 134, 135
universality
    meaning 9
    universalism, distinction 204

Vasant, F. 224
Vaughan, F. 167
Venkatachalam, R. 223, 224, 225
Verhelst, Thierry G. 6
via negativa 172, 173
vigilance, attention as 139
violence, Derrida on 53

Wallerstein, Immanuel 21, 24
Walsh, R. 167
Warren, Karen 8
Washburn, M. 167, 168, 169
Webb, E. 44, 145
Weil, S. 94, 98, 107, 123, 181, 193
    on attentive love 111-12, 137, 148, 169
    exemplar of attentive love 109-10
    on justice 110-11
    The Need for Roots 109
'West', meaning 15 n.5
'White Man's Burden' 6
Whitford, M. 139
Wilber, K. 11, 75, 162, 170
    on nondual consciousness 163-4, 165-6, 166-7
Williams, J.A. 111, 112
Wiseman, J., on globalisation 206
Wolff, F. Merrell 154

Women's Movement, India 226
Wood, J. 108
World Commission on Environment and Development 88
World Council of Churches 30
World Council of Indigenous Peoples 27
World Economic Forum 206

World Parliament of Religions 30
Wyschogrod, E. 12, 65, 68, 109, 110, 174-5

Yarralin people, spirituality 134-5
Yogacarin Paramartha 163

Zimmerman, M. 135